W9-AVT-248

THE World Cup 2022 Book

The content of this book was carefully researched. All information is supplied without liability. Neither the author nor the publisher will be liable for possible disadvantages, injuries, or damages.

Please note that at the time of publication, the information in this book was up to date. However, with competitions, the events are ever-changing, and it is possible that after printing, the information may have changed.

Shane Stay

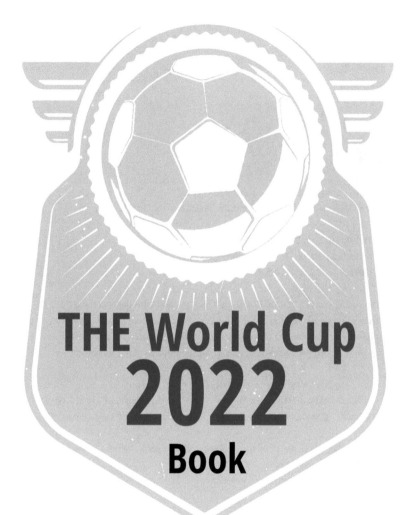

THE World Cup
2022
Book

Everything You Need to Know
About the Soccer World Cup

Meyer & Meyer Sport

British Library Cataloguing in Publication Data
A catalogue record for this book is available from the British Library

THE World Cup 2022 Book
Maidenhead: Meyer & Meyer Sport (UK) Ltd., 2022
ISBN: 978-1-78255-250-5

All rights reserved, especially the right to copy and distribute, including the
translation rights. No part of this work may be reproduced–including by photo copy,
microfilm or any other means–processed, stored electronically, copied or distributed
in any form whatsoever without the written permission of the publisher.

© 2023 by Meyer & Meyer Sport (UK) Ltd.
Aachen, Auckland, Beirut, Cairo, Cape Town, Dubai, Hägendorf, Hong Kong,
Indianapolis, Maidenhead, Manila, New Delhi, Singapore, Sydney, Tehran, Vienna

📖 Member of the World Sports Publishers' Association (WSPA), www.w-s-p-a.org
Printed by Seaway Printing, Green Bay, WI
Printed in the United States of America
ISBN: 978-1-78255-250-5
Email: info@m-m-sports.com
www.thesportspublisher.com

Credits
Cover and interior design: Annika Naas
Layout: Annika Naas
Cover and interior images: © AdobeStock
Managing editor: Elizabeth Evans

CONTENTS

INTRODUCTION

The best teams in the world will kick off the 2022 FIFA World Cup in November with more than a billion fans watching. A new champion will emerge. International soccer supremacy—and the right to be called one of history's greatest teams—is at stake in Qatar. Star-studded teams from every corner of the globe will arrive in the Middle Eastern oasis—social media will be abuzz, cameras will flicker, as countries will collide and a new champion will emerge as one of history's greatest teams!

CRISTIANO RONALDO, MESSI, NEYMAR, HARRY KANE, and MBAPPÉ are but a handful of stars that will sparkle at the 2022 FIFA World Cup in Qatar. It's an exciting time when the best players in the world flaunt their stuff in stadiums filled with eager fans. Ticket stubs will be saved, souvenirs purchased as the best nations in the world battle it out for the illustrious FIFA World Cup. The beat of Brazil's samba, the ferocity of Argentina's presence, the grace of the French, the daunting Germans, the impressive English, Mexico, the unequivocal rock stars of CONCACAF Mexico…all 32 nations will have a chance as the month-long event plays out.

The most anticipated sporting event is back. The FIFA World Cup will be played in Qatar. Proponents argue that this is a grand opportunity for the Middle East to showcase its love for soccer. Indeed, this is the first time that a Middle Eastern nation has hosted the FIFA World Cup. Critics point out issues such as allegedly accepting bribes, unsuitable weather, a lack of experience (not to mention prestige) as a top soccer-playing nation, alleged human rights violations, along with geographic and economic challenges for travelers to arrive and watch the games. Despite the criticism, however, Qatar—a small, oil-rich nation jutting out into the Persian Gulf that neighbors Bahrain, Saudi Arabia, and United Arab Emirates—will go down in history as the twenty-second nation to host the FIFA World Cup. Prior to Qatar 2022, there have been 21 World Cup champions—an elite group.

Previous World Cup winners:

2018: France	1974: West Germany
2014: Germany	1970: Brazil
2010: Spain	1966: England
2006: Italy	1962: Brazil
2002: Brazil	1958: Brazil
1998: France	1954: West Germany
1994: Brazil	1950: Uruguay
1990: West Germany	1938: Italy
1986: Argentina	1934: Italy
1982: Italy	1930: Uruguay
1978: Argentina	

Previous host nations include Russia, Brazil, South Africa, Germany, Korea-Japan, France, United States, Italy, Mexico, Spain, Argentina, West Germany, Mexico, England, Chile, Sweden, Switzerland, Brazil, France, Italy, and Uruguay.

For Qatar, 2022 will be its first opportunity to host the World Cup. Instrumental in organizing the Cup were Sheikh Mohammed bin Hamad bin Khalifa Al Thani (whose older brother is Sheikh Tamim bin Hamad Al Thani, Emir of Qatar), Hassan Al Thawadi, Nasser Al-Khater, and Colin Smith. In 2010, when FIFA announced Qatar as the 2022 host, infrastructure planning began right away. In the lead-up to the competition, many new stadiums have been erected specifically for the World Cup and with the help of German engineering. Each new stadium was made to be unique and beautiful to reflect the local culture. With the exception of Al-Shamal Stadium, which is situated in the north, the games will be played on the eastern side of Qatar.

Everything you could possibly want in a tournament is present: drama, tension, rivalries, top goal-scorers, elite defenders and goalies, midfield magicians, free-kick specialists, penalty-kick tendencies, coaches, strategies, formations, possession-based and free-flowing styles; it will be one for the record books! Later in the book, we'll get into the background of each stadium, detailed predictions for the 2022 FIFA World Cup, overviews of past World Cups, and much more.

Once again, the United States—the all-time leader in the Olympics—is competing for the World Cup.

The United States is intertwined in international sports in more ways than one.

Broadly speaking, the United States hosts the biggest competitions in the world. The upcoming 2026 FIFA World Cup will be jointly hosted by Canada, Mexico, and the United States. Notably, during the 1994 FIFA World Cup, the US set attendance records that have yet to be broken. What's more, the Super Bowl, NBA Championship, World Series, NHL Stanley Cup, and the tennis US Open are highly anticipated sporting events that captivate international audiences. These sports conjure up a myriad of athletes such as Tom Brady, Kobe Bryant, Babe Ruth, Wayne Gretzky, and Roger Federer.

The FIFA World Cup, on the other hand, is the world's passion—the most popular sporting event on earth! The amount of beer to be consumed: mind-boggling! (And the list of the many beers to be consumed would almost require its own chapter.) The amount of smartphone activity in Qatar: head-spinning! The largest sporting event the world has ever known captivates more than a billion fans!

World Cup champions make up an exclusive list. There are also the great teams, such as Brazil 1970, Brazil 2002, Italy 2006, Spain 2010, and Germany 2014. Not to mention, there are a few teams over the years that didn't hoist the trophy but gained recognition, including Brazil (1982) "arte de futbol"; Cameroon (1990), "the indomitable lions"; and South Korea (2002), the first Asian team to make the semi-finals.

The largest sporting event in history has now attracted millions of passionate soccer fans from the United States, who, to the best of their ability, are duplicating the frenzy of emotion felt around the world. Reflecting fervor worldwide, the pastime of watching a game at the local bar only seems to be intensifying in the US. It's a firm reminder that, after all, the United States— the standing record-holder for highest attendance in World Cup history (World Cup 1994)—has officially joined the world's game and has bars across the nation fully equipped for World Cup action in Qatar, and subsequently for World Cup 2026. Around the world, bars from England, Germany, Japan, Egypt, Australia, Argentina, and Brazil—every corner of the globe— will be filled to capacity with eager fans celebrating each game.

For people interested in the finer nuances, a few of the rules and procedures for the World Cup have been adjusted over the years. For example, back in 1994 there were 24 teams in the tournament. By 2018, FIFA banged the table and said 32 teams will compete. (More on this to come.)

For this World Cup, all 32 teams—from Europe, South America, North America, Africa, and Asia—went through an accelerated qualification process* due to the COVID-19 pandemic, which had set things back. Despite the pandemic, which affected people worldwide, each team worked hard to arrive at this point and become a major part of history. We'll take a constructive look at each team, the players, and coaches, and break down all aspects of World Cup Qatar. And what fun it's going to be!

Throughout my life some people have asked me why soccer is so great. They know people worship the sport; they know of its allure; yet they don't quite understand its popularity. Most people might answer something about the "beautiful game" and how "Pele learned to play with a grapefruit." But my answer would be that it's great because there is no prerequisite to qualify at the highest levels. Have you ever seen an NBA lineup? Seven feet

---

*   Qatar automatically qualified as the host nation.

tall is not normal. There aren't too many 6'9" and taller people in the world, and if they do exist, they tend to find their way onto a basketball court. That's the nature of basketball; it has always been an above-the-rim sport.

Soccer, on the other hand, is based on pure skill. You can be any height to succeed. Though, common sense has shown that players shorter than 6'3" tend to do better as such physiques have a quicker response time. Some players, such as Zidane, Henry, and Ibrahimovic do excel at heights 6'2" and above, but most tend to be under six feet. There's a famous picture of Pele, riding on the shoulders of others after winning the legendary 1970 FIFA World Cup in the Azteca before over 100,000 spectators—and he's all of 5'5", thought to be one of the best players of all time.

So in soccer, only the best stand out, and the players are elite, fit athletes who are better than the best in the world. This, I believe, in part, is why soccer is so endearing to people across continents. Of course, there is the simplicity of the game (just get the ball into the goal) combined with the complexities of the game (formations, defensive posturing, athletic one-on-one ability) that make simply getting the ball into a goal challenging. The FIFA World Cup represents the biggest stage in the world for these elite players.

When Uruguay hosted the first World Cup in 1930, it's fair to assume that no one predicted how big it would become. Nothing that came before it really compared. The most recent World Cup in Russia in 2018 carried on the multimillion-dollar tradition. Qatar 2022 will, no doubt, create new memories and new legends. To win the Cup takes a lot of skill, perseverance, and luck, whether it's the ball hitting off the post, an offside call that wasn't offside, a foul that wasn't called, or something else altogether (like the late Maradona's "hand of God"). Eventually, there will only be one team standing.

The Cup happens only once every four years. Enjoy the ride!

WORLD CUP 2022 SUPERSTARS TO WATCH

Welcome to the superstar section. These players led their respective teams through the qualifiers, which we'll get to in a bit. However much or however little you know about the game, whether a seasoned fan or new to the game, it should be known these are the top, elite, players of the world, and represent the highest echelon category of the FIFA World Cup 2022 in Qatar. While you might not agree with a certain player—or two—left off this list, this list still highlights the best of the best.

RATING KEY

All ratings are judged on a scale of 1 to 10, with 10 being the highest. All ratings are based on comparisons with legends of the game, such as Pele, Maradona, and Rivaldo. For instance, Rivaldo would represent the standards for Shot Power with a 10, as would Puskas, Podolski, Littbarski, and Igor Belanov (the canon blaster). Pele, Garrincha, Maradona, Denilson, and Ronaldinho would be the standards for Dribbling with a 10. The Nigel Tufnel factor *(This Is Spinal Tap)* does come into play here, as perhaps Denilson would earn an 11 with dribbling. (Though an 11 is very rare and should not be thrown around loosely!)

A QUICK GUIDE TO THE RATING SYSTEM

Shot Power obviously speaks to the power of a shot. How hard can someone hit it? That's the question here.

Shot Accuracy refers to the pinpoint accuracy, the placement, of one's shot.

Scoring Prowess refers to the vibe a player has, combined with their overall scoring percentage, and their likelihood to score.

Dribbling refers to a player's ability to use creative dribbling as a means to 1) defensively get away from opposition and hold the ball for possession and 2) to offensively cause problems for other teams.

Speed obviously refers to outright speed covering a distance of over 40 yards or more. A distinction should be made between speed and quickness.

Quickness refers to one's ability to maneuver fast in a short time over a range of up to 40 yards.

Agility calls into question one's ability to maneuver comfortably forward, backward, and from side to side while using speed and quickness, both with and without the ball.

Skill Level represents skill on the ball: dribbling, passing, shooting, trapping, and overall touch.

Technique refers to the elegance of one's body while executing various skills.

Passing Vision refers to a player's ability to see the field and deliver smart passes to allow teammates to continue the move.

Passing Touch refers to the "weight of the ball" with respect to delivering a pass, whether it be directly at a player or by leading them.

Passing Placement is obviously related to Passing Accuracy, but slightly different in that placement has to do with *an idea of* where a player wants to pass the ball (e.g., 10 yards in front of a teammate for them to run on to it). The next step would be the practicality of placing the ball and whether the player placed the ball with good accuracy.

Passing Accuracy refers to accurately passing the ball to a given target.

Aerial Ability refers to a player's head-ball ability particularly around goal and for both offense and defense.

Toughness refers to one's ability to bounce back from being tackled or fouled.

Will to Win refers to one's ability to win each moment on the field, be it dribbling or passing, and the overall winning vibe a player has.

Soccer IQ refers to a player's knowledge of the game and how well they read the field. Do they make their teammates look good? Is their vision good? Do they choose the right moments to dribble? Do they orchestrate possession play with superior ability? These are a few questions that come into play with respect to Soccer IQ.

LIONEL MESSI (ARGENTINA)

Shot Power: 9-9.2	*Passing Vision: 10*
Shot Accuracy: 10	*Passing Touch: 10*
Scoring Prowess: 10	*Passing Placement: 9.9*
Dribbling: 11	*Passing Accuracy: 9.9*
Speed: 8*	*Aerial Ability: 5*
Quickness: 9**	*Toughness: 9.9*
Agility: 10	*Will To Win: 10*
Skill Level: 11	*Soccer IQ: 10*
Technique: 11	

Brief Superstar Description

Rosario, Argentina—a city just a short drive northwest of Buenos Aires—became synonymous with perhaps the greatest player of all time: **Lionel Messi**. Messi might be getting older, yet, based on the passionate adoration that Argentinian fans bestow upon

---

*   As an aging player, Messi's speed has declined somewhat in recent years. In his prime, Messi's speed was 9.9.

**   As with Messi's speed, his quickness has declined somewhat. However, in his prime Messi's quickness was an 11.

him, it could be assumed that he'll return for FIFA World Cup 2026 in North America.

For years now, Messi has been the face of the German powerhouse soccer brand Adidas. "The athletic apparel company is not only the official sponsor for Argentina's national team through 2022, Messi also has a separate deal with Adidas worth $10 million a year.[1]"

His skills, shot, passes, quickness, and ability to make something happen are all at the highest level. He is not quite as quick as "Messi 2006," yet his natural talent, which comes across with ease, can hardly be repudiated. The only thing holding Messi back at this point is Father Time. Still, this great player is only in his mid-30s, the 2021 Ballon d'Or winner, and can still wheel and deal with every touch of the ball. He's never showcased fancy moves, but he has a gift to dribble around opponents with change of direction and acceleration unlike but a few others in the history of the game; he's shifty, smart, and intuitive. Always a threat. Currently, his passing ability has usurped his dribbling skill, and he places the ball into the paths of teammates with touch and precision like that of Platini and Ronaldinho. If this is his last World Cup, fans should know that he is one of the three greatest players in the history of the game along with Pele and Maradona. Messi's skills will be on full display as he carries on the rich tradition of Argentinian talent.

NEYMAR (BRAZIL)

Shot Power: 8.7-9　　*Passing Vision: 9.9*
Shot Accuracy: 10　　*Passing Touch: 9.9*
Scoring Prowess: 11　　*Passing Placement: 9.9*
Dribbling: 11　　*Passing Accuracy: 9.8*
Speed: 10　　*Aerial Ability: 8.1*
Quickness: 10　　*Toughness: 9*
Agility: 10　　*Will to Win: 9.9*
Skill Level: 11　　*Soccer IQ: 10*
Technique: 11

Brief Superstar Description

Back when Pele and Maradona roamed the field as the two greats, Puma-brand boots were on their feet. They made Puma cool. Then there was a time in the post-Maradona era when Puma was worn by many, yet a true superstar was not one of them. In 2020, **Neymar** made the bold move to vacate his time with Nike and sign with the German sportswear company dynamo: Puma. *Forbes Middle* East reported, "Earlier in August UOL announced that Neymar and Nike failed to reach a deal on how much the player would be paid by the company in exchange for renewing his contract."[2] Furthermore, "It also disclosed the relationship between the football player and Nike had been soured for months."[3] It was a huge multimillion-dollar deal for Puma who agreed to pay Neymar in the neighborhood of $29.1 million per year! Puma is, indeed, cool again thanks to one of soccer's biggest stars in the world, the goal-scoring magician from Brazil: Neymar da Silva Santos Júnior. "Neymar is a social media sensation and has the title of the second most popular athlete on social media with a total of 244 million followers on Twitter, Facebook and Instagram."[4] All things considered, "his earnings in 2020, including endorsements, were estimated to be $95.5 million."[5] The Brazilian star is also a passionate video gamer. Yet the shoes are the focal point. The shoes in question, one of Puma's proudest moments in the world of soccer, will be gliding upon the perfectly cut grass of the soccer field with grace, almost perfect technique, showmanship, dexterity, speed, and quickness. Interestingly, as one of the best players in the world for years now, Neymar has suffered injuries and is shadowed by Ronaldo and Messi, so he hasn't quite achieved the title of world's greatest player. *If* Neymar can win a World Cup for Brazil, he will go down as perhaps the greatest player in the country's history.

LUIS SUAREZ (URUGUAY)

Shot Power: 9.5
Shot Accuracy: 9.9-10
Scoring Prowess: 9.9-10
Dribbling: 9.3
Speed: 8.6
Quickness: 9.2
Agility: 10
Skill Level: 9.8
Technique: 9.8

Passing Vision: 9.4
Passing Touch: 9.4
Passing Placement: 9.4
Passing Accuracy: 9.4
Aerial Ability: 8.3
Toughness: 8.1
Will to Win: 10
Soccer IQ: 10

Brief Superstar Description

Luis "El Pistolero" Suarez is truly a gifted scorer and ranks as one of the top forwards of all time. Around the box, he pounces on scoring chances; he has a crafty dribbling touch that moves the ball with purpose into dangerous areas, usually just out of reach of an opponent; he uses his muscular frame effectively by bopping defenders with his hips to get an edge on using space to create shots on goal. And his shots on goal—lethal with accuracy and typically driven low (a goalkeeper's nightmare!). For a forward of his talent, his best years were spent with Barcelona as part of the Suarez–Messi–Neymar frontline—a rare combination of brilliant play. How far will he go this World Cup? Hard to say as his talents are underutilized with a less-than-spectacular Uruguayan side.

CRISTIANO RONALDO (PORTUGAL)

Shot Power: 10
Shot Accuracy: 9.9-10
Scoring Prowess: 10

Dribbling: 10
Speed: 9.3*
Quickness: 9.7**

---

*   During his prime Ronaldo's speed was a 10.

**   During his prime Ronaldo's quickness was an 11.

Agility: 10
Skill Level: 11
Technique: 10
Passing Vision: 9.8
Passing Touch: 9.7
Passing Placement: 9.6

Passing Accuracy: 9.7
Aerial Ability: 11
Toughness: 7*
Will to Win: 10
Soccer IQ: 10

Brief Superstar Description

Cristiano Ronaldo—a human Lamborghini—was once best known for his speed and quickness, though currently his value lies in his experience and wisdom. The brilliant winger is likely going to be linked with the greatest players never to win a FIFA World Cup. Such company includes Matthias Sindelar, Alfredo Di Stefano, Ferenc Puskas, George Best, Johan Cruyff, Socrates, a basketful of English talent since 1966 (such as Bryan Robson, Gary Lineker, and Wayne Rooney), Platini, Marco van Basten, George Weah, Carlos Valderrama, Hristo Stoichkov, and Ariel Ortega. However, this should not take away from his individual skill, which ranks among the best. As one of the richest athletes on earth, Ronaldo (Nike's billion-dollar man) has a European Championship, which he dropped out of with an injury, but he has not yet attained the ultimate prize, the FIFA World Cup Trophy. This might be the aging superstar's last World Cup, though he might have a place with Portugal in some capacity in 2026. For now, he still has that creative spark to make a play happen at any given moment, and all eyes will be focused on his every touch of the ball, which is still electric. As for free kicks, the right-footed magician always has a few tricks up his sleeve, including a deadly dipping strike that constantly causes problems for keepers.

---

*   Ronaldo is often unfairly lambasted for his toughness or lack thereof. It should be noted that despite "whining a lot" he does take a lot of fouls.

LUKA MODRIC (CROATIA)

Shot Power: 9

Shot Accuracy: 9.4

Scoring Prowess: 8.4

Dribbling: 9.3

Speed: 7.3

Quickness: 8.9

Agility: 10

Skill Level: 10

Technique: 10

Passing Vision: 10

Passing Touch: 10

Passing Placement: 10

Passing Accuracy: 10

Aerial Ability: 5

Toughness: 8-9

Will to Win: 10

Soccer IQ: 10

Brief Superstar Description

Not the quickest around, nor the fastest, **Luka Modric**—the pride of Croatia—is a passing savant. Any pass he makes looks elegant. The placement is pristine, the touch is light. His vision is phenomenal, and his ability to link passes together with precision touch, timing, and accuracy is next level. He's a gifted possession-oriented field general, full of fortitude, with a knack for making teammates look good. His vision and eagerness to share the ball make him a special threat; he reads the field and each moment of a game with an intuitive eye that allows him to control the tempo of play with dangerous consequences for opponents.

In 2018 he led Croatia to a second-place finish in the FIFA World Cup, and he holds the distinction of breaking the 10-year cycle between Cristiano Ronaldo and Messi for the Ballon d'Or which he won in 2018; in that same year, he also won the Best FIFA Men's Player award.

Furthermore, he won the 2022 UEFA Champions League final with Real Madrid. This occurred just months before the 2022 FIFA World Cup. With Modric on the field, Croatia is in a good place.

ANTOINE GRIEZMANN (FRANCE)

Shot Power: 9

Shot Accuracy: 9.9-10

Scoring Prowess: 10

Dribbling: 9.8

Speed: 9.3

Quickness: 9.6

Agility: 10

Skill Level: 10

Technique: 10

Passing Vision: 9.8

Passing Touch: 9.8

Passing Placement: 9.8

Passing Accuracy: 9.8

Aerial Ability: 7

Toughness: 8

Will to Win: 10

Soccer IQ: 10

Brief Superstar Description

Antoine Griezmann, whose countenance goes from calm and steady to outright passionate upon scoring a goal, has been steadily encroaching on France's all-time scoring list and is soon to take the number one spot which until now has been held by Henry. Griezmann has superstar playmaking ability that rests in buildup play with teammates, smart dribbling in tight areas, and a creative awareness as he finds spaces around the box to deliver telling, accurate, and cultured shots on goal. Everything with Griezmann is smart, crafty, and skillful. He's a forward with an innate sense for creating magic around the box using a one-two combination with teammates and dangerous passes.

MBAPPÉ (FRANCE)

Shot Power: 9.9

Shot Accuracy: 9.7-9.8

Scoring Prowess: 10

Dribbling: 10

Speed: 10

Quickness: 10

Agility: 10

Skill Level: 9.9

Technique: 9.9

Passing Vision: 9.6

Passing Touch: 9.6

Passing Placement: 9.6

Passing Accuracy: 9.6

Aerial Ability: 8

Toughness: 8

Will to Win: 10

Soccer IQ: 10

Brief Superstar Description

Mbappé—who is agile, in stellar shape, and about 5'10"—often bounces forward with electric, formidable, and seemingly unbeatable speed. Determined, he shakes off defenders on his way down the line into open space to create opportunity for a shot on goal, a piercing low-driven strike—a nightmare for keepers. Typically, the outcome of his dashing runs will mean a goal, leaving opposition's fans to commiserate over what just happened. Now in his early 20s and already a 2018 World Cup champion, the French star is an integral part of Les Bleus in Qatar, and his scoring prowess will be counted on both by his teammates and his supporters back home.

HARRY KANE (ENGLAND)

Shot Power: 9.9	*Passing Vision: 9.6*
Shot Accuracy: 9.9-10	*Passing Touch: 9.7*
Scoring Prowess: 10	*Passing Placement: 9.7*
Dribbling: 8.5	*Passing Accuracy: 9.7*
Speed: 7.5	*Aerial Ability: 9.4*
Quickness: 8	*Toughness: 9*
Agility: 10	*Will to Win: 10*
Skill Level: 10	*Soccer IQ: 10*
Technique: 10	

Brief Superstar Description

Harry Kane is one of those special forwards who isn't fast, but who uses his body exceptionally well to gain position on defenders, hold them off, all while constructively—and certainly methodically—setting up the next move for his teammates. Call it an "innate skill." It's certainly one coaches try to teach but to routinely pull it off is another thing altogether. When it comes to finishing, Kane is a threat to goalkeepers, and his every touch around goal is clinical, his movement is clinical, his finishing is clinical…be it on the ground or by air, Kane is going to get the ball in the net. The result often is magical.

EDEN HAZARD (BELGIUM)

Shot Power: 9.8

Shot Accuracy: 9.8-9.9

Scoring Prowess: 10

Dribbling: 11

Speed: 9.6

Quickness: 11

Agility: 10

Skill Level: 11

Technique: 10

Passing Vision: 9.7

Passing Touch: 9.7

Passing Placement: 9.7

Passing Accuracy: 9.7

Aerial Ability: 5-6

Toughness: 7.2

Will to Win: 10

Soccer IQ: 10

Brief Superstar Description

Eden Hazard has a propensity for shifting past bewildered defenders with extraordinary technique, explosive quickness, change of pace, and change of direction that is second to none. This ability sets him apart as a superstar in Qatar. When not on injured reserve, Hazard is a special talent worth the price of admission.

He has been in the "best player in the world" conversation for a few years now. However, those pesky leaders, Messi and Ronaldo, have had something to say about it still. Others in the mix have been Neymar and Mo Salah. Still, Eden Hazard is truly a great player in his own right. His skill and technique will be on full display throughout the tournament. For Hazard, Qatar represents yet another opportunity to remind everyone just how talented he is.

KEVIN DE BRUYNE (BELGIUM)

Shot Power: 10

Shot Accuracy: 9.9-10

Scoring Prowess: 10

Dribbling: 9.8

Speed: 9.2

Quickness: 9.4

Agility: 10

Skill Level: 10

Technique: 10

Passing Vision: 9.8

Passing Touch: 9.7

Passing Placement: 9.7

Passing Accuracy: 9.7　　　*Will to Win: 10*
Aerial Ability: 7-8　　　*Soccer IQ: 10*
Toughness: 8

Brief Superstar Description

His play is purely clinical. It seems anything a coach would want in a player can be found in **Kevin De Bruyne**. He's deadly on counters; he's brilliant in possession play; his passing vision, technique, placement, accuracy, and timing are immaculate. The average viewer may not see anything special, but that is often the sign of real talent—they make it look easy! Part of De Bruyne's brilliance is his ability to play with grace; every move he makes is effortless. In addition, his shot is like a bullet from a gun, and, more often than not, it's driven low, making him a real threat to his opponents.

MEMPHIS DEPAY (NETHERLANDS)

Shot Power: 9.7　　　*Passing Vision: 9.6*
Shot Accuracy: 9.6　　　*Passing Touch: 9.6*
Scoring Prowess: 9.3　　　*Passing Placement: 9.6*
Dribbling: 9.3　　　*Passing Accuracy: 9.6*
Speed: 9.6　　　*Aerial Ability: 8*
Quickness: 9.7　　　*Toughness: 8*
Agility: 10　　　*Will to Win: 9.8*
Skill Level: 10　　　*Soccer IQ: 10*
Technique: 10

Brief Superstar Description

Memphis Depay is like a middleweight boxer: fast, nimble, and powerfully built. He skillfully presses his opponents, coming at them from all angles, usually getting a shot off. With over 60 goals with Lyon (where he sat comfortably in French professional soccer from 2017-21), he eventually made the move to Barcelona in 2021 to show off his skills on a larger stage, validating his status as a superstar. Since 2013, the 5'9" forward also has scored over 30 goals for his home nation.

TIMO WERNER (GERMANY)

Shot Power: 9.9	Passing Vision: 9.6
Shot Accuracy: 9.8	Passing Touch: 9.6
Scoring Prowess: 9.7	Passing Placement: 9.6
Dribbling: 9.3	Passing Accuracy: 9.6
Speed: 9.5	Aerial Ability: 8.5
Quickness: 9.7	Toughness: 8
Agility: 10	Will to Win: 9.8
Skill Level: 10	Soccer IQ: 10
Technique: 10	

Brief Superstar Description

Timo Werner—nicknamed "Turbo Timo"—possesses speed, quickness, and good acceleration. This combination has helped him score many goals throughout his career—78 with RB Leipzig before his move to Chelsea in 2020. He's a clever and formidable German forward who can step back and join link-up play with mids and defenders during possession. All the while, his speed and awareness during the offensive buildup give him advantage over defenders around the box where his shooting is dangerous both from distance and up close.

ROBERT LEWANDOWSKI (POLAND)

Shot Power: 9.8	Passing Vision: 9.8
Shot Accuracy: 10	Passing Touch: 9.7
Scoring Prowess: 11	Passing Placement: 9.6
Dribbling: 8	Passing Accuracy: 9.6
Speed: 8	Aerial Ability: 10
Quickness: 8.6	Toughness: 8.8
Agility: 10	Will to Win: 10
Skill Level: 10	Soccer IQ: 10
Technique: 10	

Brief Superstar Description

Robert Lewandowski—lean, mean, and sporting an impressive six-pack—is a goal-scoring mega-force! He's a classical technician around goal, a clinical finisher with accuracy, a strong shot with both feet, good in the air, and he has an uncanny ability to score with confidence. Don't look for super speed, outright quickness, or fancy dribbling from him as the Polish wonder is a number nine without those attributes. Rather he's a natural scorer similar to Ian Rush. What's more, Lewandowski can successfully hold off defenders with his back to goal, allowing for a strong buildup in possession. This, in turn, creates solid chances for him to score more often. With over 70 goals for Poland, he's a scoring wizard who will go down as one of the all-time greats in his position.

GARETH BALE (WALES)

Shot Power: 9.9
Shot Accuracy: 9.9
Scoring Prowess: 9.9
Dribbling: 9.8
Speed: 9.9
Quickness: 9.6
Agility: 10
Skill Level: 9.9
Technique: 9.9

Passing Vision: 9.7
Passing Touch: 9.7
Passing Placement: 9.6
Passing Accuracy: 9.6
Aerial Ability: 9.9
Toughness: 8.8
Will to Win: 10
Soccer IQ: 10

Brief Superstar Description

Gareth Bale is an outright gamer who exhibits powerful speed down the wing, skillful play, a strong shot, and the ability to create scoring chances for himself and others. With Bale on the field, there's a feeling that he can break a play open at any given moment. While Wales might not pull its weight in the tournament, Bale will be a star to watch. Wales is a quality side, yet it's a smaller nation with a weak track record in World Cup

25

competition. If anyone can lead the team forward on a miraculous run, it will be Gareth Bale.

KOKE (SPAIN)

Shot Power: 9	Passing Vision: 9.9
Shot Accuracy: 9.5	Passing Touch: 9.9
Scoring Prowess: 5*	Passing Placement: 9.9
Dribbling: 9.8	Passing Accuracy: 9.9
Speed: 9.3	Aerial Ability: 6-7
Quickness: 9.6	Toughness: 8
Agility: 10	Will to Win: 10
Skill Level: 10	Soccer IQ: 10
Technique: 10	

Brief Superstar Description

Koke has been lauded by Xavi and others as Spain's future in the midfield. Like Xavi, he is a passer's passer, one who looks to set up teammates within Spain's dominant passing attack that favors out-possessing opponents. While Koke might not sparkle on the stage with fancy Garrincha-like dribbling moves, he will lead Spain's attack with fluid, brilliant, methodical, and technically superior passing. As he likely won't be the main goal scorer, any and all goals will likely result from his possession play.

PEDRI (SPAIN)

Shot Power: 9	Quickness: 9.6
Shot Accuracy: 9.5	Agility: 10
Scoring Prowess: 5	Skill Level: 10
Dribbling: 9.8	Technique: 10
Speed: 9.4	Passing Vision: 9.9

---

*	This is tricky for Koke. With the national team, he's not a scorer but assists his teammates in scoring. Whereas with his club side, Atletico Madrid, he's done more scoring.

Passing Touch: 9.9   *Toughness: 8*
Passing Placement: 9.9   *Will to Win: 10*
Passing Accuracy: 9.9   *Soccer IQ: 10*
Aerial Ability: 5-6

Brief Superstar Description

Typically, **Pedri** is a midfielder. Still, he's also comfortable operating out of central areas and out wide. He is almost what one could call a "free player" as he roams the field and can be found making play options in wide areas and even making penetrating runs at times. Within Spain's immaculate passing network, Pedri has the luxury to find moments here and there to punch holes in defenses around the touchline and make dangerous runs toward goal. Pedri, with his technical ability, passing skill, and field vision, is one of the world's fastest growing stars.

CHRISTIAN PULISIC (UNITED STATES)

Shot Power: 9.3   *Passing Vision: 9.7*
Shot Accuracy: 9.8-9.9   *Passing Touch: 9.7*
Scoring Prowess: 9.5   *Passing Placement: 9.7*
Dribbling: 9.8   *Passing Accuracy: 9.7*
Speed: 9.8   *Aerial Ability: 6-7*
Quickness: 10   *Toughness: 9*
Agility: 10   *Will to Win: 10*
Skill Level: 10   *Soccer IQ: 10*
Technique: 9.9

Brief Superstar Description

Christian Pulisic—a confident player—is like a mix between Landon Donovan and Clint Dempsey with a tiny hint of George Best.

Pulisic can operate in tight spaces with very defined dribbling ability, and he can also break open a 50-yard solo run to goal. Always dangerous, Pulisic is faster than Dempsey and about a half step slower than Donovan in the open field. As two of the greatest players in US history, Donovan and Dempsey are getting a run for their money with Pulisic. Donovan was an outright speedster, world-class wheels at that, and very good at going north to south. Dempsey was not fast or excessively quick but very crafty. Dempsey, like Xavi and Carlos Valderrama, had the ability to make a simple pass that had flow and created momentum for teammates; it always felt like there was something going on when he had the ball.* Bottom line: Pulisic has speed to cover the full field like Donovan and the craftiness of Dempsey. There is already talk of Pulisic being the best player in the history of the USMNT. Perhaps even better than Donovan and Dempsey.

Soaring forward in the blink of an eye, Pulisic creates opportunities to step past a defender or two, while always on the lookout for a clever pass to a teammate which places defenders on their heels.

Pulisic's natural ability to dart around sets him apart from the class.

JESUS CORONA (MEXICO)

Shot Power: 9.1	Agility: 10
Shot Accuracy: 9.3	Skill Level: 10
Scoring Prowess: 9.1	Technique: 10
Dribbling: 10	Passing Vision: 9.6
Speed: 9.3	Passing Touch: 9.6
Quickness: 9.6	Passing Placement: 9.6

---

* Was Dempsey a world-class passer of the ball like Xavi and Valderrama? Not quite in their class. For starters, he was a different position as a forward and attacking midfielder. Yet he, like many others, possessed some of their qualities with respect to passing.

Passing Accuracy: 9.6   *Will to Win: 8*
Aerial Ability: 6   *Soccer IQ: 10*
Toughness: 8

Brief Superstar Description

Within CONCACAF, Mexico—El Tri—is the coolest kid in school. When Mexico plays in the US, the fans come out in droves. If players show up to an event, a restaurant, anywhere, they are mobbed by overly enthusiastic supporters. Right now, the player on Mexico's roster with the most superstar glitter is **Jesus Corona**, or "Tecatito." The nickname refers to the beer Tecate which is different from his last name Corona, another beer. Mr. Tecatito—the elusive 5'9" winger who signed with FC Porto in 2015—is as cool as it gets in all of CONCACAF right now. When he touches the ball, electricity is in the air. His dribbling is marvelous; the feeling one gets when he heads down the line is that something spectacular could happen at any moment—and it often does. Tecatito's skill is remarkable. El Tri has a gift in Corona who works his magic out wide.

ALPHONSO DAVIES (CANADA)

Shot Power: 8.3   *Passing Vision: 8.8*
Shot Accuracy: 8   *Passing Touch: 8.8*
Scoring Prowess: 8   *Passing Placement: 8.8*
Dribbling: 8.9   *Passing Accuracy: 8.8*
Speed: 10   *Aerial Ability: 8.6*
Quickness: 10   *Toughness: 8.9*
Agility: 10   *Will to Win: 10*
Skill Level: 8.8   *Soccer IQ: 9*
Technique: 8.8

Brief Superstar Description

Alphonso Davies is fast. He's one of those speedsters with a boost, especially around the box where he has a way of zipping around defenders. He's played with the clubs Vancouver Whitecaps and Bayern Munich. He's a versatile left fullback, left wing, and he adds attacking value to his team. So far, Davies has achieved a lot, including winning the Golden Boot Award at the 2017 CONCACAF Gold Cup, becoming a 2018 MLS All-Star, and being named the Bundesliga Rookie of the Season in 2019-20. As Canada works its way through Qatar in very unfamiliar territory (a FIFA World Cup!), Davies, with Tajon Buchanan and Cyle Larin, will add punch to the offense.

SON HEUNG-MIN (SOUTH KOREA)

Shot Power: 9.4

Shot Accuracy: 9.9-10

Scoring Prowess: 9.4

Dribbling: 8.9

Speed: 9

Quickness: 9.5

Agility: 10

Skill Level: 9.5

Technique: 9.8

Passing Vision: 9

Passing Touch: 9

Passing Placement: 9

Passing Accuracy: 9

Aerial Ability: 8.6

Toughness: 8.9

Will to Win: 10

Soccer IQ: 10

Brief Superstar Description

In the company of many talented South Korean players, **Son Heung-min** is the real deal in the forward position who has been making big news in Europe with over 75 goals scored at Tottenham. He's also a scoring sensation for his national team, having hit the 30-goal mark and climbing. At 6'0" he can play forward and out wide with good speed, finishing technique, and scoring instincts that set him apart as an attacking threat.

TAKUMI MINAMINO (JAPAN)

Shot Power: 10

Shot Accuracy: 9.6

Scoring Prowess: 9

Dribbling: 9.1

Speed: 9

Quickness: 9.5

Agility: 10
Skill Level: 9.8
Technique: 10
Passing Vision: 9.8
Passing Touch: 9.5
Passing Placement: 9.5

Passing Accuracy: 9.5
Aerial Ability: 8.1
Toughness: 9
Will to Win: 10
Soccer IQ: 10

Brief Superstar Description

Japan has a team of stars among stars. While **Takumi Minamino** gets the nod, he's surrounded by a group of talent that includes goal-gobbler Yuya Osako, Takefusa Kubo, Ao Tanaka, Junya Ito, and Wataru Endo the Great. BTS stunt double in the making, Minamino earned an obscure *Guinness World Record* for the highest number of high fives in a minute, a stunt he pulled back in 2014. Who knew that was a thing? As for soccer, where high fives certainly have a place, he's known for being a versatile attacking mid and winger. The 5'9" dynamo, who was the 2013 J. League Rookie of the Year, has pace, quickness, skill, technique, vision, and field awareness that make him a major concern for defenders. He's acquired valuable field time with Cerezo Osaka, Red Bull Salzburg, Liverpool, and Southampton. He scored an important goal during qualifiers for the 2022 World Cup against Saudi Arabia on February 1, 2022, that helped get Japan to this point. In all, he's scored over 15 goals for his nation, and he looks to lead a strong team in Qatar as Japan aims to make headlines by reaching the final for the first time in its history.

MATHEW RYAN (AUSTRALIA)

Shot Blocking: 10
Positional Awareness: 9.9
Quickness: 9
Agility: 9.9
Keeper Skill Level: 9.9

Technique: 10
Passing: 7
Keeper Aerial Ability: 10
Toughness: 10
Will to Win: 10

Brief Superstar Description

Mathew Ryan—born in 1992—earns respect as goalkeeper for Australia, one of the top teams in Asia. The 6'0" standout has played with a few clubs including Club Brugge, Valencia, Genk, Brighton & Hove Albion, Arsenal, and Real Sociedad. He's had several honors that include A-League Goalkeeper of the Year in 2011-12; Belgian Professional Goalkeeper of the Year in 2013-14 and 2014-15; and winner of the Golden Glove for the 2015 AFC Asian Cup. As captain of Australia, he first debuted with his national team in 2012. Since that time, he's acquired over 65 caps standing in front of the net. He's seen every trick in the book, so it'll be tough for teams to get one past him. If Australia is to make a big run, it will have a lot to do with Ryan as the last defender.

THE 32 TEAMS OF THE 2022 FIFA WORLD CUP IN QATAR

EUROPE
Germany, Spain, England, France, Belgium, Netherlands, Croatia, Denmark, Poland, Portugal, Serbia, Switzerland, Wales

SOUTH AMERICA
Brazil, Argentina, Uruguay, Ecuador

NORTH AMERICA
United States, Mexico, Canada, Costa Rica

AFRICA
Morocco, Senegal, Tunisia, Ghana, Cameroon

ASIA
Australia, Iran, Japan, Saudi Arabia, South Korea, Qatar

OCEANIA
(Oceania did not qualify a team this year)

THE TEAMS FROM EUROPE (13)

GERMANY
World Cup titles: 4 (1954, 1974, 1990, 2014)
Overall Team Rating: 9.9

A BRIEF TEAM HISTORY
Let's take a brief look at Germany's World Cup track record:

1930: Germany didn't compete in the World Cup.

1934: Germany placed third.

1938: Germany didn't get out of the early first stage.

1950: The Germans didn't compete.

1954: World Cup champions! Coach Herberger led the squad with standouts Fritz Walter and Helmut Rahn. With steady passing, firm organization, and resolve, the Germans defeated Hungary in the final, thus establishing West Germany's first World Cup title. This first World Cup title was the start of a great run, as Germany separated itself from the rest of the world as an elite soccer-playing nation.

1958: West Germany reached fourth place in Sweden.

1962: The World Cup in Chile wasn't the best result as West Germany got knocked out in the quarter-finals.

1966: West Germany placed second. West Germany defeated the talented USSR in the semi-finals; Beckenbauer, one of Germany's best all-time players, scored an impressive long-distance shot. As for the final, West Germany faced another WWII foe, England. The classic showdown was in

Wembley Stadium before a packed house. Just a short time after the war, the two teams made the memorable walk onto the field, side by side, amid dignitaries and royalty in the stands. It was truly a game for the ages. England scored a questionable goal by Geoff Hurst, as the ball hit the crossbar and then it went just over the line. Some think not! There obviously wasn't any goal-line technology back then, and according to the referees, it was a goal. At the final whistle, the Germans came in second, losing 4-2.

1970: West Germany placed third. West Germany lost to Italy 4-3 in the semi-finals before earning the third-place title by defeating Uruguay.

1974: World Cup champions! West Germany hosted in 1974 and defeated the ultra-talented Dutch in the final. The white and black vs. the orange—a beautiful sight for fans watching on color TV! With this win, West Germany was now a two-time holder of the trophy. As a result of this victorious run in 1974, West Germany joined Uruguay and Italy as teams with two titles each. Incidentally, Brazil was out in front with three titles.

1978: The West Germans lost out early to Austria, and Coach Schon retired.

1982: Comeback time. West Germany placed second after losing to Italy in the final. Despite losing in the final, West Germany and France had a magnificent encounter in the semi-finals. Not only was it one of the great games of the tournament, it ranked as one of the best in World Cup history. Breitner and Littbarski matched wits with Platini and Giresse. The dramatic game—one that involved a French player being carried off on a stretcher because of a collision with goalkeeper Toni Schumacher—ended in a shootout which the Germans eventually won.

1986: West Germany—one of the favorites in the tournament— earned another second-place finish. Germany made it to the final with the help of midfield maestros Matthaus and Rummenigge. Under the guidance of Coach Beckenbauer, the Germans mounted an exciting comeback, tying the game 2-2. However, the magic of Maradona, with the help of Burruchaga and Valdano, was too much to handle, and Argentina won its second World Cup title in a sold-out Estadio Azteca!

1990: World Cup champions! The Germans won a third World Cup title! It was a rematch in the final against Argentina. On Italian ground, Brehme guided home a well-placed penalty kick in the lower-left corner for a 1-0 victory. The legendary skipper Beckenbauer became the first player and coach to win the World Cup.

With the collapse of the Berlin Wall in 1989, West Germany would be reunited with East Germany. However, as things played out, the familiar title of West Germany was used in the 1990 World Cup, and, later, the title Germany was used in the 1994 World Cup and all World Cups after. The demolition of the wall began in June of 1990 and was finished in 1992.

1994: Not a good World Cup for Germany as it took an unexpected defeat in the quarter-finals from Bulgaria and its star player Stoichkov, the Ballon D'Or winner of that year.

1998: Germany had a less than pleasing result in 1998 with a 3-0 defeat from Croatia in the quarter-finals.

2002: Germany got to the final and placed second with a 2-0 loss to Brazil. Certainly, for most countries, this was a good result. But German fans wanted more; they wanted first place!

2006: Germany lost in the semi-finals.

2010: Germany, again, lost in the semi-finals.

2014: World Cup champions! Yet again, Germany was on top of the world with a much-deserved title! Unexpectedly,

Germany—with talents like Schweinsteiger, Kroos, Özil, Müller, and Neuer—thumped host-nation Brazil 7-1 in the semi-finals and met a stern test in the final with Argentina, led by Messi. With a chest trap and a volley into the goal from Mario Götze, Germany attained a nerve-wracking 1-0 victory for its fourth World Cup championship.

2018: One to forget! Germany had one of its worst performances on record as it couldn't escape group play! A nightmare unfolded as the Germans finished last behind Sweden, Mexico, and South Korea.

Germany leads all nations with four World Cup second-place finishes (1966, 1982, 1986, 2002). And the Germans lead with four third-place finishes as well (1934, 1970, 2006, 2010).

UEFA EUROPEAN CHAMPIONSHIP

The Germans won the illustrious UEFA European Championship in 1972, 1980, and 1996.

In the 2020 Euro, which was held in 2021 due to the COVID-19 pandemic, Germany lost in the Round of 16 to England by a score of 2-0. Thomas Müller—an attacking mid who seems to play his best during World Cups and not so much during Euros—missed a one-on-one shot with the goalkeeper, just wide of the post, and overall the near miss kind of summed up Germany's 2020 Euro. The team didn't seem to be playing its best soccer.

With three previous Euro championships, Germany will certainly look to get back on track with a title in 2024. Incidentally, Germany will also host Euro 2024. In 2017, Germany won first place in the Confederations Cup held in Russia.

FACTS ABOUT THEIR COUNTRY

Germany manufactures beautiful cars—Mercedes, BMW, and Porsche—that are shipped all over the world. What's more, Germany is the original home of the world's greatest soccer gear—Adidas and Puma. Two brothers first founded Adidas, but then, after an alleged fight, one of the brothers moved across the street and started Puma! Some of the greatest players in the world have worn **Adidas**: Messi, Zidane, Platini, Beckenbauer. The same goes for **Puma**: Neymar, Maradona, Cruyff, Pelé.

Germany's population is about 83 million with a GDP of approximately $4 trillion.

Soccer is Germany's number-one sport. It's an important aspect of its culture, and Germans take pride in their many achievements. Lothar Matthaus leads German players with 150 caps; he represented his country on the field from 1980-2000. He also leads the world in World Cup appearances for a field player with 25. He has appeared in five World Cups; as of 2018, only one other field player has been in five Cups, and that would be Mexico's Rafael Marquez. Need a good goalkeeper? Germany has had plenty. The World Cup keeper of the tournament award has gone to Harald Schumacher (1986), Oliver Kahn (2002), and Manuel Neuer (2014). Not bad!

It took a long time for a European nation to win the World Cup on South American soil. Germany finally broke through in 2014.

Going into the 2022 FIFA World Cup, Germany's all-time top three scorers are:

1. Miroslav Klose (71)   3. Lukas Podolski (49)
2. Gerd Muller (68)

Germany proudly has two players at the top of the list of the best World Cup scorers ever:

1. Miroslav Klose   3. Gerd Muller (West
   (Germany, 16)*   Germany, 14)
2. Ronaldo (Brazil, 15)   4. Just Fontaine (France, 13)
                             5. Pelé (Brazil, 12)

---

* As of 2014, Klose holds the World Cup record with 16 goals. Will someone out-score him? It may take some time!

It will be hard for others to achieve such a record!

Alongside high-tech industrial cities like Kassel and Hanover, Germany also has stunning countryside in the north, including the forests around Berlin, and in the south where people take in the mountain ranges of beautiful Bavaria.

Germany, the land of fine beer! Tourists from around the world visit Germany with the intent of trying authentic German beer. A handful of exciting beers likely to be consumed by fans during World Cup action are brewed by:

- Oettinger Brauerei
- Krombacher Brauerei
- Bitburger
- Beck's Brewery

WHERE THE TEAM IS TODAY—TACTICS AND STRATEGIES

The dynamic Germans have a strong, "must see" team, yet again.

Defensively, Germany has had great one-on-one defenders. Its team shape is second to none as well. With both of these factors in place, Germany will trample its opponents. Germany's athletic defenders, who do such great work, have the added ability to open up for a good counterattack offensively, which is where Germany thrives.

Germany's formation may change. It might change during a game in transition from defense to offense, sending different players into the attack—this is done by many teams, if not all as part of the flow of a game.

Tactics and strategies: Whether in a 3-4-2-1, 4-3-3, or a 4-2-3-1 (a few formations used in the past), the current German team has been known for not living up to expectations (think, Euro 2020). Regardless, this German side exudes exceptional passing between teammates. Despite what formation is being used, sometimes the Germans get caught up in the attacking half with its opponent in a defensive shell, crowding the box. (Germany, Spain, and others often face this issue; it's called "being too good at possession, and the other team forms a human wall.") This is where Germany might face some challenges in terms of penetrating through the defense to create quality shots on goal. It's not quite as easy as it sounds. Even if the opponent is less than quality, it is, after all, a human wall of athletic guys doing everything they can to prevent quality scoring chances around the box. The two-man game is imperative in these situations as it creates chemistry between offensive players and will lead to more quality chances on goal. One alternative to improvising around the box is to just cross the ball into the box with a hope and a prayer—not good. To its credit, Germany tends not to blindly cross the ball into the box. What Germany does extremely well includes owning possession with technicians, artists, and competitors.

Germany—along with Spain, the Netherlands, and Brazil—are timeless. It's a team that seems to have a better understanding of *how the game should flow.* Call it athletic ingenuity—Germany has it. It will riddle opposition forces with a systematic display of possession as it connects passes with undeniable panache; across the board, players have deft touch coupled with a very good understanding of rhythm and timing.

Germany's effort in the 2014 World Cup, though not being their best performance recently, was still fluid. Passes linked together effortlessly and skillfully. They can dominate in possession. In part, their strength on offense is why Germany enters Qatar 2022 as one of the favorites.

HANSI FLICK—A BRIEF COACHING PORTRAIT

Before we get to the man of the hour, **Hansi Flick**, it would be unjust to ignore his overwhelmingly brilliant predecessor, Joachim Löw.

Löw is, was, and always will be a master of his craft, a World Cup champion from 2014! Yet even the great Löw was under immense pressure to achieve results. He came into the job with a great deal of experience, which helped guide his path through good times and bad. As a player, Löw suited up with teams such as SC Freiburg, VfB Stuttgart, and Eintracht Frankfurt. 1994-2004: Löw coached various club teams, including Stuttgart. 2004-2006: Löw became Germany's assistant coach under Jurgen Klinsmann. 2006: Löw took over as Germany's head coach and won the FIFA World Cup in 2014. This was Germany's first World Cup championship since 1990, when Beckenbauer was coach of West Germany—a 24-year wait!

In March of 2021, Löw said he would end his run as coach once the 2020 Euro concluded (in the summer of 2021, of course). All in all, he did so much as coach. He had vision, which he managed to make a reality with his group of talented players. Sure, there were a couple results that were less than spectacular—the 2018 World Cup and 2020 Euro—but the World Cup title in 2014 was the crowning achievement!

Though, as all good things come to an end, so, too, does the reign of Coach Löw, a true legend. He was replaced by Hansi Flick (born in 1965 in Heidelberg, West Germany). Roughly a year before World Cup 2022, Flick takes the job—no pressure there! Flick, though, comes from a place of confidence. He was, after all, a midfielder for Bayern Munich for over a hundred games (1985-90). As a coach, Flick has led Victoria Bammental, 1899 Hoffenheim, and Bayern Munich (2019-21). Previously, under Löw, he was an assistant coach for Germany from 2006-2014.

For a nation reeling from the 2-0 Euro defeat suffered to England, Flick is seen as the savior, or, if things don't go well, the scapegoat. It's tough to be a coach, especially for a team that is expected to win the World Cup. In spite of being an assistant for Germany all those years, he has had little time to figure out the lay of the land as head coach. For Flick, the quick introduction takes the form of World Cup qualifiers and the actual World Cup.

KEY PLAYERS AND THEIR CHARACTERISTICS
Timo Werner has lightning speed and a thunderous shot. He's a top-level forward who is always a threat around the box. His

awareness, vision, technique, touch, and instincts are elite, and, if that's not enough, he has a strong instinct for setting up teammates, which is a plus for forwards (who are too often accused of being selfish on the ball). Werner possesses an all-around game that is feared by opposing teams. After all, his ability to score and set up teammates at the drop of a hat is a deadly combination.

Serge Gnabry—who has club experience with Arsenal, West Bromwich Albion, Werder Bremen, Bayern Munich, and 1899 Hoffenheim—joined Germany in 2016 and has been lighting up the goal-scoring board with big numbers. As of fall 2021, he reached the 20-goal mark. Born in 1995, the 5'9" striker is on a path to greatness as he looks to make Qatar a tournament for the ages. He's high on the list as one of Germany's top guns to bring home the title.

After colossal individual success in World Cup 2010, **Thomas Müller**—synonymous now with Bayern Munich—has continued his scoring ways with 40 goals in total for Germany as of late 2021, and that number is only going to increase with time. There's a certain fluidity to his game, particularly when it comes to passing, that embodies great discernment for any situation; there's a flow generated when he distributes the ball, even for the most mundane passes. All in all, his presence—bestowed with the most brilliant German instruction a soccer star can have—creates harmony in the buildup play around the box, and, as a result, many scoring chances are afforded to both him and his teammates. As an unselfish player who gets on the score sheet often, Müller is a constant threat around goal and a nightmare for the opposition.

Joshua Kimmich—a talented midfielder and defender—brings stability and a touch of class to the lineup for Germany. He's been with Germany since 2016 and has acquired over 60 caps and counting. Don't expect many goals from Kimmich. If he scores, it's a bonus. What he brings to the games is his ability to dominate his section of the field which in turn brings calm and organization to the other positions. With club experience at RB Leipzig and Bayern Munich, as well as the German national team Player of the Year award in 2017, he's a proven commodity for the national team. Born in 1995, the 5'10" technician is in the prime of his career, and his presence will be crucial for Germany moving ahead in Qatar.

What can be said about **Manuel Neuer** that hasn't been said already? The one-time World Cup champion from 2014 and stellar performer for Bayern Munich has been regarded as one of the best keepers ever to play the game. At 6'4", he's an iron wall of gifted athletic ability and has won the Best European Goalkeeper award in 2011, 2013, 2014, 2015, and 2020. In addition, he took home the Golden Glove from the 2014 FIFA World Cup. Does he come off the line sporadically to distribute the ball (making announcers groan)? He sure does. When he does it, it seems like perhaps he's bored. Maybe even the best keepers in the world need a thrill from time to time.

Leon Goretzka—born in 1995—is a 6'2" midfielder who has over 40 caps with Germany since he debuted in 2014. He spent a great deal of time with Schalke 04 (2013-18) and made the switch to powerhouse club Bayern Munich in 2018. On route to a championship run in Qatar, Germany will depend on Goretzka for steadiness, distribution, organization, and calm for best results. He's good in the air, has a strong shot, and is versatile at center mid, defensive mid, and out wide. Along with Joshua Kimmich, Goretzka was behind an online effort "We Kick Corona" to help deal with the COVID-19 pandemic.

Kai Havertz—born in 1999 in Aachen, Germany—is 6'3" and an attacking midfielder who's good with both feet, technically sound, and solid in the air. He's very highly thought of as a player who is versatile, smart, and constantly a threat for defenses—one that can do just about whatever he wants. From 2016-20, he appeared in a little over 115 games for Bayer

Leverkusen, 36 goals to his credit. In 2020, he made a move to Chelsea and gained more fans in England. After plenty of experience with Germany's youth national teams, he debuted with the senior national side in 2018.

OVERALL PLAYER RATING

Timo Werner: 9.9

Serge Gnabry: 9.4

Thomas Müller: 9.9

Joshua Kimmich: 9.9

Manuel Neuer: 10

Leon Goretzka: 9.7

Kai Havertz: 9.5

KEY PLAYER STATS

(Total career goals for their country)

	Games Played	Goals
Timo Werner	52	22
Serge Gnabry	33	20
Thomas Müller	115	43
Joshua Kimmich	67	4
Manuel Neuer	112	0
Leon Goretzka	44	14
Kai Havertz	28	8

WHAT TO WATCH FOR ON TV

Leading up to and during European qualifiers for World Cup 2022, Germany had a number of player options: **goalkeepers** Manuel Neuer, Marc-Andre ter Stegen, and Bernd Leno; **defenders** Mats Hummels, Matthias Ginter, Antonio Rudiger, Thilo Kehrer, Niklas Sule, Lukas Klostermann, Emre Can, Marcel Halstenberg, Robin Koch, Jonathan Tah, Nico Schulz, and Robin Gosens; **midfielders** Joshua Kimmich, Kai Havertz, Leon Goretzka, Marco Reus, Jamal Musiala, Florian Neuhaus, Jonas Hofmann, Karim Adeyemi, Ilkay Gundogan, and Julian Brandt; **forwards** Timo Werner, Serge Gnabry, Thomas Müller, Leroy Sane, Kevin Volland, Luca

Waldschmidt, and Amin Younes.

Germany's road to Qatar played out in Group J in European qualifiers against Romania, North Macedonia, Iceland, Armenia, and Liechtenstein. It was smooth sailing. On September 5, 2021, Germany beat Armenia 6-0; on November 11, 2021, Germany defeated Liechtenstein 9-0!

The 4-2-3-1—likely the German approach—is beneficial for a number of reasons. The first of which is four defenders. This gives a solid defensive stance which is pertinent. (Three defenders isn't standing on firm ground defensively. Four defenders have depth and good shape to trap attacking players, be it in the form of individual dribblers or passing combinations from opposition forces.)

Offensively, four defenders allow for more options in possession; the majority of touches in a game go to defenders. The better shape a defense has to string passes together is paramount. So, aligning four defenders across the field is a better option than three.

The German defense has always been strong, particularly when combined with the fluid attack and frequent possession. The German national team, much more than most other nations, has seized on this little secret for generations; its understanding, decade after decade, of how defense is the foundation of offense is partly why Germany has separated itself as a world leader in soccer.

As Germany navigates through the forest of competition in Qatar, you will see much of the same from the likes of Mats Hummels, Matthias Ginter, Antonio Rudiger, Thilo Kehrer, and Niklas Sule on defense. As things flow together, there will be a give and take between defenders and the frontline that will be something to watch.

As a team coming off a disappointing 2020 Euro, Germany still has a group of leading players. Combined with past successes of the German teams of yesteryear, Germany is a favorite for a reason.

Neuer—always ready to hop off his line preemptively—

should be a force in goal, and up top will be the options of Werner, Gnabry, Müller, Kimmich, Goretzka, Sane, and Havertz. Germans aren't the flashiest dribblers in the world, but don't be fooled as great German teams have always had highly effective ball dribblers (Bernd Schneider and Lothar Matthäus). As of 2022, Kavertz, Werner, and Müller will help lead the attack with precise passing that creates effective dribbling opportunities in and around the box. Passing and dribbling go hand in hand. The use of both allows for Germany to penetrate defenses.

What's more, on top of stringent defense, good shape, possession-oriented passing, and effective dribbling, Germany unleashes a well-orchestrated counterattack. If the counter isn't on, the Germans will begin passing the ball across the field with exceptional organization. Waiting and searching for a moment to strike is practically a German calling card. Nothing screams "four World Cup championships" like a patient team, and this team is patient and confident. At this point, other nations should be nervous.

Every move Germany makes is accentuated by superior technique and a high soccer IQ. Plain and simple, this leads to success. Furthermore, Germans have a knack to get at least one goal. With strong shots around the box, combined with a gallery's worth of fine-tuned tenacity and a strong will to win each moment, Germany will hold their status as a leader in world soccer.

As four-time World Cup champions, Germany desperately wants to make history with a fifth. As everyone knows, Germany can take any team in the world. The only thing standing in Germany's way might be Germany. Qatar 2022 is a special opportunity for a comeback year. As such, Germany wants to make it a special one.

SPAIN
World Cup titles: 1 (2010)
Overall Team Rating: 9.9

A BRIEF TEAM HISTORY
Prior to the 2010 World Cup in South Africa, Spain's long-travelled road was full of disappointment.

Let's take a glance at Spain's World Cup efforts:

1930: Spain didn't compete.

1934: Spain was defeated in the quarter-finals.

1938: Spain did not play.

1950: Spain took fourth place.

1954: Spain didn't qualify.

1958: Spain didn't qualify; major let down.

1962: Spain was eliminated in group play.

1966: Yet again, Spain was eliminated in group play.

1970: Spain didn't qualify.

1974: More disappointment as Spain didn't qualify.

1978: Spain finally arrived but was knocked out in the group stage.

1982: As host, Spain was eliminated in the second group stage.

1986: Spain finally made it to the quarter-finals.

1990: Spain was knocked out in the Round of 16.

1994: Spain earned its way into the quarter-finals again.

1998: Spain couldn't escape its group.

2002: Spain was sent packing in the quarter-finals.

2006: Spain, despite having a talented team, couldn't escape the group stage. Yet something was in motion. From 2008-12, things changed big time.

2010: World Cup champions! Spain finally won the World Cup. Outside of an early loss to Switzerland, Spain—led by Xavi, Iniesta, and Puyol—seemed unstoppable. Could anyone have guessed that a smaller group of players, mainly from Barcelona, that relied on "over-possession" would win the FIFA World Cup with such clarity?

Spain didn't just win the 2010 World Cup, it accomplished the unthinkable, winning the 2008 Euro, 2010 World Cup, and the 2012 Euro! The Triple was achieved by a group of talent referred to as the "Golden Generation." A few of the core players included Xavi, Iniesta, Sergio Busquets, Puyol, Ramos, Alonso, Pedro, Silva, and Villa. It was a remarkable run similar to the back-to-back three-peats by the Chicago Bulls, Ussain Bolt's three-for-three 100-meter golds, and the medal tally of Michael Phelps. A lot of Spain's success was due to its Tiki-Taka style whereby skillful defenders knew how to incorporate everything for the midfielders to be able to incorporate everything. And what exactly does "incorporate everything" mean? Short passes done with a vibrant frequency—that was and is the essence of Tiki-Taka.*

2014: Spain was slowing down as it didn't escape its group with such elite teams as the Netherlands, Chile, and Australia. Spain's shocking departure was felt around the world.

2018: Spain lost in the Round of 16 to Russia, the host nation.

UEFA EUROPEAN CHAMPIONSHIP

Spain won the European Championship in 1964, 2008, and 2012. In 1964, Spain won the championship on home turf when it defeated the powerful USSR with goals from Pereda and Marcelino. Then, more than 40 years had passed, yet Spain couldn't capture a major trophy! Finally, in 2008, Spain captured the European Championship for the second time as it took down Germany in the final. In 2012, Spain repeated as European champions with a convincing victory over Italy in the final.

---

* The "two-man game" is essential for this style of play to work. The "two-man game" occurs when one player passes to a teammate and the ball is passed right back. This occurs often in basketball, and it creates chemistry between players, and, perhaps most important, it makes possession a lot easier throughout the duration of a game (especially around the opponent's box).

FACTS ABOUT THEIR COUNTRY

Spain—a Western European oasis of scenic views, history, architecture, cathedrals, backpackers, music, fine cuisine, and exquisite wine—has around 47 million people and an estimated GDP of $1.4 trillion.

Very often Spaniards like to kickstart the morning with a cup of coffee, and one shouldn't be surprised when the selection is a cafe con leche, which contains half-coffee and half-milk, or a cortado, which contains a shot of espresso with a little milk.

Whether it's breakfast, lunch, or dinner, one thing is certain: Spaniards look forward to soccer. The top three scorers for Spain's national team are:

1. David Villa (59)
2. Raul (44)
3. Fernando Torres (38)

Estrella Galicia is a Spanish beer sure to be enjoyed by fans watching World Cup action—and maybe even the most-spilled beer as the fans celebrate the goals!

WHERE THE TEAM IS TODAY—TACTICS AND STRATEGIES

The perfection-oriented Spanish excel with technically accurate passing and a form of Tiki-Taka one might call Tiki-Taka Light. Heavy on short passing, Spain will out-possess an opponent with complete authority, similar to Iceman (Val Kilmer) from *Top Gun*. What happens is Spain stays on you until you make a mistake! Of course, this was how Goose (Anthony Edwards) described Iceman's flying to Maverick (Tom Cruise), though it's an apropos description of the way Spain decimates opponents with over-possession. Cool, calm, collected, and one step ahead.

While Spain often has the majority of possession, opponents typically resort to a human wall situated around the box. This can get tricky for Spain—or any team for that matter—when it comes to scoring goals as a human wall is tough to penetrate. As I've predicted in the past, Spain will have difficulty moving forward in the goal-scoring department because the method of Tiki-Taka really takes a special group—with a *will* to score—to produce an *abundance* of goals. The Golden Generation possessed this quality, yet it's difficult to ask current—and future—players to get the same results.

Tactics and strategies: Spain will quite likely trap opponents with a 4-3-3 formation. Spain has an outstanding group of pass-minded technical gurus such as Busquets, Pedri, Koke, and Alba, yet there's one issue: finishing. Even though Spain will be Spain, a high-quality team of possession-oriented geniuses, it's going to have a hard time in big tournaments for the next 10 to 20 years, Qatar included.

LUIS ENRIQUE—A BRIEF COACHING PORTRAIT

Luis Enrique, a former attacking midfielder, enjoyed a club career with Sporting Gijon, Real Madrid, and Barcelona. He also represented Spain from 1991-2002 with a little over 60 caps. In 2018, Enrique planted himself on the sideline as Spain's head coach with a fashion sense—jeans, an old belt, and polo shirts—better suited for a casual walk around cafes in Barcelona than an official game; nonetheless, his soccer sense is second to none and he has every intention to make Spain world champions yet again. His task will be to keep the momentum going strong; short passing combinations, possession worth its weight in gold, and a tight defense will be front and center. Goals will be an issue. If Enrique can keep the troops focused, then good things should happen. As the coach of an elite program, his shoulders will be weighed down by expectations. Without a championship in this tournament, it might be curtains for Enrique as Spain's coach.

KEY PLAYERS AND THEIR CHARACTERISTICS

Koke—born in 1992 in Madrid—provides veteran leadership in midfield, as the Atletico Madrid standout first played for Spain in 2013. Not a big scorer for the national team, Koke provides much needed confidence on the ball with regard to possession. Spain's former midfield maestro, Xavi, has a high regard for Koke as a passer and one of the guiding forces of the Spanish national team.

Morata—who's kept good company with Real Madrid, Juventus, Chelsea, and Atletico Madrid—will hopefully be a leading force as a forward. Depending on who you ask, he's either 1) somebody who can score one day, or 2) he's an unsteady talent who is lost the next day. (Is there a grey area between the two? Perhaps.) Is he a dribbling phenom? No. Is he a brilliant passer? Not really. Is he a finisher? That's the hope. He's a technically sound, forward who links up the play and has a presence to score similar to Robert Lewandowski. Will he produce goals like Lewandowski? That remains to be seen.

Sergio Busquets—born in 1988—is a holdover from the Golden Generation. Now a veteran, the lanky Barcelona midfielder is known for connecting passes that make offensive play flow. He's not a big scorer. Rather, he's all about connectivity with passes between teammates, which he does very well; he'll pass the ball softly and early. One drawback is his propensity to not score though Spain feels secure with his veteran leadership.

Pedri—born in 2002—is an up-and-coming Spanish midfielder to keep an eye on. In 2020, he joined Barcelona and later suited up with Spain's senior side in 2021 as he competed in the 2020 Euro. Some say he's best suited in central midfield where he can operate between the lines. Keep an eye out for Pedri's versatility in midfield, outstanding technique, dribbling ability, keen sense of passing, and the ability to make teammates look good. For all intents and purposes, he should be a player of the future for Spain.

Ferran Torres is an attacking player replete with speed, skill, technique, scoring ability, aerial aptitude, and confidence that is more often than not found on the right wing. A present-day version of a winger, Torres is comfortable on the inside of the pitch as well, as he can create danger by cutting into the middle. Born in 2000, the 6'0" forward made a move from Valencia to Manchester City in 2020. He only joined Spain's senior team in 2020, and by fall of 2021, he had 22 caps and 12 goals—quite remarkable!

OVERALL PLAYER RATING

Koke: 9.7   Pedri: 9.7

Morata: 8.9   Ferran Torres: 9.7

Sergio Busquets: 9.2

KEY PLAYER STATS
(Total career goals for their country)

	Games Played	Goals
Koke	65	0
Morata	55	26
Sergio Busquets	136	2
Pedri	12	0
Ferran Torres	27	13

WHAT TO WATCH FOR ON TV
As La Furia Roja approached World Cup 2022, the options were virtually endless, wherein Spain's a country that could theoretically field three or so national teams. A few players included **goalkeepers** David de Gea and Unai Simon; **defenders** Jordi Alba, Cesar Azpilicueta, Pau Torres, Inigo Martinez, Eric Garcia, Sergio Reguilon, Marcos Alonso, Aymeric Laporte, Jose Gaya, Raul Albiol, and Sergio Ramos; **midfielders** Sergio Busquets, Koke, Pedri, Gavi, Jesus Navas, Rodri, Sergi Roberto, Pablo Fornals, Mikel Merino, Marcos Llorente, Thiago Alcantara, Fabian Ruiz, Dani Olmo, Carlos Soler, Sergio Canales, and Marco Asensio; **forwards** Ferran Torres, Rodrigo, Alvaro Morata, Bryan Gil, Yeremi Pino, Mikel Oyarzabal, Pablo Sarabia, Gerard Moreno, Abel Ruiz, Adama Traore, and Ansu Fati.

Spain's road to Qatar took shape in Group B in European qualifiers against Sweden, Greece, Kosovo, and Georgia. Notwithstanding a little resistance from Sweden, Spain comfortably led the way.

Now in Qatar, Spain is ready to capture yet another title. The players are certainly suited for the task!

Perhaps after viewing such a list of talent, it's easy to see how difficult it actually is to be head coach for a national team! It's often too easy to see a lineup just before kickoff and think: *Yeah, that's how it should be!* Well, a lot of thought went into it. Rest assured, coaches agonize over who should be on the final roster.

Spain has great individual talent, yet it's a team that follows a philosophy—team passing. Players aren't overtly flashy, so don't expect to see Denilson showboating around. When it comes to Spain, as usual, team passing is more important than any one player. All of Spain's players need to touch the ball for the unit to succeed.

Short passing will be the name of the game, as Koke, Pedri, Busquets, and company move the ball through numerous channels in the fashion of Tiki-Taka. This is, after all, Spain's calling card. (Within the Tiki-Taka approach, often two players will exchange multiple passes, which improves possession and chemistry within the passing structure, which, over the course of a 90-minute game, wears down the resolve of the opposing team. It often creates better scoring opportunities. This is where its effectiveness gets tricky. The Golden Generation had a unique understanding of Tiki-Taka, which makes them a tough group to live up to.)

For Spain's style, one has to step back in time and recognize the heavy influence of the Dutch legend Johan Cruyff. Cruyff brought his passing prowess to Barcelona, where he played and coached, and the style continued to progress at Barca under coaches Louis van Gaal and Frank Rijkaard. In turn, this Dutch wisdom trickled over to the Spanish national team; it was later adopted by Spanish coaches throughout the years, including

Vicente del Bosque, Spain's coach from 2008-16.

Koke, Pedri, and Busquets are carrying the weight of Spanish soccer history forward with grace and style. In Qatar 2022, Spain will display, arguably, the best passing in the tournament. Will goals accompany this journey? That's the million-dollar question.

ENGLAND
World Cup titles: 1 (1966)
Overall Team Rating: 9.7

A BRIEF TEAM HISTORY
Let's take a glance at England's World Cup history. As you'll see, since the 1966 championship, it's been a tough ride!

1930: England declined to participate.

1934: England declined to participate, yet again. The World Cup was hosted by Italy, under the watchful eye of Mussolini, who, incidentally, was eventually accused of being influential in rigging the tournament for the Italians. Possibly England felt some trepidation.

1938: England declined to participate, yet again! France hosted this year. Still the English decided to stay home.

1950: England took eighth overall. Brazil hosted the first post-WWII World Cup. England finally participated, but it wasn't the best result as the inventors of the sport eventually placed eighth overall. Along the way, England took a humiliating 1-0 defeat from the United States.

1954: England lost in the elimination phase to Uruguay by 4-2 at the St. Jakob Stadium in Basel, Switzerland.

1958: England earned three consecutive ties which led to a play-off loss against the USSR, eliminating England.

1962: A loss in the quarter-finals to Brazil sent England packing. Initially, England finished second in its group which included Bulgaria, Argentina, and Hungary with a win, loss, and a draw. There were important goals from Flowers, Charlton, and Greaves. Yet, even with a goal from Hitchens, England didn't have enough to hold off a 3-1 defeat from Brazil in the quarters.

1966: World Cup champions! To date, this was England's first and only World Cup title. And what a year it was! As host nation, England won its group with two wins over Mexico and France and a draw against Uruguay. England stepped around Argentina 1-0 in the quarter-finals. Then it took down Portugal 2-1 in the semis. In the much-anticipated final, the Three Lions defeated mega-rival West Germany by 4-2.
England certainly had an advantage as all its matches took place in Wembley Stadium. England's triumph was epic. In the post-1966 era, don't ask. England has almost inexplicably come up short in World Cups, particularly in 1986 with "the hand of God" from Maradona and 2010 with the "ball crossing the line" against Germany. It's been a tough road to say the least.

1970: England lost in the quarter-finals by 3-2 to West Germany. After starting out with a 2-0 lead, with goals from Mullery and Peters, England just couldn't hold off a fierce German comeback.

1974: England failed to qualify.

1978: England failed to qualify, yet again!

1982: After three wins in group play against France, Czechoslovakia, and Kuwait, England advanced in a tournament based on round-robin play, wherein England drew 0-0 with West Germany followed by another 0-0 tie with Spain, which sent West Germany to the next round.

1986: England lost in the quarter-finals to Argentina. After a win, draw, and a loss in a group with Morocco, Poland, and Portugal, England defeated Paraguay 3-0 in the second round with goals from Lineker and Beardsley. Up next was the famous loss to Argentina. In front of over 100,000 people,

Maradona leaped into the air and quickly administered "the hand of God" that pushed the ball past Shilton for a goal. Maradona followed this up with his next act that has amounted to, arguably, the greatest single goal in World Cup history as he gallantly dribbled half the field past multiple English defenders and Shilton for the eventual game-winner. Incidentally, Lineker headed in the last goal off a cross from Barnes. That was it. England was eliminated.

1990: England placed fourth overall. Despite not winning the whole thing, this was a big result for England. In group play, England had a win and two draws against Ireland, Holland, and Egypt, with goals from Lineker and Wright. In the second round, David Platt scored the winner against Belgium.

This set up an interesting contest with Cameroon in the quarter-finals. Cameroon had shocked the world with an opening-game victory over defending champs Argentina. In arguably the most exciting game of the tournament, England got out to a 1-0 lead from Platt. Then Cameroon mounted an inspirational comeback and surged ahead 2-1 with goals from Kunde and Ekeke; Cameroonian legend Roger Milla was instrumental as a sub. Cameroon was on the verge of becoming the first African team to make the semis of a World Cup. However, two late penalties from Lineker gave England the victory.

England entered the semis against the heavily favored West Germans. The game concluded as a draw and went to penalty kicks. Lineker, Beardsley, and Platt scored the first three. Subsequently there were two misses from Pearce and Waddle, which allowed the Germans to win after Brehme, Matthaus, Riedle, and Thon each scored.

1994: England failed to qualify. To add insult to injury, a year earlier, in 1993, England lost to the United States by a startling score of 2-0 in the US Cup held at Foxborough

Stadium in Boston, the sight of the Boston Tea Party of 1773. It seems England was caught off-guard, yet again.

1998: England lost in the Round of 16 to Argentina. The Three Lions were stacked with talent, including Michael Owen (who would eventually win the Ballon d'Or in 2001), Alan Shearer, David Beckham, Paul Ince, Le Saux, and Paul Scholes. In the group stage, England had wins over Colombia and Tunisia, along with a loss to Romania. Thereafter, England encountered rival Argentina that featured Ortega and Veron. It was an epic game with an impressive goal from Owen as he showcased explosive speed to put himself in a position to chip a line drive past the keeper. It wasn't enough as England lost in a penalty shootout.

2002: Out in the quarter-finals with a loss to Brazil. England's 2002 group consisted of Sweden, Argentina, and Nigeria. The Three Lions managed to narrowly escape with a win and two draws. England defeated Denmark in the second round. This led to a devastating quarter-finals loss to the eventual champions that year, Brazil. With Beckham and others, England played well but was sent packing by the samba beat of Ronaldo, Ronaldinho, Rivaldo, Roberto Carlos, and Cafu.

2006: England lost in the quarter-finals to Portugal. In a group with Sweden, Paraguay, and Trinidad and Tobago, England led the way with two wins and a draw. England had a stacked squad that included Beckham, Gerrard, Lampard, and Rooney. In the second round, England defeated Ecuador with a goal from Beckham. This led to a loss in the quarter-finals to Portugal whose roster boasted that of Luis Figo and Cristiano Ronaldo. The match ended up in penalties; misses came from Lampard, Gerrard, and Carragher. The only made penalty came off the foot of Hargreaves.

2010: England lost in the Round of 16 to Germany. England started out the tournament with a group match against the United States, with reminders of the 1950 World Cup defeat everywhere. England scored first with Gerrard. Then a bizarre shot trickled in off the foot of Dempsey, an innocent-looking shot. It came from outside the box. As the ball pathetically rolled toward keeper Robert Green, half the population of the British Isles could've checked email as the shot rolled so slowly. Next was part of the unavoidable saga English fans have endured for so long: The ball went off the goalkeeper's gloves and over the line for a goal.

England tied the United States and Algeria and defeated Slovenia. With this, England graduated from its group (which, incidentally, the United States won).

Right out of the gate, England met archrival Germany in the Round of 16. Admittedly, England had played robotically in previous games, and its star forward Rooney had been surprisingly idle. Unfortunately for English fans, Germany went ahead by two goals in the first half. Then Upson got a goal, and things were turning in England's favor. Something clicked; you could feel the momentum changing. Lo and behold, everything spun in England's favor as Lampard's excellent game-tying goal hit the crossbar and went over the line…yet it was called back! The referees didn't see in real-time what instant replay showed to be a clear and decisive goal. The game would've been tied going into halftime and who knows what would've happened from there. Subsequently Germany jumped ahead and won by a score of 4-1. England's misfortune was Germany's gain.

This 2010 English side was quite good and the second-round loss to Germany was a tough reminder as to how tricky the World Cup can be. There's hope one second and absolute despair the next. As always, English fans were optimistic with respect to the next tournament. If English fans have to wait 36 years for another title, so be it! At that point, two titles would be better than one!

2014: England finished dead last in its group. Morale was low as the Three Lions got two losses and a draw in its group with Italy, Uruguay, and Costa Rica. By the looks of it, maybe English fans will have to wait 54 years for a second and third title.

2018: England placed fourth overall. In Group G with Belgium, Tunisia, and Panama, England managed to place second, earning a spot in the coveted Round of 16. With Harry Kane leading the way, England got past Colombia. Then in the quarter-finals, England stepped past Sweden by 2-0. In the semis, the Three Lions didn't have enough to overcome Croatia.

It was a great comeback. It wasn't a first-place trophy, yet England reminded naysayers how good it is on the pitch. Many feel that momentum is leaning its way—that the 21st century is an opportunity for England to climb to the top yet again.

UEFA EUROPEAN CHAMPIONSHIP

With the exception of the 2020 Euro in which England placed second overall, the European Championship experience has been a major disappointment for the Three Lions.

Prior to 2020, England made zero appearances in the Euro final. From 1960 on, the Championship was won by the following teams: the Soviet Union, Spain, Italy, West Germany, Czechoslovakia, West Germany, France, Netherlands, Denmark, Germany, France, Greece, Spain, Spain, Portugal, and Italy.

Past European Championships and World Cups have proved disappointing for England, but, each year, England is full of hope and a roster of world-class talent. As for the second-place finish in the 2020 Euro (which technically was played in 2021, just before the 2022 World Cup), there was a strong wave of momentum building in the England camp, a clear warning sign for all competition!

FACTS ABOUT THEIR COUNTRY

The modern game of soccer as we know it today is widely believed to have begun in England in the mid-1800s. It came together as an offshoot of rudimentary forms of rugby. Initially, before rules were officially outlined with the formation of the Football Association in 1863, local villages would play a rather violent form of the game; on more than one occasion it was banned. However, it gained momentum. Eventually schoolboys were encouraged to play it as a productive outlet. It evolved and become the beautiful game beloved throughout the world.

Today, England has a population of around 56 million. England's GVA is around £1.9 trillion. For many, soccer is the sport. In particular, England's national team—also known as the Three Lions—is of paramount concern. There's a long list of great players who have worn an England jersey—Jimmy Greaves, Bobby Moore, Bryan Robson, Paul Gascoigne, Alan Shearer, David Beckham, Michael Owen, and Steven Gerrard—but only three stand on top the mountain of elite scorers. The top three scorers for England's national team are:

1. Wayne Rooney (53)   3. Bobby Charlton (49)
2. Harry Kane (50)*

English beers are plentiful. Some of which include Late Knights Worm Catcher, Harvey's Blue Label, and Fuller's London Porter. These beers (and many others) will be ready to go for World Cup action as fans watch with intrigue as Southgate and company look to make a few records of their own.

---

*   Still active, and this number will likely increase.

WHERE THE TEAM IS TODAY—TACTICS AND STRATEGIES

As of the 2020 UEFA European Championship, England was a possession-oriented dynamo. For the past 10 to 15 years, England has opted for more of a short-passing approach. Gareth Southgate has coached the squad with an eye for sharp, precision passing: England 3.0.

Diego Maradona—who foiled Shilton's dreams of World Cup glory in 1986—pointed out that England players tackle hard but with honor. In other words, you shouldn't expect cheap shots from anyone in Southgate's lineup. It's a true virtue of the players: They compete fiercely yet with sportsmanship.

For years, the English approach to soccer has been to possess the ball with purpose on the field, attacking down the line. Under Southgate, some of this has changed. Instead, this England team is likely to adopt an approach more like that of Spain. However, don't expect a full Tiki-Taka, though England's modern look is certainly a change of pace. **Tactics and strategies:** This 2022 team, which will likely be in a 3-4-2-1 or perhaps a 4-4-2 formation, is a short-passes group that may in fact use possession with purpose to appease fans who want action. But possession as a direct strategy is very much at the forefront. Of course, when possible, England unleashes a formidable counterattack that can catch any team off-guard.

GARETH SOUTHGATE—A BRIEF COACHING PORTRAIT

In 2016, **Gareth Southgate** signed to coach England, and since then he's steered the ship about as well as one could've hoped for minus an actual championship in the 2018 World Cup and 2020 Euro. Just as soon as England had a satisfactory run in the 2018 World Cup (taking fourth overall after narrowly losing to Croatia in the semis), it followed that up with an exemplary second-place finish in the 2020 Euro, barely losing to Italy in the final. Most worldwide would agree that Southgate has done well, and one could point to his highly technical approach that encompasses an appreciation of many athletic disciplines. On a visit to the United States a few years back, he watched an American football game and took notes on coaching strategies he might be able to use.

Born in 1970, Southgate started his professional playing career with Crystal Palace in 1988, then landed with Aston Villa, and eventually wound things up with Middlesbrough, a journey that ended in 2006. In addition, he was an experienced member of England's national team (1995-2004), with 57 appearances as a defender and midfielder. Perhaps best known as the only player to miss a penalty kick against Germany in the semis of the 1996 Euro in Wembley of all places, Southgate is making up for a missed shot with perseverance and resolve.

Currently England's prospects are looking good. Southgate has put together a stellar group. Southgate and the Three Lions are prepared to mount an attack in Qatar. Millions in England, with fans scattered around the world, eagerly await!

KEY PLAYERS AND THEIR CHARACTERISTICS

Harry Kane, forward extraordinaire, is captain of the team with the weight of England's hopes and dreams on his shoulders. As they say, 'Football can be fickle at the top.' On August 15, 2021, the opening line of Harry Kane's *Wikipedia* page read, quote, "Harry Edward Kane MBE (born 28 July 1993) is an English professional crybaby who sits in his room throwing a tantrum, to avoid playing for Premier League club Tottenham Hotspur and captains the England national team."[6] End quote. Minutes later, at second glance, the less than complimentary opening line was edited to something less assumptive that does not violate journalistic objectivity. While this description may have changed quickly, Kane's role in the spotlight hasn't. Whether he scores or not will be of endless discussion and critique as the 2022 World Cup progresses. As forwards go, Kane is very fascinating. He's not noticeably quick or fast, yet he has presence. He positions himself well as a link-up player and holds off opposition defenders effectively with his body. In addition, his scoring sense is world-class. Kane is simply a gamer and ready to take on the world's best in Qatar. Keep an eye on Kane as one of the elite forwards in the tournament.

Raheem Sterling is quick, shifty, and a nightmare for opponents around the box. With multiple speeds in his arsenal of quickness, Sterling can dart past defenders with ease, creating many scoring chances for both teammates and himself. In the 2020 Euro, Sterling was a star as he placed numerous balls in the net that helped England earn a second-place overall finish.

Jack Grealish—who suited up with Manchester City in 2021—has turned into a fan favorite for England due to his tenacious work effort, high skill level, and ability to make things happen. When Grealish is on the field, there's a sense that something is about to break wide open. Do some critics think he dives too much? Perhaps. However, the dynamic attacking midfielder has a big future ahead of himself and he's hoping to deliver in Qatar.

Harry McGuire is a well-traveled central defender having played with Sheffield United, Hull City, Wigan Athletic, Leicester City, and Manchester United. Since 2017, McGuire has suited up with England and now has the responsibility of guiding his nation through Qatar with his prowess in the air as the 6'4" defender will try to stop each and every attack coming his way.

Kyle Walker—born in 1990—is blazing fast. As an experienced outside defender, he'll be expected to shut down every attack coming down his side of the field. Few can get past him, and fewer still can avoid his recovery speed. In essence, should opposing teams muster up a counterattack or two, Walker will be front and center to put a lid on it fast. His résumé includes Tottenham Hotspurs and Manchester City. A veteran with the England national team, Walker joined in 2011 and has gone over 60 caps. Perhaps this will be his last hurrah at a World Cup, and perhaps with his contributions it will be as a world champion.

OVERALL PLAYER RATING

Harry Kane: 9.8   Harry McGuire: 9

Raheem Sterling: 9.3   Kyle Walker: 9.6

Jack Grealish: 9.6

KEY PLAYER STATS

(Total career goals for their country)

	Games Played	Goals
Harry Kane	72	50
Raheem Sterling	76	19
Jack Grealish	23	1
Harry McGuire	45	7
Kyle Walker	67	0

WHAT TO WATCH FOR ON TV

The England players to watch this World Cup include **goalkeepers** Jordan Pickford, Sam Johnstone, and Nick Pope; **defenders** Kyle Walker, Luke Shaw, John Stones, Tyrone Mings, Kieran Trippier, Conor Coady, Fikayo Tomori, Ben Chilwell, Reece James, Trent Alexander-Arnold, Eric Dier, Michael Keane, Joe Gomez, and last but not least, Harry Maguire; **midfielders** Phil Foden, Declan Rice, Mason Mount, Jordan Henderson, James Ward-Prowse, Jesse Lingard, Kalvin Phillips, Jude Bellingham, and Harry Winks; **forwards** Harry Kane, Raheem Sterling, Marcus Rashford, Jadon Sancho, Tammy Abraham, Ollie Watkins, Bukayo Saka, Dominic Calvert-Lewin, and Jack Grealish.

On route to Qatar, England was in Group I in European qualifiers, alongside Poland, Albania, Hungary, Andorra, and San Marino.

England—despite only winning the Cup once a gazillion years ago—is perhaps the most interesting team to watch every four years for many reasons, but the one reason that always stands out is the hope that this could be the year! England possesses world-class talent (most of whom gather crucial experience from the ultra-powerful Premier League). Players hone their natural abilities with the highest level of training available. England's fans are passionate and dedicated. The England team has so much going for it, so every year is thought to be the year.

Yet, things tend to unravel during the World Cup competition. Even Sherlock Holmes would be puzzled as to why England fails in every World Cup competition. The mystery of England's lack of championships from World Cups stumps people around the world. England fans certainly have had a lot to ponder over the years. As a result, some may prefer to lean on tangible "reasons" be they an injury, bad chemistry on the field, a problem with the referee, a cheat, or flat-out bad luck. Keegan was injured; Maradona used his hand; Lampard's shot crossed the line!

In Qatar, England intends to alter its course. Under the guidance of Coach Southgate, England has a formidable lineup with Harry Kane, Raheem Sterling, Jack Grealish, and Harry McGuire. Also in the mix are Kyle Walker (a devastatingly fast outside defender), Kieran Trippier (a well-regarded, experienced defender), John Stones (a steady defender with many caps under his belt), Luke Shaw (an adept midfielder and defender on the wing), Jordan Henderson (a team leader and midfielder with experience from Liverpool), Jadon Sancho (a skillful, crafty, and dangerous attacking mid), and Marcus Rashford (a fast, experienced, and dangerous forward). With the talented Jordan Pickford in net, England will be a force to reckon with.

Watch for many short passes as England has centered its approach on a thoughtful buildup in the attack while relying on relentless defense around its own box. In transition, England's counterattack is forceful with speed and crisp passes. All in all, England poses a dangerous combination with counters, possession passing, and firm defense. Add to this the invisible yet ever-present momentum. With its recent second-place finish at the 2020 Euro, the Three Lions are favorites in Qatar. Could this be the year? It's certainly shaping up that way.

FRANCE

World Cup titles: 2 (1998, 2018)
Overall Team Rating: 9.7

A BRIEF TEAM HISTORY

Let's take a quick glance at France's World Cup record:

1930: In this, the opening World Cup, France didn't get past the group stage.

1934: France lost in the opening round.

1938: France made the quarter-finals.

1950: Didn't compete.

1954: France didn't get out of its group.

1958: France took third overall, much better!

1962: France didn't make it through qualifications.

1966: France didn't get out of its group.

1970: France didn't make it through qualifications.

1974: France, yet again, didn't make it through qualifications.

1978: In Argentina, France didn't get out of its group.

1982: France got fourth overall. With Platini (who, perhaps, is the best player in France's history), Giresse, Tigana, and Rochteau, France gracefully advanced its way to the semis before dramatically losing in penalty kicks to West Germany.

1986: France placed third overall.

France—the Euro 1984 champions—entered the World Cup in Mexico with confidence. Its 1986 lineup was similar to that of 82, and the French showcased brilliant soccer that defeated the previous World Cup champs, Italy, in the second round. This led to a classic quarter-final showdown with a stacked Brazilian side. From the attack of Josimar, Junior, Muller, and Careca, Brazil went ahead 1-0 with a definitive goal from Careca that nearly broke the net in two. Socrates and Brazil were after more goals; perhaps instead of following the samba beat, Brazil should have tightened up possession of the ball for a victory. From a blunder in front of the Brazilian net and a possible foul on the goalkeeper that was overlooked, Platini equalized, tapping the ball in at the far post. French keeper, Joel Bats, saved a crucial penalty kick off the foot of substitute Zico, which kept France in the game. Finally, in a penalty shootout (which happened to be on his birthday), the sure-footed Platini missed his shot. Nonetheless, France won the shootout and earned a place in the semi-finals against West Germany. France, just inches away from the elusive final, put in a good effort but West Germany prevailed. Eventually, France defeated Belgium in the consolation match to earn a third-place finish.

1990: France didn't qualify.

1994: France didn't qualify, yet again!

1998: World Cup champions! As host nation, France toppled Brazil in the final 3-0 with help from team leaders Zidane and Deschamps.

2002: France couldn't escape its group! From world champs to utter despair! What a quick turnaround!

2006: France placed second overall. When discussing, or debating, the best French player of all time, two camps are formed: Platini and Zidane. For one last go-around, Zidane—Zizou—led the French attack with the electric Ribery and Henry, not to mention a stellar defense behind them. In the final match, France and Italy squared off in a classic midfield battle that ended 1-1. A true steward of drama, Zidane was ejected for headbutting Italian defender Materazzi in the chest. (Allegedly, it was over words regarding Zidane's sister.) Unfortunately for France, Italy won in a shootout.

2010: France couldn't escape its group. An escapade fraught with disaster. The French team suffered inner turmoil in 2010 as players united behind a teammate that was sent home after words with a coach. A protest ensued as the team declined to practice. A disgusted coach threw his whistle to the ground. Tempers flared. Patrice Evra led the players as they retreated to a bus and shut the doors. Eventually, in true French form, the players delivered a letter to the head coach, and they asked him to read it out loud. Bottom line: Things were not going well for France! Hence an early exit from the tournament. This was the pinnacle, the World Cup; national pride was on the line; the whole world was watching; all the training, practice, commitment, money, investment, media, sponsorship, passion, and time that went into this effort. To have it end so abruptly and in such disappointing fashion, what was the point? A cynical headline could have read: 'We might have fallen flat on the field but score one for democracy!'

2014: France didn't make it past the quarter-finals.

2018: World Cup champions! Indeed, the French are defending champions in Qatar! The FIFA World Cup title from 2018 was well deserved as France convincingly dismantled Croatia in the final match. On the way, France initially landed first in its group that included Denmark, Peru, and Australia. In the Round of 16, Les Bleus snuck past Portugal 2-1. For the quarter-finals, Varane and Griezmann gave France a 2-0 win over Uruguay. Then a 1-0 victory over Belgium sent France into the final whereby a 4-2 win over Croatia was enough to earn a second World Cup championship.

With Griezmann and Mbappé leading the way, offense was flying high. France is expected to do big things in Qatar 2022, and, who knows, maybe a repeat title for number three.

UEFA EUROPEAN CHAMPIONSHIP
In 1984 and 2000, France won the European Championship. Instrumental in 84 was Platini, star of the show, and Zidane was a guiding force at the turn of the century. At the 2016 Euro, which France hosted, the team came so close to winning a third but fell short in the final against Portugal.

FACTS ABOUT THEIR COUNTRY
France boasts some of the best wine and cuisine in the world. For years, France has been a unique attraction for tourists. It's a country known widely for the Lascaux cave paintings, the Carnac stones, democracy, Joan of Arc, Napoleon, Descarte, Voltaire, Cezanne, Monet, Matisse, Debussy, the Tour de France, the Roland-Garros French Open, fine clothing such as Lacoste (founded in 1933), Cannes Film Festival, Emanuel Macron, and the enigmatic Daft Punk! To this day, France is still a center of art and culture. Currently, France has a population of around 67 million people, with a GDP of around $2.9 trillion.

Soccer is one of France's best athletic success stories, with two Euros and two World Cups to date. France has the distinction of scoring the first-ever goal in World Cup history at the 1930 FIFA World Cup in Uruguay. The goal was scored by Lucien Laurent.

Just Fontaine holds a special record: In the 1958 FIFA World Cup, he scored 13 goals! (Fontaine outdid Sandor Kocsis—of Hungary—who scored 11 goals in the 1954 FIFA World Cup. Since Fontaine's flurry of brilliance, the closest challenger has been Gerd Müller of West Germany with 10 goals in the 1970 FIFA World Cup.) Over the years, Les Bleus has fielded some elite scorers. France's top all-time scorers are:

1. Thierry Henry (51)   2. Olivier Giroud (48)*

---

*   Still active, and this number will likely increase.

3. Antoine Griezmann (42)*   **5.** Karim Benzema (37)**
4. Michel Platini (41)

As for the top three players in French history, you might get another story. Some would say:

1. Platini   **3.** Henry
2. Zidane

While others might emphatically say:

1. Zidane   **3.** Henry
2. Platini

Most players end their international career on a normal note, i.e., playing for their home country. Platini, on the other hand, decided to do things differently. After a distinguished career with France in the 1970s and 80s in which he captained the team, he opted to play his last international game for Kuwait in 1988! Go figure.

Certainly, the French are known for world-class wine. However, a handful of beers that might make a few rounds include Duyck Jenlain Ambree, La Choulette Blonde, and Kronenbourg 1664.

WHERE THE TEAM IS TODAY—TACTICS AND STRATEGIES

France is currently one of the top teams in the world. It earned second place in the 2016 Euro, first place in the 2018 FIFA World Cup, and suffered a Round of 16 loss to Switzerland in the 2020 Euro. Despite the latter result, France has high hopes for Qatar 2022.

Tactics and strategies: France will conceivably opt for a 4-2-3-1. In this case, if you were to take the center attacking

---

*   Still active, and this number will likely increase.

**   Still active, and this number will likely increase.

mid and draw him back a bit, this formation could be construed as a 4-3-3. As such, France in a 4-3-3 isn't out of the question. Perhaps still, France may use a 3-5-2.

Defensively, France falls on opponents extremely well with Kante, Pogba, Rabiot, Pavard, and Varane. France often has the ability to swarm its opposition, and this leads to well-conducted counterattacks. In fact, because of a fluid style, the French excel at counterattacking, and if the field opens up, watch out! Many quality scoring chances will present themselves. For those watching live, you'll feel the roar of the crowd grow livelier with each pass nearing the goal.

At its best, offensive French soccer is marked by poetic fluidity in the buildup to goal. Everything clicks.

At its worst, well, pack your bags and good luck next time! Part of the beauty of watching France is that you don't know which version you're going to get. As evidenced from past Cups, the French are either genius or a group-stage bust. Come World Cup time, there's always something brewing in the French camp: Whether it's a debilitating protest—testing the grounds of liberty—à la 2010 or a situation like in 1982 when a player was reprimanded and not allowed to play for allegedly having an affair with Platini's wife.

In the attack, France's dynamic lineup plays with calm fluidity, capitalizing on a structured passing system that, at times, comes across like a top-level pickup game. More often than not, France's play is brilliant. This makes France one of the most exciting teams in the tournament. When it's all said and done, France in 2022 should not disappoint.

DIDIER DESCHAMPS—A BRIEF COACHING PORTRAIT
Didier Deschamps played as a midfielder in his day with clubs Nantes, Marseille, Bordeaux, Juventus, Chelsea, and Valencia. He also captained France to the 1998 FIFA World Cup championship. As of 2018, he coached France to the World Cup

title! This accomplishment is a rare distinction that sets him apart from all other coaches in Qatar.

For France to be successful in this competition, Deschamps must balance the right lineup, formation, and game plan with chemistry, good spirits, patience, combination passing, and firm defense. France's combination passing might just be the key to success. The team must dominate tight spaces and pass the ball within inches of the opposition. When France is operating on all cylinders, this passing is a thing of beauty. Deschamps, the conductor of this orchestra, somehow has to keep things rhythmic. If he can, it will be very interesting to see how far Les Bleus can get.

KEY PLAYERS AND THEIR CHARACTERISTICS

Kylian Mbappé—who typically goes by just Mbappé—has risen to become one of the biggest stars in French soccer history. Speed is the name of the game for Mbappé. One must admit, he's got a unique running motion as his legs spring "upward" in an odd way for his stride; nonetheless, his speed is breathtaking at times. He's worth the price of admission. With scoring partner Griezmann by his side, France is looking to be very dangerous for opponents.

Paul Pogba has become known for "off-field shenanigans" perhaps more than his actual play. Be it the 2018 World Cup with his video diaries or a post-goal celebration that seems to linger on for 10 million years, Pogba looks for any chance to control the moment. Celebrations are nothing new in soccer as Junior and Brazil took delight for minutes on end during the 1982 World Cup, irritating opponents. Perhaps Pogba has been watching the VHS tape *G'olé!* with commentary by Sean Connery. Maybe not. Depending who you ask, Pogba is either a fan favorite or highly overrated. Like Giroud, he receives a fair share of criticism. Regardless, the midfielder with Manchester United is one of the guys France is hoping will bring home another title. The bottom line is Pogba, with his central midfield vision, distribution, and organization, in tandem with Kante, will be a vital part of France's progression.

Hugo Lloris—born in 1986—has played keeper with Nice, Lyon, and Tottenham Hotspur. He won the prestigious UNFP Player of the Month award during his time with Lyon in September 2009 in Ligue 1; also in Ligue 1, he earned Goalkeeper of the Year in 2009, 2010, and 2012. With Tottenham—having joined in 2012—he's played in over 300 games! Quite remarkable. At around 6'2", Lloris dominates his net with a keen sense of positional awareness combined with athleticism and well-rounded technique. He joined France in 2008, and, as they say, sometimes it takes 10 years to get something done. Despite the pain and anguish that was the World Cups 2010* and 2014** (which was felt by pretty much every French player and fan across the land), he became a FIFA World Cup champion in 2018! What's more, he has over 130 caps for France to date. His accolades have increased over the years. A repeat World Cup title in Qatar would solidify his place on the Mount Rushmore of goalkeepers.

Giroud has many goals under his belt, a leader in the history of French goal-scoring, as a matter of fact. Yet the tall, 6'4" forward receives plenty of criticism from the French as some feel his play is inconsistent. He's not much of a dribbler, nor is he going to create his own shot except once in a blue moon. Rather he depends upon teammates for precise passing to set him up around the box whereby he exudes a keen sense of scoring, coupled with good technique and overall accuracy. He's good in the air as well. However, as a well-traveled forward in his

---

* In the 2010 FIFA World Cup, France endured stinging defeats from Mexico and South Africa, and Le Bleus did not escape its group.

** In the 2014 FIFA World Cup, France took a tough 1-0 loss in the quarter-finals to rival Germany.

mid-30s, fans may not expect to see the Giroud of old. Though, as a veteran presence with the squad, there might just be some surprise moments from the classic scorer.

Antoine Griezmann—whose superlative arsenal of talent landed him a lucrative spot with FC Barcelona in 2019—has proven to be a superb threat in the attack, be it creative dribbling, insightful passing, or a presence around goal that seems to invite scoring chances. The left-footer always seems to be in the right place, and he will be an impact player in Qatar—one to take note of.

OVERALL PLAYER RATING

Mbappé: 9.8   Olivier Giroud: 9

Paul Pogba: 9   Antoine Griezmann: 9.9

Hugo Lloris: 9.9

KEY PLAYER STATS

(Total career goals for their country)

	Games Played	Goals
Mbappé	56	27
Paul Pogba	91	11
Hugo Lloris	139	0
Olivier Giroud	112	48
Antoine Griezmann	107	42

WHAT TO WATCH FOR ON TV

As the 2022 World Cup approached, France had a number of players to call on, some of which included **goalkeepers** Hugo Lloris and Steve Mandanda; **defenders** Benjamin Pavard, Presnel Kimpembe, Raphael Varane, Leo Dubois, Lucas Digne, Lucas Hernandez, Clement Lenglet, Kurt Zouma, and Ferland Mendy; **midfielders** Adrien Rabiot, Paul Pogba, Aurélien Djani Tchouaméni, Jordan Veretout, Thomas Lemar, N'Golo Kante, Corentin Tolisso, Moussa Sissoko, and Steven Nzonzi; and **forwards** Antoine Griezmann, Mbappé, Kingsley Coman,

Olivier Giroud, Ousmane Dembele, Marcus Thuram, Nabil Fekir, Anthony Martial, Moussa Diaby, Wissam Ben Yedder, and Karim Benzema.

On route to Qatar, France was in Group D in European qualifiers, alongside Ukraine, Finland, Bosnia, and Kazakhstan.

Mbappé, Griezmann, Benzema, Kante, Pogba, Pavard, Rabiot, Varane, and Giroud make up part of the engine that will keep France running at optimal speed. With Lloris in the net, it's a team that has a strong chance to repeat as World Cup champions. On the way to this achievable goal, France will rely on free-flowing soccer mixed with continual possession. Add to this a strong, athletic, defense that leads to an energetic counterattack with speedy wings, and France is a top-shelf power that will be tough to beat.

In the late 1970s, with the emergence of midfield magician Michel Platini, France stepped up to a new level of international soccer. Prior to Platini's arrival, France's relationship with the World Cup was less than enriching. Since Zidane in 1998 and Griezmann in 2018, France has two World Cups…as a team on the verge of a third.

As with Brazil, Argentina, Germany, and Italy, France is must-see on TV. Fans will be tuning in by the millions to see if Les Bleus can make history as back-to-back champions. The only two nations to accomplish this have been Italy (1934, 1938) and Brazil (1958, 1962). As such, the pressure will be on; France will be center stage and certainly under scrutiny.

Will France pull it off? It's very possible. Realistically, France is one of the top five teams to win the whole thing in Qatar!

BELGIUM
World Cup titles: 0
Overall Team Rating: 9.7

A BRIEF TEAM HISTORY
Belgium's early World Cup days were, well, not too great. Let's take a look at Belgium's World Cup record:

1930: Belgium couldn't get past the first round.

1934: Belgium couldn't get past the first round.

1938: You guessed it; Belgium couldn't get past the first round.

1950: Belgium didn't compete.

1954: Belgium didn't get out of its group.

1958: Didn't qualify.

1962: Didn't qualify.

1966: Didn't qualify.

1970: Belgium couldn't get out of its group.

1974: Belgium didn't qualify.

1978: Belgium didn't qualify, yet again!

1982: Belgium made it to the second group phase.

1986: Belgium earned fourth place overall. In the semi-finals, the Belgians put up a good fight but lost to the supremely talented Argentines, led by Maradona who eventually won the title.

1990: Belgium made the Round of 16.

1994: Yet again, Belgium made the Round of 16.

1998: Belgium couldn't escape its group.

2002: Made the Round of 16.

2006: Didn't qualify.

2010: Didn't qualify.

2014: Belgium made the quarter-finals. The Belgians had a strong unit this time around, with De Bruyne and Eden Hazard, and the result was much better than previous Cups.

2018: Belgium placed third overall. This time, still with De Bruyne and Eden Hazard, Belgium surged ahead and nearly made the final.

UEFA EUROPEAN CHAMPIONSHIP
Recently, Belgium lost to Italy in the quarter-finals of the 2020 Euro. Belgium is hoping to take this defeat and use it as a learning tool for a victorious run in Qatar.

FACTS ABOUT THEIR COUNTRY
Belgium has a population of around 11 million people, with an estimated GDP of $500 billion. Belgium's top scorers of all time:

1. Romelu Lukaku (68)*
2. Eden Hazard (33)**
3. Bernard Voorhoof and Paul Van Himst (30)

Many Belgians that travel or live outside their country find a way to watch their team in action. During past World Cups, Goal, a soccer bar in Los Angeles, has played host to many Belgian expat fans that have congregated en masse to cheer their team on. Essentially, as you can imagine, things have gotten rowdy. Blame the beer, blame the game…either way, Belgians are ready to rock! According to Jay, who worked at Goal during the 2014 World Cup, when Belgium played the United States in the elimination round, "…it was as chaotic and awesome as I've ever seen this bar before." He added, "We sold more Stella and Palm than you can imagine." Belgian beers are top level, sought after throughout the world. Duvel, Vedett, and so many others will likely fill the pubs come game time!

WHERE THE TEAM IS TODAY—TACTICS AND STRATEGIES
Belgium has been one of FIFA's top teams for years now. Its high-ranking status has been due, in large part, to the prowess of Eden Hazard, De Bruyne, and Lukaku. Add to the mix Hazard's younger brother Thorgan as well as Axel Witsel and

---

*   Still active and this number will likely increase.

**   Still active and this number will likely increase.

Jan Vertonghen. Their experience and playmaking abilities have kept Belgium in the upper echelon of elite teams. In years past, Belgium has been ranked favorably in the top 20 or so, and that may be the case again sometime soon. For now, though, Belgium is flying high and expected to show very well in Qatar 2022.

Tactics and strategies: Belgium will likely mobilize with a 3-4-2-1 (or possibly a 4-2-3-1 or 4-4-2). It's a team that passes through the channels with ease, marksmanship, and fluidity. This sets up very auspicious dribbling opportunities for De Bruyne and the Hazard brothers, Eden and Thorgan. Stylistically, Belgium resembles Spain with a touch of Netherlands and a twist of France. Key contributors to watch for: Courtois (one of the best keepers in the world), defender Jan Vertonghen, midfielder Axel Witsel, attacking mids Eden Hazard and De Bruyne, along with striker Lukaku.

ROBERTO MARTINEZ—A BRIEF COACHING PORTRAIT

Spanish-born **Roberto Martinez** has coached Swansea City, Wigan Athletic, Everton, and Belgium. His jaunt with Everton lasted from 2013-16. Then he sauntered over to Belgium in 2016.

As a player, Martinez was a defensive midfielder with a number of teams, including Wigan Athletic and Swansea City. Belgium's swift and accurate passing structure, one that is possession-oriented and gives the stars opportunities to go at defenders, showcases Martinez's influence as coach.

After having replaced the previous coach, Marc Wilmots, Martinez has brought impressive results. At the 2018 FIFA World Cup, Belgium took third overall. Leading up to the 2022 World Cup, Belgium has been ranked by FIFA as the world number one.

Still, good times don't last forever, especially in soccer, as Belgium suffered a quarter-finals loss in the 2020 Euro to the eventual champions, Italy. However, Belgium has a lot going for it in World Cup 2022. Should this be Martinez's last tournament with Belgium, he will still end on a high note. He's guided the team with a possession-based approach rooted in the soccer-philosophy of Johan Cruyff, and Belgian soccer has flourished. To end as FIFA World Cup champions will be asking a lot though. For a nation that, at its best, has placed second in the 1980 Euro and third in the 2018 World Cup, it is perhaps destined to finish slightly behind the pack despite being ranked number one in the world. An interesting question arises: If Belgium falls short of a World Cup championship, is Martinez to blame? Probably not. He's been an important piece of the puzzle for Belgium. As such, he's established pivotal building blocks for his successor to rise even higher.

KEY PLAYERS AND THEIR CHARACTERISTICS

Jan Vertonghen is a unique, multitalented, veteran defender who has the ability to cleverly dribble away from pressing forwards. What's more, his passing touch is very good. He is also, as good defenders should be, a well-trained tackler of the ball. He calmly cleans up messes and lends a steady presence to transition offense whereby his overall skillset helps put things in motion. As such, he's a crucial figure for Belgium.

Eden Hazard—who's climbed the charts from Lille to Chelsea to mega-power Real Madrid—is like poetry in motion when he's not injured. He's an attacking player's attacking player—quick, elusive, explosive, possesses good instincts, immaculate technique, and is always a threat. Step aside Jimmie Walker, he's redefined "Dyn-o-mite!" If you were to combine the styles of Arjen Robben with Messi, you'd have Hazard. The 5'8" dynamo, thought of as Europe's best talent for a time, the guy who could potentially take the throne from Messi and Cristiano Ronaldo as the best player in the world, is a one-on-one nightmare for opposing coaches. Good luck to whoever's going to guard him! If he's not side-stepping defenders, he's retaining possession extremely well. He constantly keeps the opposition off-balance, creating scoring chances for his team. You can count on Eden for a goal; he's easily one of the tournament's All-Star XI.

Kevin De Bruyne has established himself, alongside Eden Hazard, as one of the elite attacking midfielders in Europe. In World Cup 2014, De Bruyne scored a decisive goal against the US in the second round. As for World Cup 2018 in Russia, he scored an important goal in the 2-1 quarter-final victory over Brazil and helped Belgium earn a third-place finish in the tournament. De Bruyne wisely signed with Manchester City in 2015 where, to date, he's flourished as a salient EPL talent. His shooting ability is superb, with an inclination to keep shots driven low to the ground (which is very difficult for keepers to handle). He's not what you would call quick, but he's quick enough. Perhaps this has enabled him to fine-tune his dribbling skills, which are very effective, and he possesses the highly valued combination of being a lethal dribbler and passer. This skill opens avenues for him and teammates to enjoy many lucrative scoring chances.

Romelu Lukaku—Belgium's all-time leading scorer— has a great skill of playing with his back to goal while being defended. He posts up around the box and receives passes while holding off a defender, gaining crucial territory to either set up his own shot or pass it off to someone else. With this type of play, a lot can develop in the attack and this approach should be beneficial. Lukaku—a power forward with experience from Everton, Manchester United, Inter Milan, and Chelsea—is a fan favorite, and supporters of Belgium are placing their hopes—and maybe a few bets—on his scoring many goals.

OVERALL PLAYER RATING

Jan Vertonghen: 9.5   Kevin De Bruyne: 9.8
Eden Hazard: 9.8   Romelu Lukaku: 9

KEY PLAYER STATS
(Total career goals for their country)

	Games Played	Goals
Jan Vertonghen	138	9
Eden Hazard	119	33
Kevin De Bruyne	91	24
Romelu Lukaku	102	68

WHAT TO WATCH FOR ON TV

As a number-one team in the world, Belgium had a pool of talent leading into World Cup 2022 that was off-the-charts impressive. Some of the players included **goalkeepers** Thibaut Courtois, Simon Mignolet, and Koen Casteels; **defenders** Toby Alderweireld, Jason Denayer, Dedryck Boyata, Jan Vertonghen, Thomas Foket, Timothy Castagne, Thomas Meunier, and Thomas Vermaelen; **midfielders** Kevin De Bruyne, Axel Witsel, Youri Tielemans, Yannick Carrasco, Hans Vanaken, Leander Dendoncker, Leandro Trossard, Alexis Saelemaekers, Dennis Praet, Nacer Chadli, Adnan Januzaj, Thorgan Hazard, and Eden Hazard; **forwards** Dries Mertens, Jeremy Doku, Christian Benteke, Dodi Lukebakio, Charles De Ketelaere, Michy Batshuayi-Atunga, and Romelu Lukaku.

On route to Qatar, Belgium was in Group E in European qualifiers, alongside Czech Republic, Wales, Belarus, and Estonia.

One-on-one situations are where Belgium thrives. First you have to contend with Eden Hazard taking guys on with quicker-than-lightning acceleration, changing direction, and leaving defenders in the dust. Then there's Lukaku posting up around the box, with his back to goal, pushing defenders back, getting himself deep into enemy territory to allow for a shot or to set up teammates—a technique that reverberates Brazilian futsal strategy.

The passing is on point (accuracy, timing, rhythm, and combinations); the dribbling from Hazard is worth its weight in gold; the precision teamwork is off the charts; yet Belgium will likely fail with respect to actually winning the World Cup. Why? There's something about Belgium: Its soccer pedigree is good, but it just can't get over that hump of a major title. Talk about Netherlands and Spain being "the two best teams to never win a World Cup!" At least Spain finally got one. As for the Netherlands, well, it got second behind Spain at the 2010 World Cup and is still looking for that magical title. To its credit, Netherlands at least won the 1988 Euro—a major tournament. Belgium, on the other hand: zilch. No World Cup. No Euro. Sure, Les Diables Rouges came in second at the 1980 Euro, and the 80s saw many talented players such as Eric Gerets, Jan Ceulemans, Jean-Marie Pfaff, and the sparkling midfield star Enzo Scifo— but no championship as of yet.

The Belgian Football Association dates back to 1895, and it's been influential in the sport ever since. This current team that landed in Qatar, an elite group of talent, is carrying on the tradition with aplomb. With so much talent on the field, accentuated by a wall in goal with Courtois, one might think that Belgium's time has finally come. This is the year! This team certainly is one that could bring it all home. But despite all its experience and recent successes, this likely isn't going to be Belgium's year. Don't be too fooled by FIFA's ranking of Belgium. Certainly, it's a team to watch, but something with Belgium (good ranking or not) fails come World Cup time. It's one of those soccer mysteries.

NETHERLANDS
World Cup Titles: 0
Overall Team Rating: 9.5

A BRIEF TEAM HISTORY
The World Cup record of Netherlands is interesting, to say the least. It's a lot of not showing up at all juxtaposed with sporadically doing extremely well. Let's take a look!

1930: Netherlands didn't compete.
1934: Made the Round of 16.
1938: Made the Round of 16.
1950: Didn't compete.
1954: Didn't compete.
1958: Didn't qualify.
1962: Didn't qualify.
1966: Didn't qualify.
1970: Didn't qualify, again!
1974: Finished in second place!
1978: Finished in second place!
1982: Didn't qualify.
1986: Didn't qualify.
1990: Made the Round of 16.
1994: Made the quarter-finals.
1998: Earned fourth overall.
2002: Didn't qualify.
2006: Made the Round of 16.
2010: Finished in second place!
2014: Earned third place.
2018: Didn't qualify.

UEFA EUROPEAN CHAMPIONSHIP

The big year! Netherlands won the Euro in 1988. Engineered in midfield by the one and only Ruud Gullit, the Dutch soared ahead of the pack with the exploits of Marco van Basten and Frank Rijkaard. In the semis, the Dutch got past a superbly talented West Germany on German soil by a close score of 2-1. Netherlands ended up surpassing the mighty Soviet Union 2-0 in the final with a goal from Gullit and a sublime volley from the young phenom, van Basten (a once in a lifetime goal that appeared lucky and brilliant at the same time). Coach Rinus Michels, a true master of the game, celebrated a well-deserved victory as Netherlands danced away with its first major title.

As for the next 20 years or so, at its best, Netherlands made the Euro semis in 1992, 2000, and 2004. Most recently in the 2020 UEFA Euro, Netherlands—stacked with talent as per usual—was disappointingly defeated 2-0 in the Round of 16 by the Czech Republic. How did one of the "nail in the coffin" goals emerge? Simple, messy, defensive errors—a momentary lapse resulting from a lack of concentration, organization, and, some may say, common sense. So no, the championship trophy has not returned to Amsterdam.

FACTS ABOUT THEIR COUNTRY

The Netherlands—a tiny coastal nation in Western Europe—might be known for waterways and boat-making, yet there's also a large street party you may or may not have heard of. Jeff Scott wrote for *CNN*: "Every April, the Dutch host the biggest street party in Europe. Previously Koninginnedag (Queen's Day), the festival is now Koningsdag (King's Day) in honor of King Willem-Alexander."[7] If the Dutch team brings home a FIFA World Cup championship, there will be a street party like never before! The current population of Netherlands is around 17.6 million, and its GDP is about $1 trillion.

The Dutch national team soccer program formed in 1905, and today the team is commonly referred to as "The Flying Dutchmen." Despite Dutch soccer being so well regarded around the world, the Netherlands has only one major championship to date: the 1988 UEFA Euro. In fact, the Dutch are still chasing that elusive FIFA World Cup title. So far it has placed second on three occasions: 1974, 1978, and 2010. Who has sponsored the Dutch national team uniform over the years? Good question. Interesting answer.

1966-74: Umbro led the way.   1991-96: Lotto.
1974-90: Adidas took the lead.   1996-today: Nike.

Arguably the best player in Dutch history, some say the world, would be attacking midfielder Johan Cruyff, who scored 33 goals for his country from 1966-77. Some of the best scorers in the history of the sport have come from Netherlands, including Abe Lenstra, Marco van Basten, Dennis Bergkamp, and Ruud van Nistelrooy. The top three scorers for the Dutch national team are:

1. Robin van Persie (50)   3. Patrick Kluivert (40)
2. Klaas-Jan Huntelaar (42)

WHERE THE TEAM IS TODAY—TACTICS AND STRATEGIES

Dutch passing schemes are always top level. Players produced by the Netherlands are credited—rightfully so—with elite skill and technical ability. On top of that, the players combine elite passing combinations. As Dutch coaches have exported valuable training techniques around the world—including its famous approach to passing—one might assume that its secrets are out. Can opposing forces then swindle the Dutch out of victories using the very tactics Dutch coaches have been schlepping around the globe all this time? It's very possible. In fact, the international landscape has gotten much more homogenized over time.* In spite of this salient obstacle the Dutch have created, with ill effects to its own fortune, if the team can exude what it does best, the very thing other nations have been stealing, then good things should occur. In the best-case scenario, the Dutch can beat all the wannabes at its own game: elite passing.

Tactics and strategies: As per design, like a passing-clinic paradigm stenciled on blueprints sent from above, the Netherlands—often in a 4-3-3—will put forth a full-on assault by way of brisk, timely, and accurate passing. Each player seems to possess the same trapping and distributing technique that creates holes in the wall of any defense. In doing so, the Flying Dutchmen will utilize the wings with darting runs combined

---

* This is particularly true from circa 1990 to the present.

with one–twos to cause havoc around the box. This buildup leads to crafty dribbling around the scoring areas as the Dutch will seize on any opportunity to exploit its opponents' weaknesses around goal. When done correctly, Dutch passing rings out like a harmonious symphony of chords, all coming together the right way. When not done right, the Dutch look disjointed, out of sync, and rushed. Whatever the case may be, the Netherlands will live and die by its passing prowess.

LOUIS VAN GAAL—A BRIEF COACHING PORTRAIT

Louis van Gaal has followed an interesting coaching path. From 1991 to today, his stops have gone as follows: Ajax, Barcelona, Netherlands, Barcelona, AZ (a pro Dutch team), Bayern Munich, Netherlands, Manchester United, and, as of 2021, Netherlands again! Prior to his arrival, the coaching position for the Dutch national team was recently held by Guus Hiddink, Danny Blind, Ronald Koeman, and Frank de Boer.

As a 6'1" midfielder in his day, van Gaal—born in 1951—was associated with Ajax, Royal Antwerp, Telstar, Sparta Rotterdam, and AZ. As coach of one of the best nations to never win the World Cup, van Gaal wants to make history as the first. With a talented team that persevered in the European qualifiers, the task at hand is very much in reach.

KEY PLAYERS AND THEIR CHARACTERISTICS

Memphis Depay, an attacking forward extraordinaire, is set to gobble up space with defined dribbling ability mixed with one–twos around the box, a constant threat for defenses. At club level, Depay has spent time with PSV Eindhoven, Manchester United, Lyon, and he recently landed with Barcelona in 2021 alongside teammate de Jong. From club to country, Depay is a closely guarded man as he combines skill, quickness, and speed to create scoring chances. Most of Netherlands's attack will be focused on him. A marvelous talent, it seems as though Dutch scientists had been surreptitiously developing him in a low-key KNVB lab facility leading up to his national team debut in 2013. The 5'9" Barcelona star has a strong group of teammates on his side. He has many options, including the likes of Wijnaldum and de Jong, to combine with to penetrate the opposition. If Netherlands can get its act together and win the World Cup in 2022, Depay will be front and center. He's a standout performer, a game-changer, and a star to watch in Qatar.

Matthijs de Ligt—born in 1999—transitioned from Ajax to Italian super-club Juventus in 2019. The previous captain of Ajax has turned into a fixture for the Dutch national team. As a smart passer with great technique, the young star will help guide things from the back with a sophisticated air. He was part of Ajax's great 2018-19 UEFA Champions League adventure and is ready to make 2022 a championship year for Netherlands.

Georginio Wijnaldum is a midfielder with great attacking ability with over 80 caps for his country. Dating back to 2011, which was his first game with Netherlands, Wijnaldum brings experience and leadership to the table, a valuable combination the team is leaning on.

Virgil van Dijk is a gamer. Virgil, a center back for English soccer-giant Liverpool, placed second in the 2019 Ballon d'Or voting behind Messi. As a standout for Netherlands, van Dijk— who's 6'4"—is strong defensively, possesses speed (to spare) and skill (which he conducts with ease), and is a great asset in the air for corner-kicks. A vast amount of the team's success will be placed on his shoulders.

Frenkie de Jong, a reliable center mid, took the leap in 2019 from Ajax to Barcelona. His vision combined with a sharp ability for connecting with teammates exudes the protocol of the aforementioned clubs. Not a big scorer, the midfield maestro is more of a distributing genius. Since 2018, he's acquired over 30 caps for Netherlands. He's a vital part of the Dutch engine that keeps passes moving throughout; he and the other passing savants are looking to make waves in Qatar like never before. He'll be responsible for much of Netherlands's success.

OVERALL PLAYER RATING

Memphis Depay: 9.3   Virgil van Dijk: 9.5
Matthijs de Ligt: 9.4   Frenkie de Jong: 9.2
Georginio Wijnaldum: 9

KEY PLAYER STATS

(Total career goals for their country)

	Games Played	Goals
Memphis Depay	79	41
Matthijs de Ligt	37	2
Georginio Wijnaldum	86	26
Virgil van Dijk	47	5
Frenkie de Jong	43	1

WHAT TO WATCH FOR ON TV

Netherlands typically has a gazillion players to choose from. Leading up to and during European qualifiers for World Cup 2022, Netherlands had options that included **goalkeepers** Tim Krul, Justin Bijlow, Jasper Cillessen, and Maarten Stekelenburg; **defenders** Matthijs de Ligt, Joel Veltman, Patrick van Aanholt, Kenny Tete, Hans Hateboer, Stefan de Vrij, Daley Blind, Denzel Dumfries, Nathan Ake, Owen Wijndal, and Virgil van Dijk; **midfielders** Georginio Wijnaldum, Guus Til, Davy Klaassen, Ryan Gravenberch, Frenkie de Jong, Marten de Roon, Donny van de Beek, Tonny Vilhena, and Kevin Strootman; and **forwards** Ryan Babel, Quincy Promes, Calvin Stengs, Luuk de Jong, Steven Berghuis, Donyell Malen, Wout Weghorst, Steven Bergwijn, and Memphis Depay.

On route to Qatar, Netherlands was in Group G in European qualifiers, along with Norway, Turkey, Montenegro, Latvia, and Gibraltar.

In Qatar, Matthijs de Ligt, Stefan de Vrij, and Daley Blind should likely be overseeing things with superior vision from central command (a.k.a., the defense) combined with captain, defense superstar, and runner-up for the 2019 Ballon d'Or, Virgil van Dijk. This is a dream come true for any coach and a nightmare for opposing teams, hunkered down, wondering what to do. Certainly, the Netherlands has a defense like a fortress of trees. Adding even more firepower up front is Memphis Depay, Georginio Wijnaldum, Davy Klaassen, and Frenkie de Jong. The linkup play, combination passing, and overall flair will be off the charts. Talent of this sort leads to excitement…and expectations! Dutch fans couldn't ask for a better opportunity to win the FIFA World Cup. Despite not making the 2018 FIFA World Cup, Dutch soccer is roaring back on the scene.

With Netherlands, at its best, practically every pass is like a brushstroke on a canvas painting, with each player in harmony together as *one artist*. At its worst, the *artist* in question can get caught up with something else, as is often the case with Dutch artists. You never can tell with these guys. Maybe it just depends on the day. Regardless of the outcome this time around, the Dutch are a team to watch considering the exquisite technique combined with a top soccer IQ. The final equation for fans, journalists, and historians alike is going to rest in the hands of a formidable group that is on the verge of winning its first FIFA World Cup title to mount on the trophy case back in the KNVB headquarters.

On route to this goal, Netherlands will most likely operate out of a 4-3-3 (or perhaps a 4-2-3-1).

The history of Dutch soccer has a long, substantial list of excellent players to lean on such as Abe Lenstra, Johan Cruyff, Ruud Gullit, Frank Rijkaard, Ronald Koeman, Marco van Basten, Ronald de Boer, Frank de Boer, Ruud van Nistelrooy, Arjen Robben, and many others that have adorned the vibrant orange uniform.

Despite its amazing talent, the FIFA World Cup hasn't exactly been a good friend to the Dutch unless you consider three second-place finishes a sparkling companionship. Bottom line: the Dutch team of 2022 can change all that in seven games!

CROATIA
World Cup titles: 0
Overall Team Rating: 9.4

A BRIEF TEAM HISTORY
Let's take a look at Croatia's World Cup record.
1930: Not yet Croatia proper.
1934: Not yet Croatia proper.
1938: Not yet Croatia proper.
1950: Not yet Croatia proper.
1954: Not yet Croatia proper.
1958: Not yet Croatia proper.
1962: Not yet Croatia proper.
1966: Not yet Croatia proper.
1970: Not yet Croatia proper.
1974: Not yet Croatia proper.
1978: Not yet Croatia proper.
1982: Not yet Croatia proper.
1986: Not yet Croatia proper.
1990: Not yet Croatia proper.
1994: Not yet Croatia proper.
1998: Finished third overall!
2002: Group stage.
2006: Group stage.
2010: Didn't qualify.
2014: Group stage.
2018: Finished second overall!

UEFA EUROPEAN CHAMPIONSHIP

Croatia's best results in UEFA Euro action are from 1996 and 2008 in which it got to the quarter-finals, and then from 2016 and 2020 when it reached the Round of 16.

FACTS ABOUT THEIR COUNTRY

Croatia is a small nation just east of Italy with a population of around 4 million people and an estimated GDP of $63 billion.

You're not going to find baseball or American football in Croatia. Basketball, yes. But above all, you'll find soccer ruling the streets and fields alike. From Boban to Modric, the honor of wearing the Croatia jersey is beyond compare. Likewise, to be a leading scorer for Croatia is to be in good company. The all-time top three scorers for Croatia's national team are:

1. Davor Suker (45)   3. Ivan Perisic (32)*
2. Mario Mandzukic (33)

As fans watch the 2020 FIFA World Cup, awaiting the next goal, a few beers likely to be tossed back include Lasko, Karlovacko, and other domestic creations for the grand occasion.

WHERE THE TEAM IS TODAY—TACTICS AND STRATEGIES

Do not underestimate the Croatians. **Tactics and strategies:** Of the teams in the mix for a stellar push in the elimination rounds, Croatia is set on being in the driver's seat with a 4-2-3-1 (or perhaps a 4-3-1-2, which essentially amounts to a 4-3-3). Assuming this remains the case, Modric is key in the midfield with distribution as he orchestrates Croatia's play throughout the tournament. All things rest on his foot. Essentially, if you take him out of the equation, it's rough sailing for Croatia. With Modric pulling the strings, this allows Perisic, Rebic, Kramaric, and Kovacic to excel with scoring chances. Also important in the mix is Brozovic, a driving force in midfield.

---

*   Still active and this number will likely increase.

Croatia has skillful buildup play in possession and strings together short passes very efficiently. It's a team that looks to score, and weapons are lurking around each corner with Perisic on the wing, Kramaric thundering in, and the accurate and dangerous precision shooting of Modric. **In an article for** *BBC News*, **Guy De Launey explained:** "Everyone seems to have an opinion about sport. Ask three people about their views on a particular team, player or competition and the chances are they will give totally different answers."[8] As De Launey pointed out, "But ask a Croatian why their small country excels on the international sporting stage, and the response is surprisingly uniform."[9] The response essentially is Croatians are full of talent. After watching the current national side, one would have a hard time disagreeing. For dangerous teams that are fun to watch, this Modric-led symphony is about as close to a masterpiece as you can get! When it gets momentum, which is often, Croatia is apt to score, or at the very least, it can keep opposing teams in precarious situations. The latter is a good plan, too, as good possession combined with scoring threats is a long-term solution that Croatia is happy to have on its side.

ZLATKO DALIC—A BRIEF COACHING PORTRAIT

Zlatko Dalic took the coaching position in 2017. He had a big start as Croatia surged ahead in World Cup 2018 by earning second-place overall. With a defeat to France in the final, the small nation with soccer on its mind came oh-so-close to being champions. It was a history-making run that Dalic is hoping to duplicate, but this time with the championship in hand. The team is certainly talented and experienced which will help in this regard. Of further note, at the 2020 UEFA Euro, which, of course, took place in 2021, Croatia found its way to the Round of 16. Given the team's talent level, it was a somewhat disappointing headline but nonetheless the ramifications of that result should serve as motivation for a group that can use that experience in the grueling rounds of competition that the World Cup has to offer.

Dalic's approach will rest heavily on smart—constructive—passing that is best exemplified by the genius that Modric brings to the table, supplemented by a supporting cast that, in its own right, is superb. It's a small nation that juggles the reality of being an underdog with big expectations. Oftentimes, expectations can be a burden as is the case with Brazil, who is the opposite of an underdog and has big expectations surrounding it wherever it plays; high expectations can psychologically cause players to rush things and press for goals when patience and possession would otherwise lead to better scoring chances. It will be interesting to see if Dalic and his crew can balance the attack with patience and let the game flow as opposed to frantically pushing forward with a rushed effort. If Croatia can use patience and skillful buildup play as a virtue, then good things should follow. As for Dalic, it'll be his job to guide this orchestra with a nuanced touch.

KEY PLAYERS AND THEIR CHARACTERISTICS

Luka Modric—a superstar in Qatar—is the general in midfield and surrounded by extreme talent that has the potential to find its way into the final game easily. Having said that, it's a crowded tournament of talent and other nations could also find a path to championship glory just as easily. Though few teams in World Cup 2022 have the likes of Modric, a Ballon d'Or winner. His passing touch is phenomenal which has been highly appreciated by fans of Real Madrid, where Modric has played a starring role since 2012. Like Xavi, he knows exactly when and how to pass to someone so they can shoot. And not just shoot, but shoot well. Now in his mid-30s, Modric has, perhaps, one last chance to bag the FIFA World Cup for Croatia which would be a perfect ending to his stellar career.

Ivan Perisic is a threat out wide. He's just plain good and always on the verge of scoring—a complete nightmare for defenses. The 6'1" winger, who's typically found on the left, has impressive speed, ambition, skill, and a keen insight to breaking free into space whereby he often finds dangerous opportunities to either shoot or set another player up in the box. His left foot is deadly, and he's backed it up with over 30 goals since first joining Croatia in 2011. When it comes to dribbling on the wing, he has some tricks that are strengthened with a burst of speed that's hard to keep up with as well as the ability to tap it long for a move toward the touchline. As a veteran presence, Croatian fans are confident in his ability to guide the team forward with favorable results.

Mateo Kovacic—Croatia's midfielder wonder alongside Modric—is highly regarded as a multi-threat with excellent passing, dribbling, defensive anticipation, and, of course, tackling (where he excels). He is in such high regard that he's landed with three of the top clubs in the world: Inter Milan, Real Madrid, and Chelsea. Was he brought in to score? No. Don't accuse Kovacic of being a big scorer. Rather, he's a setup guy. His exceptional dribbling ability allows him to get free from pesky defenders who eventually succumb to his formidable speed and unwavering ambition. In addition, his defensive play is feisty, which lends him well to strong tackles as he slides in from all angles with an eye to disrupt an attack from ever getting started. Kovacic is a big reason for Croatia's success. He'll be pivotal in Qatar.

Andrej Kramaric—who was born in 1991 and first appeared with Croatia in 2014—is a potent 5'10" forward with telling experience from playing with Leicester City in 2015-16. What's more, he's spent a lot of time recently with 1899 Hoffenheim, and he's thundered home over 75 goals since 2016. He has the ability to bring the game to him, keeping defenders on their toes because he can break free for a goal at any moment. He's able and ready as a lone gun up top and out wide on the wing. His aptitude in this regard is a bonus for Croatia as it looks to surge forward in Qatar with his scoring touch.

Marcelo Brozovic—of Inter Milan notability—is a guiding force in midfield, one that is crucial for Croatia's success in

Qatar. In some circles, he's thought of in the same way as Frank Lampard—a solid two-way performer who offers skilled passing, dribbling, tackling, and the ability to cover ground from box to box. He should, quite adeptly, supplement Modric throughout games and open up passing lanes for teammates—such as Perisic—to find avenues to goal. With Brozovic, Kramaric, Kovacic, Perisic, and Modric working in concert together, it's a special time for Croatian soccer.

OVERALL PLAYER RATING

Luka Modric: 10   Andrej Kramaric: 9.3

Ivan Perisic: 9.6   Marcelo Brozovic: 9.3

Mateo Kovacic: 9.3

KEY PLAYER STATS

(Total career goals for their country)

	Games Played	Goals
Luka Modric	152	22
Ivan Perisic	113	32
Mateo Kovacic	81	3
Andrej Kramaric	71	19
Marcelo Brozovic	74	7

WHAT TO WATCH FOR ON TV

Croatia had a full pool of players to choose from as World Cup 2022 was approaching. A few of them were **goalkeepers** Dominik Livakovic, Simon Sluga, Lovre Kalinic, and Ivica Ivusic; **defenders** Domagoj Vida, Dejan Lovren, Borna Barišić, Duje Ćaleta-Car, Josip Juranović, Joško Gvardiol, Šime Vrsaljko, and Dario Melnjak; **midfielders** Luka Modric, Marcelo Brozović, Mario Pašalić, Nikola Vlašić, Luka Ivanušec, Mateo Kovačić, Milan Badelj, and Marko Rog; and **forwards** Ivan Perisic, Andrej Kramaric, Ante Rebić, Mislav Oršić, Marko Livaja, Antonio-Mirko Čolak, Josip Brekalo, Ante Budimir, and Bruno Petković.

On route to Qatar, Croatia was in Group H in European qualifiers, alongside Russia, Slovakia, Slovenia, Malta, and Cyprus.

Croatia's skillful approach—with brilliant passing interplay—is a hallmark of this unique group of talent that's on a collision course with history. Can Croatia break through the glass ceiling and win the FIFA World Cup? Can it reach the ultimate goal? If so, this is the team to get it done. Everyone watching in Croatia—from spellbound kids all the way to adults that lived through the 90s and witnessed firsthand the brilliant teams of that era—knows as much. With Modric, Perisic, and Kramaric, wave after wave of relentless attacks will flow, causing opponents to fall back and regroup. This team plays with a pride and honor that shows in every step. Electricity will be in the air with practically every touch of the ball. Now with a strong World Cup résumé—a third- and second-place finish—expectations are high, and each goal will be worth its weight in gold.

Strong defense, tough tackles, quick counters, solid possession, and guile around goal will be the calling card for Croatia on route to what it believes is a reachable goal: a team dance on the winner's podium.

DENMARK
World Cup titles: 0
Overall Team Rating: 9.2

A BRIEF TEAM HISTORY
Let's take a brief look at the World Cup record of the Dazzling Danes.

1930: Denmark didn't compete.
1934: Didn't compete.
1938: Didn't compete.
1950: Didn't compete.
1954: Didn't compete.

1958: Didn't compete.

1962: Didn't compete.

1966: Didn't compete.

1970: Didn't compete.

1974: Didn't compete.

1978: Didn't compete.

1982: Didn't compete.

1986: Made the Round of 16. Out of nowhere, Denmark said, "You know what, enough's enough." And things changed big time. This was a monumental year for Denmark which had a remarkably vibrant squad led by Preben Elkjaer, Michael Laudrup, and Frank Arnesen. Denmark made a huge impression with eye-opening wins over Uruguay and West Germany in the group stage. However, Spain was too much for the debutants in the Round of 16.

1990: Denmark didn't qualify.

1994: Didn't qualify.

1998: Denmark advanced to the quarter-finals.

2002: Made the Round of 16.

2006: Didn't qualify.

2010: Denmark couldn't escape its group.

2014: Didn't qualify.

2018: Denmark made the Round of 16. Denmark had a long haul before getting to Russia in 2018. In the European qualification games, its group included Poland, Montenegro, Romania, Armenia, and Kazakhstan. Denmark finished in second place behind Poland and had a two-game playoff with Ireland (who had finished second in its group behind Serbia). On November 11, 2017, Denmark and Ireland tied 0-0 in Copenhagen. Then on November 14, 2017, Denmark brought its A-game with a 5-1 victory in Dublin. This allowed the Danes to compete in World Cup 2018.

On the grand stage in Russia, Denmark found itself in Group C, which consisted of France, Peru, and Australia, and it took second place. Right out of the gate, in the Round of 16, Denmark lost in penalty kicks to Croatia. This summed up its World Cup ride in 2018.

As one can imagine, World Cup 2022 is an epic opportunity for the Danes to make up for lost time.

UEFA EUROPEAN CHAMPIONSHIP

Denmark won the Euro championship in 1992. To date, this has been Denmark's biggest triumph. Most recently, in the 2020 competition, Denmark was confronted with major adversity. After its star player, Christian Eriksen, went down in the first game with a medical injury, which was surreal and likely the most dramatic event to ever occur in a Euro tournament, Denmark rallied with a lot of emotion and eventually made it to the semi-finals. At this point, despite a great effort, the Danes lost 2-1 to England.

FACTS ABOUT THEIR COUNTRY

Beautiful castles, green hills, majestic coastal views, and domestic beer that's top shelf, Denmark has it. Denmark has a population of around 5.8 million people with an estimated GDP of $370 billion. It's a small geographic section of Europe that juts out from the northern part of Germany into the southern tip of Scandinavia; as such, Denmark has the North Sea to its west and the Baltic Sea to its east.

From this small little area, soccer brand Hummel—which has headquarters in Denmark—has made a big impression with players and fans over the years. With an undertone of national pride, Hummel has been heavily involved with the Danish national team. Here's a list of kit brands over the years for Denmark:

Hummel (1979-2004)   Hummel (2016-present)
Adidas (2004-16)

The leading scorers in Denmark's history are:

1. Poul Nielsen and Jon Dahl   2. Pauli Jorgensen (44)
   Tomasson (52)   3. Ole Madsen (42)

A few brews to be enjoyed by fans during the World Cup include: Albani Giraf Gold and Carls Porter.

WHERE THE TEAM IS TODAY—TACTICS AND STRATEGIES

The Danes are organized, well positioned, firm on defense, and possess smart, very patient short-passing schemes (with impressive technical undertones of futsal and indoor soccer).

Denmark has benefitted from a resurgence of talent in recent years. The Danes have produced highly skillful teams such as the 1992 Euro champs and the Dazzling Danes of the 1986 World Cup. Despite this reservoir of talent, which has risen to the surface today, the ability to rein in a World Cup title has been elusive for the Hummel-wearing technicians. This is where the current team has an opportunity to right the wrongs of the past, mitigate the deleterious effects from not playing in a World Cup before 1986, change the course of history, and make Denmark a world champion.

Tactics and strategies: On this quest to win a World Cup, one that is very attainable, Coach Kasper Hjulmand and team will probably operate out of a 3-4-3, perhaps a 4-1-4-1, or maybe even a 5-4-1. These formations were seen at one time or another during World Cup qualifiers in Europe's Group F. Possibly this musical chair approach to formations will only strengthen the awareness of players should they have to adjust in the World Cup, but employing three defenders is never a good idea—the strength in defense is diminished and the options for backline possession are limited. Perhaps Denmark will rely on the innate quality bestowed upon the current players from the 1992 Euro championship run, as if by telepathy. Teams such as Brazil or Italy know full well that relying on past success is a mysterious process that has no guaranteed outcome. On a smaller scale, Denmark certainly has this on its side. Denmark is on the cusp of something great every time it enters a tournament. It's definitely a plus for Denmark to have a Euro title within its inner soccer DNA. Will a World Cup championship come to fruition? That's another question. Good luck, Denmark.

KASPER HJULMAND—A BRIEF COACHING PORTRAIT

Kasper Hjulmand took over as Denmark's coach in 2020. Prior to Hjulmand, Morten Olsen held the job from 2000-2015. In December 2015, it was made known that Age Hareide, a former Norway national team player, was the new coach, and he led the squad from 2016-20. (For a short stint, thanks to some wrangling between the Danish Football Union and the players, John Jensen, a former Danish national team player, stepped in as caretaker in 2018 for a friendly game between Denmark and Slovakia.)

Now with Qatar in view, Denmark's present coach, Kasper Hjulmand is ready to make history. Kasper H—born in 1972—played for a time with the University of North Florida and then subsequently spent time with Danish sides Randers Freja, Herlev IF, and B.93. Since 2008, he's spent a significant amount of time coaching at FC Nordsjaelland and, to a lesser extent, Mainz 05. Despite his experience with teams that aren't exactly household names, Kasper H has managed to prove his worth and instrumentally position himself as national coach for one of the top squads in the world. To see such a rise is astounding. Under the guidance of Kasper H, Denmark is a passing team that moves the ball across the field well with an eye to penetrate dangerous areas around opposing defenses with skill, smarts, and dexterity. One drawback is that Denmark doesn't use the two-man game approach—as so elegantly punctuated by Spain—and this very well might be an issue as the World Cup progresses. Without a steady flow of two-man game passing, the possession of a team tends to fall apart around the opposing team's box; it will be interesting to see how Kasper H adjusts if this turns out to be the case. Another problem is the lack of a star player to lean on for goals. The team approach formula of Kasper H will be at the forefront, and the indoor-esque skill his players tend to exude will be pivotal for scoring chances and success.

KEY PLAYERS AND THEIR CHARACTERISTICS

He has a presence. You don't want to mess with this guy. **Simon Kjaer**—blonde, all of 6'3" who has over 115 caps and counting as a center defender—brings energy, passion, tattooed arms, and hard tackles to defense…which often leave attackers on the ground, wondering what happened. Denmark's captain and the soul of its defense has played for a number of clubs, the most recent of which include Sevilla, Atalanta, and A.C. Milan. Born in 1989 in Horsens, Denmark, Kjaer enters Qatar in his early 30s, and this might just be his last hope to bring home a World Cup title.

Pierre-Emile Kordt Højbjerg—born in 1995—is a talented midfielder who brings club experience from Bayern Munich, Southampton, and recently Tottenham Hotspur. He played his first game for Denmark in 2014 and since then has gathered over 50 caps. His EPL experience along with that of his national team will be crucial for Denmark moving forward. In addition, his defensive presence and transition passing will account for a much-needed flow in play for his side to have positive results.

Thomas Delaney—born in 1991—is a 6'0" midfielder tasked with the responsibility of guiding Denmark forward with distribution, possession, organization, and defensive work and the ability to somehow tie it all together with goals. He has a wealth of experience from the club side of things, having suited up with Copenhagen, Werder Bremen, Borussia Dortmund, and Sevilla. His experience with Denmark dates back to 2013, and currently he has over 60 caps for his home nation. Much of Denmark's success will rest on his shoulders.

Yussuf Poulsen—born in 1994 in Denmark—is a 6'4" forward who joined the national team in 2014 and has over 65 caps to date. He's played in over 240 games for RB Leipzig where he's acquired over 65 goals since 2013.

Martin Braithwaite—born in 1991—is a formidable 5'10" forward with experience from the venerated Barcelona and has over 55 caps for Denmark since his debut in 2013. Playing for such a team as Barcelona, one of the best in the history of the sport, brings an interesting bag of expectations from fans, as they'll certainly be counting on Braithwaite for goals. Can he live up to it? Can he handle the pressure? He has a talented group of teammates around him, including top forwards Andreas Cornelius and Yussuf Poulsen, that will help alleviate some of the mounting pressure.

OVERALL PLAYER RATING

Simon Kjaer: 9.3   Yussuf Poulsen: 9

Pierre-Emile Kordt Højbjerg: 9   Martin Braithwaite: 9.2

Thomas Delaney: 9.2

KEY PLAYER STATS

(Total career goals for their country)

	Games Played	Goals
Simon Kjaer	119	5
Pierre Højbjerg	58	5
Thomas Delaney	69	7
Yussuf Poulsen	68	11
Martin Braithwaite	60	10

WHAT TO WATCH FOR ON TV

Denmark's team has always been high quality, yet it hasn't quite lived up to its neighbor Germany. Where Germany has led the world in soccer for years with four World Cup titles and multiple Euro wins, Denmark has only achieved one Euro.

Yet Denmark remains a threat to Germany and every other team around the world. The Danes are still just slightly behind the top-brass in the world, yet each World Cup provides a new opportunity to grab all the marbles.

It's interesting to think that World Cup qualifiers are, in fact, part of the World Cup! As such, qualifiers are extremely important. Leading up to and during European qualifiers for World Cup 2022, Denmark enjoyed the services of **goalkeepers** Kasper Peter Schmeichel, Frederik Riis Rønnow, and Jonas Lössl; **defenders** Simon Kjaer, Nicolai Boilesen, Mathias Jørgensen, Henrik Dalsgaard, Joachim Andersen, Jannik Vestergaard, Joakim Mæhle Pedersen, Andreas Christensen, and Jens Stryger Larsen; **midfielders** Thomas Delaney, Daniel Wass, Mathias Jensen, Christian Nørgaard, Mikkel Damsgaard, Lasse Schöne, Lukas Lerager, and Pierre-Emile Højbjerg; and **forwards** Martin Braithwaite, Yussuf Poulsen, Kasper Dolberg, Pione Sisto, Mohamed Daramy, Jacob Bruun Larsen, Andreas Skov Olsen, Jonas Wind, Andreas Cornelius, and Robert Skov.

On route to Qatar, Denmark was in Group F in European qualifiers, alongside Scotland, Israel, Austria, Faroe Islands, and Moldova.

Denmark's World Cup journey in Qatar will be highly influenced by all the players that were part of the ride.

A big loss for the team came when **Christian Eriksen** endured a medical injury during the 2020 UEFA Euro. As a player, he has been superb. His club career has included high places: Ajax, Tottenham Hotspur, Inter Milan. As of 2022, the star player had an impressive 38 goals for his nation. Since his medical injury in the 2020 Euro, he's made a comeback. Eriksen's presence in Qatar would be a plus, as he is a talented scorer. When it's all said and done, it will be up to the current team to figure out ways to bring in substantial scoring chances.

A few players ready for the challenge are defender Simon Kjaer, midfielders Pierre-Emile Kordt Højbjerg and Thomas

Delaney, forwards Martin Braithwaite, Kasper Dolberg, Andreas Cornelius (a 6'5" power forward), and Yussuf Poulsen (who has a knack for scoring). Denmark usually doesn't score a huge number of goals, with the exception of Eriksen, who, up until recently, has accounted for the majority of the team's scoring. He will most definitely provide inspiration as the Dazzling Danes push forward in Qatar.

For soccer connoisseurs, the Danes are fun to watch. Outdoor soccer tactics mixed with skillful elements of indoor play about the pitch. It's a team that gracefully combines technical ability and short passing. Denmark, at its best—annihilating an ill-prepared team like Israel 5-0 on September 7, 2021, during qualifiers—will work the ball with precision and timing around the field. This approach tends to get most players touches on the ball. At its worst, Denmark can struggle to find answers as it lacks a true superstar to singlehandedly take over a game. Though keep in mind, this is part of Denmark's strength. It's a true team effort.

POLAND
World Cup titles: 0
Overall Team Rating: 8.9-9.1

A BRIEF TEAM HISTORY
Let's take a brief look at the World Cup record of Poland.
1930: Poland didn't compete.
1934: Didn't qualify.
1938: Made the Round of 16.
1950: Didn't compete.
1954: Didn't qualify.
1958: Didn't qualify.
1962: Didn't qualify.
1966: Didn't qualify.

1970: Didn't qualify.
1974: Poland placed third.
1978: Couldn't escape its group.
1982: Poland placed third.
1986: Made the Round of 16.
1990: Didn't qualify.
1994: Didn't qualify.
1998: Didn't qualify.
2002: Couldn't escape its group.
2006: Couldn't escape its group.
2010: Didn't qualify.
2014: Didn't qualify.
2018: Couldn't escape its group.

UEFA EUROPEAN CHAMPIONSHIP
The Euro hasn't exactly been Poland's tournament of choice. The best result was a quarter-finals appearance in 2016.

FACTS ABOUT THEIR COUNTRY
Poland, whose capitol is Warsaw, has a population of about 38.2 million people and an estimated GDP of $720 billion. Who has the most goals for Poland's national team?

1. Robert Lewandowski (76)*
2. Wlodzimierz (maybe we'll call him "W") Lubanski (48)
3. Grzegorz (maybe we'll call him "Greg") Lato (45)

Beers from Poland?

Lech	Tyskie
Żywiec	Żubr
Okocim	

---

*   Still active, and this number will likely increase.

WHERE THE TEAM IS TODAY—TACTICS AND STRATEGIES

Tactics and strategies: During an important World Cup qualifier for Qatar, Poland went with a 3-1-4-2 against England in a 1-1 tie on September 8, 2021. This was just about a year before the 2022 World Cup. On November 15, 2021, still during qualifiers, Poland was seen using a 3-1-4-2 in a 2-1 loss to Hungary that took place in Warsaw. Despite the loss, Poland was determined to make it through qualifiers, though not without a struggle. The 3-1-4-2 is nothing more than a 4-4-2 in disguise. Expect more of the same from Poland in Qatar.

Poland's fight through the qualifiers was won by one man: Robert Lewandowski. Lewandowski, Bayern Munich's star, is the man. He's thought of by many as the best striker in the world. With Lewandowski in place, scoring goals from all angles as he does, Poland always has hope. With a superstar in its arsenal, this is one of those teams that is going to depend on its star as long as it can. The attack revolves around Lewandowski. One issue for Poland will be to keep everyone involved, though. If the attack only goes through Lewandowski, then other players won't have touches on the ball. With the high stakes of a World Cup, all players must be involved for Lewandowski to succeed. If everyone does well, he'll do well. It's a team balancing act. If Poland struggles, it will be because too much attention has been paid to its star. Success will come from balance in the attack.

As a weaker side in the tournament, Poland has its work cut out for it. It's not just a group with names that are hard to pronounce. It's a steady team with hard workers. It's a very determined team, one that has strong will and a lot of fight. Poland's a contender, though it's flirting with disaster in each game.

Poland's attack is very deliberate. It focuses a lot of attention down the wings, pushing the ball about with crisp attention to pace, detail, and forward movement. A lack of creative dribbling will restrict much of Poland's potential success. Without a flashy side to its game, Poland will have a difficult time advancing in Qatar. Polish fans will dream of a result akin to that of Italy in 1982, in that Lewandowski would be the beneficiary of many goals, much like Paolo Rossi, thanks to his teammates and a lot of hard work. That dream could become a reality as both Lewandowski and Rossi rank as elite scoring forces that can carry a team. But for Poland to accomplish such a feat, the conditions have to be just right.

Despite being a quality side, Poland is a few steps behind the leaders of world soccer such as Brazil, France, and Germany. At times, as if trying to outdo the somewhat low expectations, Poland rushes the attack a bit. It plays like a team trying to catch the leaders. If it can overcome this temptation and concentrate more on steady possession play, then good things should come its way.

CZESLAW MICHNIEWICZ—A BRIEF COACHING PORTRAIT
One obvious issue that will negatively affect Poland is that on January 23, 2022, its coaching position was vacant! This set back, so close to the competition, was not a good sign. However, in February of 2022, **Czesław Michniewicz** was brought in to save the day! Czesław—born in 1970—has had a number of different coaching jobs, including coach of Legia Warsaw (2020-21). His last-minute appointment to lead Poland into the 2022 FIFA World Cup should be the ride of a lifetime for the former goalkeeper.

KEY PLAYERS AND THEIR CHARACTERISTICS
Robert Lewandowski won The Best FIFA Men's Player award in 2020 and 2021, a distinguished honor, one of many accolades he's received over the years. He is one of the world's best living strikers. If you're looking for a guy that scored 41 goals in a Bundesliga season, you've got him. Lewandowski represents Bayern Munich as not just an all-time great German league forward, which is saying something, but an all-time great in the history of the sport. His scoring touch is uncanny; it's as though the ball is destined for the net when he gives it forward

momentum. From head balls to one-touch finishes, from all angles to shots of varying types around the box—he has power, touch, technical ability, accuracy, and an overall game IQ that sets him apart. He's a finisher. Plain and simple.

Kamil Glik—born in 1988—is Poland's vice-captain with a ton of experience from Torino, Monaco, and Benevento. The 6'3" center defender represents Poland with over 85 caps, a handful of goals. He'll keep the passing in a constant flow throughout the backline, while his leadership and defending abilities will help guide his national team to perhaps a miraculous World Cup championship!

Krzysztof Piątek—born in 1995—is a 6'0" striker who brings valuable experience from Genoa, A.C. Milan, and Hertha BSC. In 2018, he joined Poland's senior national team whereby he's surpassed 20 caps and has turned into one of the team's top scorers.

A forward that will give you strong minutes with an appetite for goals is **Arkadiusz Milik**. The 6'1" star has spent time with quality teams, including Bayer Leverkusen, Ajax, Napoli, and Marseille. With Napoli, he's powered in over 35 goals. As for Poland, where he's appeared since 2012, he's gone past 15 goals and is looking for more. His instincts to score are superb, along with his touch and ability to set up a shot. He's a player opposing teams should keep an eye on.

Kamil Grosicki—born in 1988—steps up as a 5'11" winger who has played in over 115 games for Hull City with a substantial 24 goals. This would be his longest stint with a club, lasting from 2017-20. When it comes to Poland, he's a vet's vet. His first match was in 2008. Subsequently, he's attained over 80 caps with over 15 goals.

Grzegorz Krychowiak—born in 1990—stands out as a veteran presence for Poland. The 6'1" defensive mid has racked up a number of games with different clubs that include the likes of Bordeaux, Reims, Nantes, Sevilla, PSG, West Bromwich Albion, Lokomotiv Moscow, and Krasnodar. With Lokomotiv

Moscow he tallied up a little over 18 goals, more than usual. During his 80-plus games with Poland, he's tapped in a few goals, but he's known more for his defensive work in midfield, stopping opponents and distributing the ball throughout the pitch. In Qatar, should he score, it would be nice. However, he'll be expected to keep a tidy ship for Poland to have any success.

Piotr Zieliński—born in 1994—gives comfort to Poland's lineup as a 5'10" midfielder who has traversed the fields of glory with the impressive Italian sides of Udinese, Empoli, and Napoli. As for Napoli, the midfield sensation joined in 2016 and hit the 200-game mark. With such experience at a high level, Poland's in good hands. After joining Poland's senior national team in 2013, he's gone over 65 matches played, with a handful of goals.

OVERALL PLAYER RATING

Robert Lewandowski: 10   Kamil Grosicki: 9
Kamil Glik: 9   Grzegorz Krychowiak: 8.9
Krzysztof Piątek: 9   Piotr Zieliński: 9.2
Arkadiusz Milik: 9

KEY PLAYER STATS

(Total career goals for their country)

	Games Played	Goals
Robert Lewandowski	132	76
Kamil Glik	96	6
Krzysztof Piątek	23	10
Arkadiusz Milik	62	16
Kamil Grosicki	86	17
Grzegorz Krychowiak	91	5
Piotr Zieliński	72	9

WHAT TO WATCH FOR ON TV

Leading up to and during European qualifiers for Qatar, Poland used the efforts of **goalkeepers** Wojciech Szczęsny and Łukasz Fabiański; **defenders** Tomasz Kędziora, Jan Bednarek, Maciej Rybus, Tymoteusz Puchacz, Bartosz Bereszyński, Kamil Glik, and Arkadiusz Reca; **midfielders** Karol Linetty, Mateusz Klich, Jakub Moder, Przemysław Frankowski, Piotr Zieliński, Kamil Jóźwiak, Grzegorz Krychowiak, Przemysław Płacheta, Sebastian Szymański, Kamil Grosicki, and Bartosz Kapustka; and **forwards** Robert Lewandowski, Arkadiusz "Arek" Milik, Karol Świderski, Krzysztof Piątek, Dawid Kownacki, Jakub Świerczok, and Adam Buksa.

On route to Qatar, Poland was in Group I in European Qualifiers, alongside England, Albania, Hungary, Andorra, and San Marino.

Poland's big chance is now. Lewandowski, the team's superstar, is about to have his last World Cup. He was born in 1988. His career has only a few more years. Furthermore, in terms of style, Poland is walking on thin ice with its star. If it relies too much on him, the other players might get lost in the shuffle. If it doesn't involve him enough, it could be an opportunity lost. This is part of Poland's dilemma. While Lewandowski leads the cause, Poland has a squadron of talent that might not be household names. There are a number of highly talented players that get lost in Lewandowski's broad shadow. A good playmaker, midfielder **Mateusz Klich** is one. He'll be an important part of the lineup along with Kamil Glik, Krzysztof Piątek, Arkadiusz Milik, Kamil Grosicki, Grzegorz Krychowiak, and Piotr Zieliński.

The pressure is on. Poland has gotten third place in World Cup competition before. Yet, most people around the world don't think of Poland as a legitimate World Cup threat. Sure, it's a competitive team, a meager contender. Still, Poland is a nation of ultra-proud soccer fans who are dreaming of a big win for their team. Then there's reality and Poland's existing World Cup record. Poland was a dangerous squad in the 70s and 80s, no doubt. Yet it's always come away empty handed. For Poland, this is an opportunity to prove everyone around the world wrong. This is an opportunity, with one of the greatest forwards to ever adorn a pair of cleats, to risk everything, throw caution to the wind, and take it all!

PORTUGAL

World Cup titles: 0
Overall Team Rating: 9.3

A BRIEF TEAM HISTORY

Let's take a brief look at the World Cup record of Portugal.

1930: Portugal didn't compete.

1934: Didn't qualify.

1938: Didn't qualify.

1950: Didn't qualify.

1954: Didn't qualify.

1958: Didn't qualify.

1962: Didn't qualify.

1966: Portugal finished third. By way of the fleet feet and scoring talent of Eusebio, Portugal finally achieved success in World Cup competition.

1970: Didn't qualify.

1974: Didn't qualify.

1978: Didn't qualify.

1982: Didn't qualify.

1986: Portugal couldn't escape its group.

1990: Didn't qualify.

1994: Didn't qualify.

1998: Didn't qualify.

2002: Couldn't escape its group.

2006: Portugal earned fourth place. Figo and a young Cristiano Ronaldo helped Portugal surge forward with a fourth-place finish.

2010: Made the Round of 16.

2014: Couldn't escape its group.
2018: Portugal made the Round of 16.

UEFA EUROPEAN CHAMPIONSHIP
Cristiano Ronaldo and Nani led Portugal to the 2016 UEFA Euro championship. To date, this is the only Euro title for Portugal.

FACTS ABOUT THEIR COUNTRY
Portugal, a beautiful country overlooking the Atlantic Ocean, has a population of around 10.3 million people and an estimated GDP of $257 billion.

At the 2006 World Cup, Portugal received FIFA's "Most Entertaining Team Award." History was made in 2016 as Portugal won its first UEFA Euro championship. In 2017, Portugal earned third place in the Confederations Cup held in Russia. Who are the top three scorers in the history of Portugal's national team?

1. Cristiano Ronaldo (117)*   **3.** Eusebio (41)
2. Pauleta (47)

Portugal has fantastic vineyards, and when it comes to beer you can enjoy quality tasting with a number of choices, including:
Super Bock   Coral   Sagres

WHERE THE TEAM IS TODAY—TACTICS AND STRATEGIES
The 2016 UEFA Euro champs play a fluid style that pounces on counterattacks and emphasizes short-passing combinations to free up runners down the wings. The attack will be concentrated on using scoring legend Cristiano Ronaldo.

Tactics and strategies: Portugal will most likely field a 4-3-3 or a 4-2-3-1. In most scenarios, the ideal situation for Portugal is to involve its star forward Ronaldo who thrives out wide. As one of the

---

* Still active, and this number will likely increase.

world's greatest players in history, the team will rely heavily on his involvement. Without Ronaldo, should he suffer an injury, the team is in trouble. The more touches he can get, the better. Don't get too excited, though. When one player is overly ball-centric, it can have a negative result that other players feel blocked from expressing themselves. When such a situation dictates that the offense revolves around one player as much as possible, then it discourages teammates from passing to others, making what might be "the right pass in that moment" which potentially extinguishes proper flow in possession. It's a tricky balancing act. However, Ronaldo, by and large, is a good team player. If things don't go well with this plan in motion, the team might panic. Even at this level, with seasoned professionals left and right, panic can set in; after all, millions are watching with expectations on the line. Urgency and panic combine to form a terrible nightmare for any team down a goal or two. This is where the cool hand of Ronaldo comes into play, coupled with the expert leadership of veteran coach Fernando Santos.

FERNANDO SANTOS—A BRIEF COACHING PORTRAIT

Fernando Santos—born in 1954 in Lisbon, Portugal—joined Portugal as the head coach in 2014. Prior to this assignment, he was coach of Greece from 2010-14. In his days as a player, Santos suited up as a defender and played professionally from 1973 to 1987 with Portuguese clubs Estoril and Maritimo.

For the rest of his life, Santos is riding high on one of the biggest achievements a coach could ask for: the UEFA Euro. He delivered for his home country in grand fashion as the Portuguese defeated a highly favored French side in 2016, in France, even after Ronaldo had to exit the game injured. It was a testament to the resolve Portugal embodied which can be attributed to the wisdom and experience that Santos brings to his team.

The Euro is one thing, a monumental achievement no doubt. Yet the World Cup is the grand prize. Santos has brought his beloved Portugal back to the big show after navigating through European qualifiers in Group A against challengers Serbia, Ireland, Luxembourg, and Azerbaijan.

Santos led Portugal through the 2018 World Cup in Russia; however, the Portuguese lost in the Round of 16. With renewed energy, Santos has the honor—yet again—to guide his team through the 2022 World Cup in Qatar for the eighth time in his nation's history.

KEY PLAYERS AND THEIR CHARACTERISTICS

Cristiano Ronaldo—who's chiseled like an Olympic statue, the billion-dollar man, Nike's gem signing—has accolades that read like an ancient Egyptian pharaoh's wall carving. The UEFA Euro champion and Ballon d'Or winner on five occasions (2008, 2013, 2014, 2016, 2017) is regarded by most as one of the best of all time and certainly the lead contender for best winger of all time in league with other great outside dynamos like Bruno Conti, Denilson, Franck Ribery, and Arjen Robben. After his professional debut with Sporting CP, which didn't last long, he was soon gobbled up by Manchester United where he quickly sent shock waves throughout the soccer world with his electric pace, dynamic and eye-opening skill, powerful shot, and a will to score. Since his glory days in northwest England (2003-09), he's administered a statesmen-like persona, humble, dignified. All the same, he also made questionable decisions—such as disguising himself like a vagrant in downtown Madrid to fool passersby with soccer tricks—and, for the most part, paraded around like a peacock in a tuxedo, with much success, at Real Madrid and Juventus before returning to where he started: ManU. Say what you will about Ronaldo, he's soccer royalty with both virtues and faults. His day-to-day life reads like Michael Jordan during his peak wherein he couldn't even visit a mall, and, at times, had to shop after hours. Part of the intrigue toward Ronaldo is based on his fairy-tale–like success; for years he has been listed among the highest paid athletes in the world.[10] It seems like every ad available—print, digital, TV, billboards—has included him. His jersey sales, like that of Messi, Beckham, Zidane (and a few others), have been astronomical. Ronaldo's soccer journey has been epic. Ronaldo is determined as ever to make his mark on the FIFA World Cup stage with perhaps one last hurrah in Qatar for a chance to seize the ultimate prize: the very elusive Jules Rimet Trophy that has escaped his grasp all these years.

Bruno Fernandes—born in 1994 in Maia, Portugal—is an attacking mid who spent his formative years with quality club sides including Novara, Udinese, Sampdoria, Sporting CP, and in 2020 the 5'10" playmaker joined the lucrative Manchester United. In 2017, Fernandes earned his first cap with Portugal. As a seasoned midfielder, a championship in Qatar is within reach so long as he and Bernardo Silva, Andre Silva, and Ronaldo are on the same page. Distribution from Fernandes will be critical for team success. He's a risk taker, a quick box-to-box mover and shaker, one that shoots from outside the box, and one that has been criticized for turnovers, though he makes up for it with an all-around effort. Certainly, given his background, he's up for the challenge.

Bernardo Silva—born in 1994 in Lisbon, Portugal—brings a lot of swagger as an outside mid and winger, one that has been flaunting his stuff with renowned world-leader Manchester City since 2017. The 5'8" Portuguese star—who has acquired over 60 caps for his national team since 2015—will likely play the role of outside midfielder. He's a versatile talent that's been utilized from time to time as a center mid, second striker, attacking mid, false 9, outside wing-back, and a deep-lying playmaker. As a graceful and creative player that can dribble with dangerous results, retain possession, and penetrate defenses with smart plays, Silva can also score, which is something Portuguese fans are hoping for.

Andre Silva is 6'1" and is an extremely dangerous forward with experience from quality sides Porto, A.C. Milan, Sevilla,

Eintracht Frankfurt, and RB Leipzig. Since 2016, his opening game with Portugal, he's tallied over 18 goals for his nation. With this ability, he'll be expected to deliver a one-two punch with Ronaldo. In his mid-20s, Andre Silva is ready to generate action for his nation on route to a history-making title run. Can he do it? Of course, he won't be acting alone. Yet this is one of those career-defining opportunities as Ronaldo is still in the mix. Silva has a lot to prove, as do his teammates. He'll have to elude his markers, find spaces in-between defenders, and seize on half-chances to produce goals. This could be the big year. He has a prime opportunity to grab hold of the ultimate prize and make history. For the sake of Portuguese fans, hopefully he can deliver.

OVERALL PLAYER RATING

Cristiano Ronaldo: 10   Bernardo Silva: 9.2
Bruno Fernandes: 9.2   Andre Silva: 9.2

KEY PLAYER STATS

(Total career goals for their country)

	Games Played	Goals
Cristiano Ronaldo	189	117
Bruno Fernandes	46	8
Bernardo Silva	70	8
Andre Silva	51	19

WHAT TO WATCH FOR ON TV

A few Portuguese players that were available leading up to and during European qualifiers for World Cup 2022 included **goalkeepers** Rui Patrício, Anthony Lopes, and Diogo Costa; **defenders** Pepe, Jose Fonte, Ruben Dias, João Cancelo, Nélson Semedo, Nuno Mendes, Raphaël Guerreiro, Ricardo Pereira, Cédric Soares, and Luís Neto; **midfielders** Bruno Fernandes, Otávio Monteiro, Sérgio Oliveira, João Moutinho, William Carvalho, Danilo Pereira, João Mário, Renato Sanches, Rúben

Neves, and João Palhinha; and **forwards** Cristiano Ronaldo, Bernardo Silva, Andre Silva, Joao Felix, Gonçalo Guedes, Pedro Gonçalves, Pedro Neto, Rafael (AKA "Rafa") Silva, Rafael Leão, Diogo Jota, and Francisco António Machado Mota de Castro Trincão.

On route to Qatar, Portugal was in Group A in European qualifiers, along with Serbia, Ireland, Luxembourg, and Azerbaijan.

A Seleção—AKA *Os Navegadores*—are feeling a sense of urgency. After all, Portugal's greatest player—Ronaldo—might be participating in his last World Cup. When he goes, will Portugal return to the lost decade of the 1970s? The struggle for Portuguese soccer to be great—which indeed it has become—has been memorable. From Eusebio to Figo to Ronaldo, Portugal has produced *talento de alto nível* (top-level talent). It hasn't been an easy ride. What's more, there is reason for concern as Ronaldo's inevitable departure might leave his nation with a void in the superstar category. Correction. His departure *will* leave a void! Despite his current teammates being very good, it will be next to impossible to replace him. For now, though, with Ronaldo in place, the team will do everything possible to include him in every play. It's a symbiotic relationship in that if he does well, Portugal does well; and if the team does well, he does well.

With Bruno Fernandes, Bernardo Silva, and Andre Silva on the field, things are looking good. A few other players that will be pivotal in Portugal's success include midfielders Joao Mario (Benfica), who is approximately 5'10" and brings good experience to the table, along with veteran team leader Joao Moutinho (Wolverhampton Wanderers), who is 5'7"; forwards Diogo Jota (Liverpool), who is a talented 5'10" option in the attack, along with Mr. Magic, the highly skillful 5'11" Joao Felix (Atletico Madrid); and 6'2" defender Pepe (Porto).

At this point, now in his late 30s, Pepe is reaching the end of his career. Sidebar to readers: The tricky thing about a book—

which you're reading, versus a print magazine or some online publication that can change details on a whim—is that this book was printed just slightly before World Cup teams officially announced final rosters; the timeline is extremely close to the actual World Cup so therefore a book has to be printed and distributed before that time and someone like Pepe, given his age, might have been left off the final roster. Having said that, he probably was included and the longtime defender—who spent the majority of his club career with Real Madrid—is a guidepost for the squad in tight moments. He's a player that should help ease pressure as the tournament progresses.

Notwithstanding Ronaldo's age, which brings with it a slight decline in speed, look for Portugal to loft well-guided, intelligent, crosses into the box for him to guide home with superior jumping ability. As for set-pieces, step aside. He's taking it. His guided free kicks can knuckle in the air with great velocity. This causes great worry for keepers. Add to this Ronaldo's dribbling prowess (which electrifies audiences), his strong shot, and distribution around the box, and you have a potent attack that should cause major concern for other teams throughout the tournament.

SERBIA
World Cup titles: 0
Overall Team Rating: 8.7

A BRIEF TEAM HISTORY
Let's take a brief look at the World Cup record of Serbia.

1930: Competing under the umbrella of the Kingdom of Yugoslavia, fourth place.

1934: Didn't qualify.

1938: Didn't qualify.

1950: Competing under the umbrella of Yugoslavia, eliminated in the group stage.

1954: Quarter-finals.
1958: Quarter-finals.
1962: Fourth place.
1966: Didn't qualify.
1970: Didn't qualify.
1974: Couldn't get past the second group stage.
1978: Didn't qualify.
1982: Couldn't get past the group stage.
1986: Didn't qualify.
1990: Couldn't get past the quarter-finals.
1994: Didn't compete, under the umbrella of FR Yugoslavia.
1998: Made the Round of 16, competing under the umbrella of FR Yugoslavia.
2002: Didn't qualify, competing under the umbrella of FR Yugoslavia.
2006: As Serbia and Montenegro, the team couldn't escape the group stage.
2010: As Serbia, the team couldn't escape the group stage.
2014: As Serbia, the team didn't qualify.
2018: As Serbia, the team couldn't escape the group stage.
Serbia's first World Cup as "Serbia" was in 2010.

UEFA EUROPEAN CHAMPIONSHIP
As Serbia, a record in the UEFA Euro is yet to come about. Surely, down the road, expect good things from Serbia in this regard.

FACTS ABOUT THEIR COUNTRY
Serbia's population is around 6.8 million people and a GDP of about $52 billion. Not bad for a small country. Serbia is an interesting place tucked away just east of Italy. Writing for *CNN*, Mary Novakovich pointed out that "Serbia is a destination that tends to escape the attention of many travelers."[11] There's an understatement. Novakovich goes on to highlight some of the innate charm of the nation: "Serbia's landscapes range from

the endless plains of Vojvodina in the north—the country's breadbasket and wine cellar—to the dramatic mountains and gorges of the national parks in the south, west and east of this former Yugoslav republic. The legacies left by former rulers the Habsburgs and the Ottoman Turks can be found in everything from architecture to the cuisine, where East really does meet West."[12] In the heart of Serbia lies the drumbeat of passionate soccer fans. By and large, it's a nation with soccer on its mind. Aleksandar Mitrovic (46)* is the leading scorer for their team. Many Serbians will likely have Jelen Pivo beer in their hands during World Cup games.

WHERE THE TEAM IS TODAY—TACTICS AND STRATEGIES

Tactics and strategies: Serbia will likely go with a 3-4-1-2, or a similar 3-4-3 formation.

To win the World Cup outright will take a substantial effort from Serbia, one that might require the equivalent of 36 saves from the Serbian goalkeeper in each game. Serbia has very little experience in World Cup competition. The small nation is up against a swarm of experienced teams that hold multiple World Cup titles. What's more, despite doing well in European qualifiers, Serbia will have to stand up to the pressure of center stage in a World Cup, a much different place.

With the noteworthy offensive talent of Aleksandar Mitrovic, Zoran Tosic, and Dusan Tadic, Serbia is looking to build on successful outings as it enters a new World Cup phase of its international soccer agenda. After years under the umbrella of Yugoslavia, which provided a formidable program, Serbia has a good place to start.

Part of its challenge in Qatar will have to do with psychology. It's a team that can't allow itself to get psyched out by the moment, the opposing team, or the grand stage. It has the

---

*   Still active, and this number will likely increase.

talent, but the question is, how can it blend all its strengths into one successful product? Once the game starts, it's easy to say "keep possession strong" and go from there! The pressure is on, and Serbia will have to grapple with staying cool under pressure. A dilemma. In fact, a myriad of middle-of-the-road teams suffer from this dilemma. Serbia and Japan fall into a similar category. Both teams are talented, and both could theoretically be dark horses in the World Cup. However, a big problem arises when both teams meet other more experienced sides, such as Germany and Brazil. The experienced teams have a psychological edge as longstanding international powerhouses and, in some cases, former World Cup champions. As such, as games draw closer to a finish, Serbia might start to unravel on defense and rush things on offense. Never a good place to be in the 82nd minute! Hopefully, for Serbia's sake, cool heads will prevail and show the world that it belongs with the best. As a small nation with big ambition, Serbia has a lot riding on this World Cup.

DRAGAN STOJKOVIC—A BRIEF COACHING PORTRAIT
Dragan Stojković—born in 1965—was a midfielder in his playing days. He first appeared with the Yugoslavia national team in 1983, and he eventually earned 84 caps, 15 goals. As of 2021, he assumed the position of head coach for Serbia, just a year or so before the 2022 FIFA World Cup. In Qatar, he'll be leading a nation hungry for a big moment on the grandest of stages. Hopefully, Dragan and company will be able to pull off a dark-horse performance for the ages with a championship at the end. How likely this scenario will be is another story altogether. For now, everything is looking up as the team earned its way through the most competitive qualifier in the world, Europe. Dragan hasn't coached too many teams, yet his experience is deep and cultivated, having led Japanese club Nagoya Grampus and Chinese club Guangzhou R&F. With Serbia in Qatar, his approach will likely revolve around passing combinations that

accentuate the dynamic play of Aleksandar Mitrovic, Dusan Tadic, and Dušan Vlahović.

KEY PLAYERS AND THEIR CHARACTERISTICS

Aleksandar Mitrovic is a 6'2", impactful target forward who positions well and, to the delight of Serbian fans, can finish around goal. He signed with Newcastle United in 2015, as they recognized his scoring touch; eventually Fulham saw the same, and he signed there in 2018. Since his first game with Serbia in 2013, he's been a big-time scorer with over 40 goals to date and counting; Serbians are hoping for this trend to continue in Qatar.

Luka Jović—born in 1997—AKA ultra-forward, the man with a plan, is 6'0" and has lots of experience with Red Star Belgrade, Benfica, Eintracht Frankfurt, and Real Madrid. He joined Serbia in 2018 and will be called upon for greatness in Qatar.

Dusan Tadic—born in 1988 in Yugoslavia—is an elusive midfielder who joined Southampton in 2014 and Ajax in 2018. The 5'11" all-around talent did well in EPL before moving on to Netherland's best club. He's a steady scoring option for Serbia with a good shot from outside, and since his national team debut in 2008, he's netted over 15 goals. In addition, he's a playmaker; whether it's dribbling past opponents or delivering a clever back-heel, Serbia has a better chance to win with Tadic on the ball.

Dušan Vlahović—born in 2000—is a tough forward to contend with. At 6'3", he'll provide challenges in the box for defenders on crosses and set-pieces. He has a strong shot and should be a valuable linkup target for his teammates in Qatar. As of early 2022, the majority of his club experience has been with Fiorentina, where he attained over 95 appearances, with 44 goals. Also, in 2022, he joined Juventus where he's scored over 5 goals. He debuted with Serbia in 2020. So far, he's delivered on goals, and Serbian fans will be expecting big results from him in Qatar.

OVERALL PLAYER RATING

Aleksandar Mitrovic: 9.4   Dusan Tadic: 9.4
Luka Jović: 9.2   Dušan Vlahović: 9.3

KEY PLAYER STATS

(Total career goals for their country)

	Games Played	Goals
Aleksandar Mitrovic	74	46
Luka Jović	26	9
Dusan Tadic	88	18
Dušan Vlahović	14	7

WHAT TO WATCH FOR ON TV

Leading up to and during European qualifiers for World Cup 2022, Serbia had a ton of players that participated, including **goalkeepers** Predrag Rajković, Marko Dmitrović, and Mile Svilar; **defenders** Matija Nastasić, Nikola Milenković, Stefan Mitrović, Uroš Spajić, Filip Mladenović, Miloš Veljković, Strahinja Pavlović, Mihailo Ristić, and Aleksandar Kolarov; **midfielders** Dusan Tadic, Filip Kostić, Nemanja "Neno" Gudelj, Nemanja Maksimović, Sergej Milinković-Savić, Saša Lukić, Darko Lazović, Andrija Živković, Marko Grujić, Uroš Račić, Mijat Gaćinović, Aleksandar Katai, and Luka Milivojević; and **forwards** Aleksandar Mitrovic, Luka Jović, Dušan Vlahović, and Dejan Joveljić.

During European qualifiers for the 2022 FIFA World Cup, Serbia was in Group A with Portugal, Ireland, Luxembourg, and Azerbaijan. It largely had to jostle with Portugal and Ireland for group supremacy. It was an exciting, strenuous ride that turned out better than Serbia could've hoped for.

Now in the World Cup, Serbia has a lot of work ahead. As mentioned earlier, with immense pressure to perform on the biggest stage, Serbia does not want to find itself in a situation—down a goal or two—when the easy stuff becomes difficult, then the hard stuff becomes nearly impossible. Staying cool under pressure is key. Midfield interplay and active movement toward goal will define Serbia's chances to win. The combination of Serbian legends Jović and Mitrovic is vital for any possible success. They have linked up numerous times in the past, and their chemistry should be on full display. Whether the defense can avoid sloppy errors on the backline is another story. Should the coaching staff and players correct tiny issues here and there, Serbia will be a team to reckon with for this World Cup.

SWITZERLAND
World Cup titles: 0
Overall Team Rating: 8.7

A BRIEF TEAM HISTORY
Let's take a brief look at the World Cup record of Switzerland.
1930: Switzerland didn't compete.
1934: Switzerland made the quarter-finals.
1938: Switzerland made the quarter-finals.
1950: Didn't escape its group.
1954: Switzerland made the quarter-finals.
1958: Didn't qualify.
1962: Didn't escape its group.
1966: Didn't escape its group.
1970: Didn't qualify.
1974: Didn't qualify.
1978: Didn't qualify.
1982: Didn't qualify.
1986: Didn't qualify.
1990: Didn't qualify.
1994: Finally, back in the World Cup, Switzerland made the Round of 16.
1998: Didn't qualify.
2002: Didn't qualify.
2006: Made the Round of 16.

2010: Didn't escape its group.
2014: Made the Round of 16.
2018: Made the Round of 16.

UEFA EUROPEAN CHAMPIONSHIP

Switzerland's best result in the Euro was the recent 2020 competition in which it reached the quarter-finals. Not exactly turning the world upside down. As a soccer nation on the rise, perhaps the Swiss will provide more excitement down the road.

FACTS ABOUT THEIR COUNTRY

The beautiful mountainous nation of Switzerland has a population of about 8.5 million people and an estimated GDP of $749 billion. Switzerland is the birthplace of Roger Federer, Erich von Däniken, and Giorgio Tsoukalos. The Large Hadron Collider—a particle accelerator—rests on the French-Swiss border near Geneva. Who are Switzerland's top scorers?

1. Alexander Frei (42)   **2.** Kubilay Türkyilmaz and Max Abegglen (34)

Welcome to a few Swiss beers:
Erdinger   Vollmond

WHERE THE TEAM IS TODAY—TACTICS AND STRATEGIES

Tactics and strategies: Switzerland will most likely use a 4-2-3-1 or perhaps a 4-3-2-1 formation; a 4-3-3 wouldn't be out of the realm of possibilities either. Switzerland, for the most part, has always been a solid team. Though, it could be argued, in the past 20 years or so, it has really upped its game and presents more of a threat these days than ever before.

What Switzerland has going for it, that is a common theme in each game, is a unified team effort with solid players across the board who have confidence and resolve, even against a strong opponent. It's a team that doesn't get extremely rattled when things are looking bleak. This is important, as teams around the world—such as Panama and Canada—can't say the same. In terms of strategy, Switzerland is already on the right path—its players are ready, confident, poised, and experienced within the realm of European club competition.

As defense goes, the Swiss need to be sure marking is strong and team shape stays in place so it can press high around the halfway line as much as possible. If anything were to hold this group back, it will come in the form of petty errors around its own box, errors that allow opposition to get half-chances and tap-ins around goal. These types of mistakes often occur during corner kicks, and, as such, the Swiss need to clamp down on the little things to avoid problems.

On offense, Switzerland will remain steadfast in a relentless pursuit of combination passing that creeps toward the goal in a relatively innocuous manner that just might catch you off-guard. It's a constructive, thoughtful approach that enables the Swiss to stay in games as a legit threat.

As much as possible, the Swiss pursue a counterattack, and this will be of great importance for success. Also, Switzerland will rely on set-pieces around the box for strong chances. All in all, this is a team that resides in the upper middle-of-the-road. As such, do not count the Swiss out.

MURAT YAKIN—A BRIEF COACHING PORTRAIT
Murat Yakin—born in 1974 in Basel, Switzerland—took over the position of head coach for the Swiss in 2021, just a year prior to FIFA World Cup 2022. One might argue this wasn't much prep time for Yakin. As for Swiss naysayers in rival Luxembourg, they probably can't wait to see him fail. Nonetheless, Yakin has the opportunity of a lifetime to take his beloved national team as far as one might expect in Qatar. Unfortunately, judging from past Swiss forays into World Cups, one would not expect a championship game between Brazil

and Switzerland! However, this is exactly why Yakin is sitting pretty. While expectations from fans are relatively low, optimism remains high; as such, he can swoop in and catch many teams off guard. Yakin played a large part of his professional career with Grasshoppers, a franchise known for catching opposition off guard. As an experienced center defender, Yakin also played a great deal with the Swiss national team from 1994-2004, amassing an impressive 49 caps and four goals. Charged with coaching the national team under a tight timeline, Yakin has a lot put on his plate. Though, Swiss fans won't expect him to change the world in one tournament. On a positive note, Switzerland has recently mounted a major attack on international soccer; it is a team to be reckoned with on any given day. Certainly, Switzerland has always been a competitive side, one capable of an upset or two; for instance, it was mildly astounding to see Switzerland defeat Spain—the eventual World champions— in the 2010 World Cup. When it's all said and done, Yakin's journey in Qatar will depend a lot on how things play out in the Group stage. Here's the thing: The Swiss are a top-level side. Yet the team has limitations. Yakin will have to prove to spectators that his team and approach are more than a footnote in the paper. While sports betters might not be putting much faith in Switzerland, the element of surprise will be Yakin's best weapon.

KEY PLAYERS AND THEIR CHARACTERISTICS

Xherdan Shaqiri—born in 1991—is a hard-working 5'7" midfielder with experience from FC Basel, Bayern Munich, Inter Milan, Stoke City, Liverpool, and Lyon. He has established his leadership within Switzerland's ranks since his first appearance in 2010. You'll get a straightforward effort from him, as he'll leave nothing on the table. Perhaps down the road, you're looking at Switzerland's next head coach.

    Renato Steffen—born in 1991—will be found out wide, and his work ethic will be counted on for Swiss success if the team should go deep in the tournament. At 5'7", Steffen has been around a bit with experience from FC Thun, Young Boys, FC Basel, and VfL Wolfsburg. Steffen made his first appearance for Switzerland in 2015.

Mario Gavranović has plenty of club experience from Schalke 04, Mainz 05, FC Zurich, and Dinamo Zagreb. The 5'9" forward is a veteran as he first suited up for Switzerland in 2011; he'll be useful for Swiss success as, to date, he's amassed over 15 goals for the national team.

Ruben Vargas—born in 1998—provides quickness, speed, versatility, and endurance for the Swiss. Vargas is that punch Switzerland needs. As a very effective outside midfielder, he provides the spark necessary to keep opponents off balance. He's what you might call a "young veteran" as he joined Switzerland for the first time in 2019. He should be instrumental throughout the tournament.

Haris Seferovic—born in 1992—gives Switzerland experience and goals. As a well-traveled pro, he joined Benfica in 2017 and has scored over 50 times. The 6'2" forward first appeared for his nation in 2013 and since has tallied over 20 goals.

Breel Embolo—born in 1997 in Cameroon—will be found up top and Swiss fans are counting on him for goals. When he was young, his mom relocated from Cameroon to Switzerland. As a youth player he found success with FC Basel, signing a pro contract with the team at age 16. Now, the 6'0" forward has club experience from FC Basel, Schalke 04, and Borussia Monchengladbach. With the Swiss national team, his first showing was in 2015, and he's acquired over 50 caps since.

Granit Xhaka—born in 1992 in Basel, Switzerland—is one of the more experienced Swiss players on the roster. The 6'1" midfielder has suited up with FC Basel, Borussia Monchengladbach, and Arsenal. With Arsenal, he's played in over 185 games. He's played for the national team since 2011 and has slotted in over 10 goals. Should he be injury free, his fortitude and wisdom will come in handy for the Swiss.

OVERALL PLAYER RATING

Xherdan Shaqiri: 8.9

Haris Seferovic: 9.1

Renato Steffen: 8.9

Breel Embolo: 8.6

Mario Gavranović: 8.9

Granit Xhaka: 9.1

Ruben Vargas: 8.9

KEY PLAYER STATS

(Total career goals for their country)

	Games Played	Goals
Xherdan Shaqiri	106	26
Renato Steffen	25	1
Mario Gavranović	41	16
Ruben Vargas	24	4
Haris Seferovic	86	25
Breel Embolo	56	9
Granit Xhaka	104	12

WHAT TO WATCH FOR ON TV

As Switzerland battled it out in European qualifiers, a few players that were part of the journey leading up to World Cup 2022 included **goalkeepers** Yann Sommer, Jonas Omlin, Gregor Kobel, and Yvon Mvogo; **defenders** Nico Elvedi, Loris Benito Souto, Kevin Mbabu, Silvan Widmer, Manuel Akanji, Ricardo Rodriguez, Eray Cömert, Fabian Schär, and Ulisses Garcia; **midfielders** Fabian Frei, Denis Zakaria, Remo Freuler, Michel Aebischer, Renato Steffen, Djibril Sow, Xherdan Shaqiri, Steven Zuber, Granit Xhaka, and Edimilson Fernandes; and **forwards** Haris Seferovic, Breel Donald Embolo, Mario Gavranović, Christian Fassnacht, Albian Ajeti, Ruben Vargas, Cedric Itten, Andi Zeqiri, and Noah Okafor.

Prior to landing in Qatar, Switzerland had to fight its way through European qualifiers, always a tough task, in Group C with Italy, Northern Ireland, Bulgaria, and Lithuania.

Switzerland's style lies somewhere between France, Spain, and Sweden. It's a thinking team, with solid athletes to boot. Don't expect anything overtly fancy, but do expect a solid, professional performance. Without true star power, it's a team that utilizes a good balance between long balls and short-passing possession across the field. This is a good start.

Switzerland wants to escape the quagmire of average performances in the modern World Cup era. Each year, essentially, it's a program intent on improving. Bit by bit, it's getting there. But what would mean success for Switzerland? Definitely a semi-finals appearance. With each step of the way, the Swiss are trying desperately to avoid the "fizzle-out syndrome," which teams like Mexico and Australia often suffer from. In other words, Switzerland does well up to a point before falling apart. A few things the Swiss need to concentrate on are attention to detail, strong passing combinations, strategic—and confident—dribbling, and anticipation on defense. These factors will help shape a better outcome. What's more, as a team of skilled players, things are heading in the right direction. Another thing the Swiss must watch out for are turnovers. Without a true superstar, the Swiss need to invest in team unity more than ever.

Essentially, Switzerland is one of the least likely teams to be found in the semi-finals. Though one could still count the Swiss among the upper-middle pack. Traditionally, Switzerland has been a strong sparring partner for the world's elite; though, in Qatar, expect to see Switzerland attempt to break out of this mold with vigor, passion, confidence, and a chip on its shoulder. In essence, Switzerland is aware of every glamour team with the slightest public posture. With full intent, like a true steward of the underdog cause, the Swiss want to knock them out. When it's all said and done, sparks will fly with Switzerland.

WALES
World Cup titles: 0
Overall Team Rating: 8.6

A BRIEF TEAM HISTORY
Let's take a brief look at the World Cup record of Wales.
1930: Wales didn't compete.
1934: Didn't compete.
1938: Didn't compete.
1950: Didn't qualify.
1954: Didn't qualify.
1958: Made the quarter-finals.
1962: Didn't qualify.
1966: Didn't qualify. (You might want to get a sandwich.)
1970: Didn't qualify.
1974: Didn't qualify.
1978: Didn't qualify.
1982: Didn't qualify.
1986: Didn't qualify.
1990: Didn't qualify.
1994: Didn't qualify.
1998: Didn't qualify.
2002: Didn't qualify.
2006: Didn't qualify.
2010: Didn't qualify.
2014: Didn't qualify.
2018: Wales didn't qualify.

UEFA EUROPEAN CHAMPIONSHIP
Wales reached the semi-finals in the UEFA Euro 2016. To date, this has been its best result.

FACTS ABOUT THEIR COUNTRY

Wales, a beautiful tourist destination, has a population of about 3 million people and a GDP of around 77.5 billion pound sterling. On a map it sits on the western side of England.

When was the first match Wales played? Who was it against? It was in 1876 against Scotland. Who has the most goals all-time for Wales?

1. Gareth Bale (39)*

Looking for beer in Wales? Here are a few!

Polly's Brew	Bluestone Brewing
Tiny Rebel	Tudor Brewery
Axiom Brewing Company	Wrexham Lager Brewery

WHERE THE TEAM IS TODAY—TACTICS AND STRATEGIES

Tactics and strategies: Wales was seen using a 3-5-2, a 5-4-1, and a 4-4-2 in the buildup to Qatar.

Defensively, Wales has stability offered up from Benjamin Davies and Christopher Gunter. By and large, the Welsh defenders play professionally in the UK, so they are accustomed to a brisk pace. Any team that plays up-tempo will be speaking the language of Wales and its defenders should be comfortable. Should Wales face a team that slows things down, such as Spain, there might be trouble brewing.

Offensively, Wales is going to lean on the crafty play of Aaron Ramsey, Harry Wilson, Daniel James, Joe Morrell, Joe Allen, and the big 6'5" Kieffer Moore up top will come in handy for posting up, crosses, and set-pieces. One obvious attacking force Wales will funnel the ball to is Gareth Bale. With Bale dashing up and down the wing, as he does so well, this team could do some damage.

---

* Still active, and this number will likely increase.

No one can accuse the Welsh of lacking ambition. It's easy to attack Wales as the team has only been to two World Cups. But once you get started, you quickly realize that Wales is nobody's fool. These Welshmen make up some of the best talent in the United Kingdom. This nation's soccer playing dates back to the late 1800s. The nation may be small, but it's a quality side. Certainly, when you think of Wales you don't think of a team destined to win. It'll be very difficult for Wales to squeak its way out of the group stage. However, when you look again, you realize that this Welsh side—led up top by Bales and Ramsey— might be more of a prospect than first appearances would suggest.

This is not a classical long-ball team, nor is it a short-passing guru but rather a combination of the two. Wales is more than comfortable in a half-field possession game. The guiding hand of Coach Giggs has done wonders. This is a cohesive group that has the added dimension of its superstar, Bale.

This team, with its up-tempo attitude, warrants a second look. That will begin immediately in the group stage when it'll become very clear as to whether or not Wales has what it takes to make history.

RYAN GIGGS—A BRIEF COACHING PORTRAIT

One could look at previous Welsh coaches and thank them for being so experienced and for doing a good job with what they had. But let's face it, however good these coaches were, Wales hasn't seen a World Cup since 1958! The fact that Wales is in the 2022 FIFA World Cup is kind of a big deal. And who better to guide the team through the World Cup than its current coach. **Ryan Giggs**—born in 1973 in Wales—is best known for his time with Manchester United. He played in a handful of games: 672. No big deal. He scored a couple goals: 114. Again, not that big a deal. In fact, most people in Britain can claim that! Giggs—a former winger who had dribbling skills that could make your head spin—is also considered one of the best ever to come out of Wales. One thing Giggs would definitely like to add to his résumé would be a World Cup win for Wales.

As coach, he's made history by leading Wales to its second-ever World Cup! The last one was in 1958 whereby Wales lost in the quarter-finals, 1-0, to Brazil thanks to a goal from Pelé. Next on Giggs's list of things to accomplish would be a World Cup championship. This Welsh team is different. There is Gareth Bale and Aaron Ramsey, for starters. But as the old saying goes, good players don't necessarily make good coaches. Anyone with the offensive talent that Giggs possessed must, in all likelihood, be an asset as coach. Furthermore, during his time at Manchester United, Giggs received so much knowledge of the game from the great Sir Alex Ferguson. In other words, despite the saying, Wales has a special vibe right now. Other teams should proceed with caution.

Just keep in mind that Giggs is using the talent he has, the potent combo of Bale and Ramsey, along with keeping the defense consistent for an all-around approach that will keep opponents on edge. Wales is deceptively powerful, and it can strike at any moment. **Rob Page** also helped with coaching. Page—born in 1974 in Wales—is a former defender that played for Wales (1996-2005). As caretaker, he and Giggs have set the team up for success. This is a team that can be very dangerous.

KEY PLAYERS AND THEIR CHARACTERISTICS

Gareth Bale—born in 1989—has the green light to guide the national team forward. Fans are hoping that his brilliance, which is widely admired, will land Wales in the final for a fairy-tale-esque victory march. If anyone could bring home the title, it would be Bale. He has showcased his talents for the whole world to see at Real Madrid and Tottenham for over a decade now. At around 6'1" he soars down the wing with bursts of speed that leave opponents in the dust. His pace is staggering. His finishes are clinical. His eye for setting up teammates is outstanding. Currently, as a veteran who's been with Wales since 2006, despite injuries, he's taking the field with more than 100 caps and over 35 goals. He'll be a guarded man in Qatar, but if Wales can get him into a groove, then good things will be around the corner.

One of the midfielders equipped with world-class talent that will feed the ball to Bale is Aaron Ramsey. Ramsey has shown off his gift for ball-handling and distributing (with precise accuracy) throughout his career, and that has landed him at Cardiff City, Arsenal, Nottingham Forest, and Juventus. As for the latter, he signed with the Italian giant in 2019 where he's played in over 45 games to date. Like Bale, Ramsey goes back a few years with Wales. His first match was in 2008. Since then, he's acquired more than 70 caps, while hitting the 20-goal mark. If you're wondering why Welsh fans are excited about the prospects in Qatar, it would be because of Bale and Ramsey.

Harry Wilson—born in 1997—is a 5'8" winger who began playing with Fulham in 2021 where he's acquired more than 20 appearances and a handful of goals. In 2013, he debuted with Wales. Since that time, he's played in over 30 matches for his nation, racking up a few goals as well. As a winger, he adds a little punch to the lineup which is what the Welsh need for success.

Daniel James—born in 1997—is a 5'7" winger who has spent time with Swansea City, Manchester United, and Leeds United. The quick winger debuted for Wales in 2018 and should be a good option for Giggs throughout the tournament.

Joe Morrell—born in 1997—brings distribution and crafty play as a 5'6" center mid with experience from Portsmouth as of 2021. He's quietly been turning heads since his debut with Wales in 2019, and he's collected over 20 caps.

Another 5'6" midfielder comes in the form of **Joe Allen**. After hauling in over 125 games with Swansea City, Allen played in 91 games for Liverpool (with four goals) before finding a home with Stoke City in 2016 where he's appeared in over 190 matches. He was on the 2012 Great Britain Olympic squad. As for Wales, he's gathered up more than 65 caps since his debut in 2009. As a firm veteran for the team, he'll be counted on for leadership, organization, and some savvy on this quest for the World Cup title.

On the front line, Wales has a bit of an aerial target in **Kieffer Moore**, a 6'5" striker who has landed with Wigan Athletic and Cardiff City. With Wales, he's been around since 2019 and he's exceeded 20 games with over five goals. He should be a stellar target for the Welsh. If he can establish a good holdup game with his back to goal, it should serve Bale and Ramsey well in the attack. Of course, knocking in a few goals wouldn't hurt the cause either.

OVERALL PLAYER RATING

Gareth Bale: 10
Aaron Ramsey: 9.8
Harry Wilson: 9
Daniel James: 9

Joe Morrell: 9
Joe Allen: 9.3
Kieffer Moore: 8.8

KEY PLAYER STATS

(Total career goals for their country)

	Games Played	Goals
Gareth Bale	106	39
Aaron Ramsey	75	20
Harry Wilson	39	5
Daniel James	36	5
Joe Morrell	28	0
Joe Allen	72	2
Kieffer Moore	26	8

WHAT TO WATCH FOR ON TV

On the way to Qatar, Wales had many players available during European qualifiers that included **goalkeepers** Wayne Hennessey and Daniel Ward; **defenders** Christopher Gunter, Benjamin Davies, Connor Roberts, Christopher Mepham, Joseph Rodon, Neco Williams, James Lawrence, Rhys Norrington-Davies, and Thomas Lockyer; **midfielders** Aaron Ramsey, Joseph Allen, Harry Wilson, Jonathan Williams, Joe Morrell, Brennan Johnson, William Vaulks, Ethan Ampadu, Dylan Levitt, Matthew Smith, David Brooks, and Benjamin Woodburn; and **forwards** Gareth Bale, Daniel James, Kieffer Moore, Tyler Roberts, Thomas Lawrence, Rabbi Matondo, and Hal Robson-Kanu.

During European qualifiers for FIFA World Cup 2022, Wales was in Group E with Belgium, Czech Republic, Belarus, and Estonia.

With a strong defensive line, Wales is in good standing. For starters, it has the services of **Benjamin Davies**—who has over 155 games with Tottenham—to keep things steady. Along with other experienced backs, such as Chris Gunter, Wales is a formidable side that can hold its own despite not being a legendary World Cup nation. The trick will be to keep the possession continuous flow going.

Another part of the puzzle is to somehow keep the ball flowing to Gareth Bale. As always, the problem with having a superstar is that sometimes teammates try to get them the ball too often. If Wales can get the ball to Bale often, while also getting everyone else multiple touches, then a good flow should result. Harmony in possession will be a key factor for the Welsh as it will allow Bale to have "quality" touches that aren't "rushed touches". There are plenty of options that will help with possession, including Aaron Ramsey, Harry Wilson, Daniel James, Joe Morrell, Joe Allen, and Kieffer Moore.

As a nation that's only in its second World Cup, Wales has nothing to lose. Many teams in Qatar, such as Germany, Brazil, and Argentina, have reputations on the line. The Welsh will play with honor yet if it loses out in the group stage, no one will really create much of a fuss. If Brazil were to lose in the group stage, the world might as well flip upside down! Yet with any small-nation team that has a core group of skilled players, you never know.

With Giggs as the coach, this is a team that intrigues many fans around the world. The possibilities are endless. Likely, when it's all said and done, Wales will just be a footnote in the loss column. But perhaps Wales could be a dark horse, waltzing its way to the championship podium.

THE TEAMS FROM SOUTH AMERICA (4½)

BRAZIL
World Cup titles: 5 (1958, 1962, 1970, 1994, 2002)
Overall Team Rating: 9.8

A BRIEF TEAM HISTORY
What some may forget is that it took a little while before the samba beat officially played. Prior to 1958, Brazil had some adversity in World Cup competition. Let's take a brief look at the World Cup record of Brazil.

1930: Brazil was out in the group stage.

1934: Brazil made it to the Round of 16.

1938: Brazil earned third overall.

1950: Brazil earned second overall.

1954: Quarter-finals, that's it.

1958: World Cup champions! This was the breakout year as youngsters Pele and Garrincha took center stage to help deliver Brazil its first title.

1962: World Cup champions! Like a dream, Brazil followed up its first title with another in Chile. With an injured Pele resigned to the bench, Garrincha stole the show with lightning quickness, dribbling that bordered on magic, goals, and style.

1966: Brazil was out in the group stage.

1970: World Cup champions! Brazil earned its third World Cup title with Pele, Rivellino, Tostao, Jairzinho, and Carlos Alberto. Jairzinho scored in every match; quite a feat.

1974: Brazil earned fourth place.

1978: Brazil earned third overall.

1982: Brazil was out in the second round.

1986: Brazil lost in the quarter-finals to France. This quarter-final loss to France was a classic World Cup game—titans, drama, intrigue, penalty kicks, penalty misses. Platini, Giresse, Tigana, and Rocheteau barely outdid a quick, fast, and tenacious samba side that included Socrates, Careca, Junior, and Zico.

1990: Brazil suffered a Round of 16 loss to Argentina. With the help of a brilliant assist from Maradona and a winning goal from Claudio Caniggia, Brazil's bitter rival Argentina barely won the match by 1-0.

1994: World Cup champions! Put another one on the shelf for Brazil. Romario, Bebeto, and Dunga led the way as Brazil won its fourth title on American soil.

1998: Brazil gathered a second-place finish.

2002: World Cup champions! The three Rs—Rivaldo, Ronaldo, and Ronaldinho—reigned supreme and were too much to handle as Brazil waltzed past Germany 2-0 in the final.

2006: Brazil lost in the quarter-finals to France.

2010: Brazil lost in the quarter-finals to Netherlands.

2014: Brazil hosted and came away in fourth place.

2018: Brazil lost in the quarter-finals.

SOUTH AMERICAN COMPETITIONS

Brazil won the Copa America* (previously known simply as the South American Championship) in 1919, 1922, 1949, 1989, 1997, 1999, 2004, 2007, and 2019.

---

* There have been a few names for this competition. The South American Championship (also known as the South American Football Championship) began in 1916. It was called the Copa America in 1975.

OLYMPIC GOLD

Brazil made up for its 2014 FIFA World Cup blunder—when it lost to Germany 7-1 in the semi-finals—by finally winning the gold medal for soccer in the 2016 Olympics. Brazil's history with soccer has been so lucrative, yet there had never been a gold medal for the men. During the Olympic games—hosted by Brazil that year—the locals were dead set on the men's soccer team. Swimming, gymnastics, track and field—forget about it! Brazilians were watching Neymar and the team chase history. A perfect championship game culminated with Brazil vs. Germany in the gold-medal match. It was a brilliant match, two equally talented sides going at it for all the marbles. Neymar led the way as Brazil got its first gold for men's soccer. With that, a weight was lifted. Brazil finally added the Olympics to its list of accomplishments, alongside the World Cup and South American championships that have brought so much pride to its people over the years.

FACTS ABOUT THEIR COUNTRY

In Brazil, pre-historic evidence of human activity dating back 11,000 years has been found, and, furthermore, there's pottery from around 6,000 BC that's also been discovered. The Portuguese first established a presence in Brazil back in 1500 AD. (This came only eight years after Columbus sailed the Atlantic on behalf of Ferdinand of Aragon and Isabella of Castile.) As the New World was being settled, Brazil was always an exotic land steeped in mystery. *The Lost City of Z*—a book by David Grann—elucidates the adventures of British explorer Colonel Fawcett who mapped the untamed terrain of Bolivia, Peru, and western Brazil in the early 20th century. Fawcett mysteriously disappeared while he was searching for a mythical lost city of gold.

Today's Brazil, the largest geographic nation in South America, has a population of around 210 million people and a

GDP of about $1.4 trillion. The largest city is Sao Paulo, with a population of approximately 12.3 million. Rio de Janeiro—Brazil's most popular city—is a close neighbor just north up the coast a ways. Rio is extremely famous for its Carnival, held once a year and visited by millions. And, by the way, you'll find the best coffee in the world in Rio, too! Soccer rules the landscape in Brazil. With five World Cup championships, Brazilian players are highly sought after around the world. Who has the most caps for Brazil? Cafu, with 142. Brazil's top three leading scorers of all time are:

1. Pele (77)
2. Neymar (74)*

3. Ronaldo (62)

Pele has many accolades, and one of the most notable would be the three World Cup titles he was involved with from 1958, 1962, and 1970.

Ballon d'Or (Brazilian winners)

Ronaldo (1997)
Rivaldo (1999)
Ronaldo (2002)

Ronaldinho (2005)
Kaka (2007)

FIFA World Player of the Year (Brazilian winners)

Romario (1994)
Ronaldo (1996)
Ronaldo (1997)
Rivaldo (1999)

Ronaldo (2002)
Ronaldinho (2004)
Ronaldinho (2005)
Kaka (2007)

FIFA World Cup (Brazilian titles)

1958
1962
1970

1994
2002

---

* Still active, and this number will likely increase.

For Brazilians there is a lot to celebrate every time a World Cup comes around. Brazil has exquisite food as it's well known for steaks and exotic pizza varieties. Surely fans will be delving into such cuisine, and people watching the matches on TV will likely enjoy domestic beer, including Eisenbahn.

WHERE THE TEAM IS TODAY—TACTICS AND STRATEGIES

Brazil's last major title was in 2019 with its ninth Copa America championship. A few players that came up big were Coutinho, Everton, Casemiro, Firmino, Dani Alves, Willian, Marquinhos, Gabriel Jesus, Thiago Silva, Alex Sandro, Arthur, and Richarlison. Neymar was absent with an injury. Yet, without its biggest star and one of the best players in Brazil's history, the team managed to pull it together for a colossal win.

This is not to say that Brazil is nothing without Neymar as there are plenty of other stars within the national team program. This is a virtue of Brazil, and it always has been. For years there was a suggestion—more like a conversational joke—that Brazil could and should bring a B team to the World Cup. The idea being that there's so much talent, either the A or B teams could deliver a championship. Still, a team that has Neymar is just going to be better all around. This 2019 Copa America championship is fresh in the systems of Brazilian players, and it should guide them well with confidence and experience throughout the 2022 FIFA World Cup. Brazil is ready as ever. The team is strong, vibrant, full of excitement, and as usual it will be the centerpiece attraction in Qatar and the world as all cameras will be on the Verde-Amarela—"The Green and Yellow."

Brazil may have come up empty-handed in the 2021 Copa America with a narrow 1-0 loss to Argentina in the final, but its defense throughout the 2021 World Cup qualifiers was strong. Make no mistake: Despite being known for their offense, Brazilians are natural defenders, too. Brazil's current defense is rooted in quick double teams, as usual, in which Brazil swarms opponents.

Tactics and strategies: As used in South American qualifiers for the World Cup, Brazil will probably go with a 4-4-2, perhaps a 4-2-2-2; though it's not unlikely to see a 4-3-3, which the team used in the final of the 2021 Copa America against Argentina. In earlier games in the 2021 Copa America, Brazil went with a 4-2-3-1 (which is nothing more than a 4-3-3 in disguise).

In South American qualifiers for the World Cup, Brazil crushed it, dominated the pack. Brazil's players were just better than opposing forces, notwithstanding Argentina. As per usual, Brazil is a favorite in the World Cup, a must-see attraction.

Brazil's relentless attack features the current Puma king of kings, Neymar Jr., along with a band of talent fully equipped with a PhD in samba and a touch of classic European organization throughout the channels.

A few players to keep an eye on: Gabriel Jesus, Richarlison, Fred, Coutinho, Lucas Paqueta, and winger Vinicius Junior who joined Real Madrid in 2018. Additionally, there's Casemiro, a 6'1" defensive mid with Real Madrid, and reliable defenders Thiago Silva (of Chelsea), left-back Alex Sandro, and Danilo.

TITE—A BRIEF COACHING PORTRAIT

Tite is in a very good position to win a world-record sixth title for Brazil. Esquadrão de Ouro—"The Golden Squad"—already has five, and a sixth would be rare air. Brazil might just be on track to follow a familiar trend. The 1994 World Cup championship was the first for Brazil since 1970, some 24 years earlier. Now, with 2002 being the last World Cup title, Brazil is 20 years off that mark and many feel that Tite and Brazil are owed. Another interesting parallel is that in 2002, the World Cup was hosted in the exotic, non-traditional soccer territory of East Asia—South Korea and Japan. Here we are in Qatar, another exotic location that's also a non-traditional soccer territory. It's all lining up, perhaps, for another Brazilian run at the trophy. With Tite in charge, things are looking up.

Back in the day, Tite played as a midfielder with a handful of Brazilian clubs from 1978-89. Apart from coaching Brazil, a post he's had since 2016, Tite has led a number of teams, including Gremio, Internacional, and Corinthians.

Tite navigated Brazil through South American qualifiers with a steady hand. With some flair, strong defense, and organization, the international soccer community, which makes up over a billion people worldwide, will be on high alert to see if he can deliver a record sixth championship in Qatar.

KEY PLAYERS AND THEIR CHARACTERISTICS

The kids are getting tattoos these days. **Neymar**—one of the world's biggest stars—went all-in on tattoos. If there's a tattoo, Neymar's got it! And if there's a skill in soccer, he's got that, too! He is, without a doubt, a magician on the field, one of the all-time greats. He's like poetry in motion. With skill, technique, touch, vision, quickness, speed, dribbling ability, scoring ability from all angles, he's virtually unstoppable. When it's all said and done, he's a little bit of Pele, Garrincha, Ronaldinho, and Robinho all rolled into one. At times he comes across as a kid doing immaculate skateboard tricks, and with the flip of a switch he's heroically charging forward, bouncing off defenders on route to goal, taking fouls, hitting the turf, dirtying his uniform. His dribbling in tight spaces is like a dance; he can break free with big swooping 40- to 60-yard runs with ease. He's been narrowing in on the record for scoring and caps for Brazil's national team ever since he joined the team in 2010. Before long, he'll be the last samba dancer standing. Like the aforementioned Brazilian legends, Neymar also shares a trait with Maradona. When he has the ball, there is just a feeling in the air that something big is about to happen.

Thiago Silva—born in 1984—broke into Brazil's lineup as a central defender back in 2008, and since then he's broken the 100-cap mark. The steady defender is about 5'11", and in recent years his club experience has consisted of A.C. Milan, Paris Saint-Germain, and Chelsea. Now in his late 30s this will likely be his last World Cup. Brazilian fans are depending on his experience for results throughout the tournament as they put their faith in him to assuage opposing forces as they unleash attacks. His vision, touch, and passing are high level, and he's one of the top defenders performing in Qatar.

Gabriel Jesus—born in 1997 in Sao Paulo—is about 5'9", and he's the spark Brazil needs; he's the Robin to Neymar's Batman. True, Jesus could handle it on his own, but with Neymar guiding the way, Jesus is a perfect partner to break down defenses left and right as the games go on. Do Neymar and he have a matching tattoo of a boy looking at a favela? Apparently so. Jesus first debuted with Brazil in 2016 and quickly became a star. Since 2017, Jesus—who's featured in the FIFA EA Sports video game "calling on the phone" as his celebration—has been lighting up the stage with Manchester City where the dazzling attacking force has surpassed 55 goals in the EPL. With speed, deft moves, creative ingenuity, and a will to score, Jesus is versatile and can play as a straight-up scorer, a false nine, or as a winger. Video gamers around the world call on his talents to score goals in electronic land just as Brazilians back home will be watching intently for the real thing to produce on the biggest stage in Qatar.

Couthinho has a serious cannon of a shot—he's ruthless around the box, and with just a slight gap he'll pummel a drive low and hard at keepers that can penetrate even the strongest wrists. He's well traveled with Inter Milan, Vasco da Gama, Espanyol, Liverpool, Barcelona, and Bayern Munich. A veteran with Brazil, having first thrown on the yellow shirt in 2010, Coutinho combines his dynamic presence with valuable experience that'll keep opposing coaches up at night. Known as a versatile attacking midfielder with a creative eye, Coutinho was referred to as the "Little Magician" around Liverpool. He's good with both feet—though cutting in from the left side of the box to strike with his right is when he's most dangerous.

Richarlison—a forward to watch out for—joined Brazil in 2018 and has already gone past the 10-goal mark. He made a move to Everton in 2018 where he's found success with over 40 goals. It will be interesting to see how well he fairs in Qatar. Born in 1997, the 6'0" forward has a chance to tally up goals this World Cup. Will he deliver? That's another question.

Lucas Paqueta—born in 1997 in Rio de Janeiro—is a 5'11" midfielder that debuted with Brazil in 2018. Since then, he's led the national team in midfield with over 30 caps and a handful of goals. In addition, he's played with Flamengo, A.C. Milan, and Lyon. He brings creativity and organization to the fold. He should be a vital force from midfield as Brazil advances forward in Qatar.

Casemiro—a 6'1" defensive midfielder—will be relied upon for his exquisite midfield play that has earned him a place with Real Madrid back in 2013. In 2011, he debuted with Brazil. Now, as a veteran presence, Casemiro will lead his national team throughout the field with tackles—known in some circles as "The Tank" and "destroyer"—and necessary passes as he connects from deep with forward-lying teammates to best accentuate Brazil's talented forwards. The rhythm to Brazil's attack is key as the passing sets this in motion. One of the generals behind this is Casemiro, and he will be expected to jumpstart the offense for his team in Qatar.

OVERALL PLAYER RATING

Neymar: 10   Richarlison: 9
Thiago Silva: 9.7   Lucas Paqueta: 9.4
Gabriel Jesus: 9.7   Casemiro: 9.5
Coutinho: 9.7

KEY PLAYER STATS
(Total career goals for their country)

	Games Played	Goals
Neymar	119	74
Thiago Silva	107	7
Gabriel Jesus	56	19
Coutinho	68	21
Richarlison	36	14
Lucas Paqueta	33	7
Casemiro	63	5

WHAT TO WATCH FOR ON TV

At his disposal, Tite had many options leading up to and during the 2022 World Cup qualifiers, including **goalkeepers** Alisson, Weverton, and Ederson; **defenders** Danilo, Thiago Silva, Marquinhos, Miranda, Lodi, Militao, Sandro, Emerson, and veteran presence Dani Alves; **midfielders** Casemiro, Coutinho, Fred, Lucas Paqueta, Arthur (just Arthur), Allan (just Allan), Bruno Guimaraes, Fabinho, Gerson, Everton Ribeiro, Edenilson, and Douglas Luiz; and **forwards** Hulk, Matheus Cunha, Pedro, Everton, Firmino, Richarlison, Vinicius Junior, Antony, Raphinha, Gabriel Jesus, Gabi, and Neymar. (Obviously some of these players aren't strictly "forwards" or "midfielders" and they can play multiple positions and roles.)

Prior to landing in Qatar, Brazil floated its way through South American qualifiers against Argentina, Uruguay, Ecuador, Colombia, Paraguay, Peru, Chile, Bolivia, and Venezuela. Welcome to "the globalization of soccer!" One would assume that a team that has many nicknames would be a very popular team. This would be the case with Brazil, or, as some say, Selecao "The National Team"; Canarinho "Little Canary"; Verde-Amarela "The Green and Yellow"; Esquadrão de Ouro "The Golden Squad"; while some simply refer to the traveling circus that is Brazil as "Jogo Bonito." The latter translates to the "beautiful game" which is what Brazil is known for bringing to the table. In the past three decades or so, however, Brazil has been criticized for losing touch with the Jogo Bonito aspect of its arsenal of talent. Why might this be? Roughly speaking, since the 1980s, Brazilian talent began making the leap over to Europe for professional contracts with high-end clubs and a deluge of players has followed since. So Brazilian players—who would otherwise exude Jogo Bonito tendencies—have been molded into technical "robots" as they've been trained in the ways of European club team systems. This is not to say that European clubs are just "robot factories," but certainly the highly structured approach to the European club game does not foster a free-flowing artsy approach that traditional Brazilian players exuded. So, all the training Brazilian players have received within the structure of European clubs—which emphasizes stringent passing combinations and defense versus self-expression—carries over to the Brazilian national team when the players return home to represent their country. Hence, what we have is a homogenized style of play across the board, worldwide. The international influx of players going into Europe isn't just affecting Brazil, but *every* nation around the globe. Is the style of any international team really distinct anymore? It's a very interesting dilemma. A larger discussion than can be included in this book. As for Brazil, the *stylistic difference* between the Brazilian national team and a European counterpart isn't very extreme; in fact, these days there are more similarities than differences. The globalization of soccer.

But maybe for this World Cup, Brazilian players will revert to their original Brazilian ways and showcase what everyone hopes to see: flamboyant, free-flowing, graceful, tantalizing, skillful, dazzling soccer!

In Qatar, Brazil has a dynamic attack. By and large, the core unit revolves around Neymar, Gabriel Jesus, Richarlison,

Gabi, Lucas Paqueta, and Casemiro. In the event of injuries and last-minute decisions (from Tite), things can change as the tournament progresses, but one should expect this core unit to guide the way, especially under the influence of Neymar.

Brazil is still Brazil with that magical touch, and yet it's also a hybrid of the new refined European approach to the game, one that leans on module-like possession, with all individual parts coming together to form a substantial whole. Yet fans around the world yearn for that classic samba rhythm. Can Brazil deliver what fans want?

When Careca scored against France in the 1986 FIFA World Cup quarter-final, it was as if the ball crashed through the net, he hit it so hard. In that moment, the passion and joy of his and his teammates'—and that of Brazil's fans—celebration could be heard around the world like a sonic boom. Today, with Neymar leading the charge, things are no different. Millions of Brazilians back home will be watching each game, celebrating each goal with deafening noise. On route to these wall-shaking goal celebrations, Brazil will administer quick, accurate, technically sound passing, which will open up pockets of space for Neymar—and others—to exploit with masterful dribbling. The combination passing that Brazil thrives on creates opportunities on the wings for outside mids and outside defenders to strategically rush forward into dangerous positions. These outside defenders, made famous by Brazil over the years, are chosen as attackers that add enormous value to the offense; their attacking skills grant them opportunities to not just blindly cross the ball but rather to reach for scoring chances themselves. Having strong goal-scoring opportunities in both offense and defense sets Brazil apart from the majority of teams in Qatar.

With defense, midfield, and forward lines operating in full harmony, Brazil will be at its most dangerous. Brazil is a favorite for a reason, and the five-time world champion will put on a show for the ages.

ARGENTINA
World Cup titles: 2 (1978, 1986)
Overall Team Rating: 9.9

A BRIEF TEAM HISTORY
Let's take a brief look at the World Cup record of Argentina.

1930: Argentina earned second place.

1934: Argentina didn't compete.

1938: Didn't compete.

1950: Still didn't compete.

1954: You guessed it, didn't compete.

1958: Argentina lost in the group stage.

1962: Argentina lost in the group stage.

1966: Argentina got to the quarter-finals.

1970: Argentina didn't qualify.

1974: Argentina made it to the second round.

1978: World Cup champions!

1982: Argentina made it to the second round.

1986: World Cup champions! Argentina won its legendary second title under the leadership of Diego Maradona, who essentially carried the team on his shoulders with goals and amazing play that cemented him as one of the greatest ever. The 1986 squad had a special run, no doubt. Defenders Oscar Ruggeri, Jose Luis Cuciuffo, and Jose Luis Brown were the foundation from which the mids Hector Enrique, Julio Olarticoechea, and Ricardo Giusti could supply passes and support to Maradona and Valdano. The 80s were such a different time. idealistic world of a World Cup in which nations actually exuded a particular style. The globalization of pro club soccer—i.e., an influx of foreign players into clubs around the world—was just beginning to soar in big numbers. Interestingly, Giusti ventured only so far as Argentina for his pro team experience (Newell's Old Boys, Argentinos Juniors, Independiente, and Union de Santa Fe).

Most remember Jorge Burruchaga for his crafty presence and championship-winning dream goal—a one-on-one breakaway with the keeper—that he slotted past Schumacher. Yet it's easy to overlook the enigmatic, fully bearded Sergio Batista—whose jersey number was 2—who was sort of the gel as a loyal defensive midfielder. What was his role exactly? Outside of collecting loose balls and breaking up plays, he was essentially a human wall; you pass it to him, he'll pass it right back. Perfect, a little bit of Spain 2010 before Spain 2010. He provided simple little passes that quietly set everything up. In a way, Argentina felt like a beautiful South American explosion of creative self-expression—free-flowing soccer that revolved around the magical wand of Maradona.

1990: Argentina earned second place. Maradona and dynamic attacking force Claudio Caniggia led Argentina to the final only to lose by a score of 1-0 to West Germany.

1994: Argentina made it to the Round of 16.

1998: Argentina made it to the quarter-finals.

2002: Argentina couldn't escape its group. Tough year.

2006: Lost in the quarter-finals.

2010: Lost in the quarter-finals, yet again.

2014: Argentina, once again, earned second place.

2018: Out in the Round of 16.

SOUTH AMERICAN COMPETITIONS

Argentina has won the Copa America (previously known as the South American Championship) 15 times: 1921, 1925, 1927, 1929, 1937, 1941, 1945, 1946, 1947, 1955, 1957, 1959, 1991, 1993, and 2021.

FACTS ABOUT THEIR COUNTRY

Argentina is a beautiful country in the south of South America that has an estimated population of 45.6 million people and a

GDP of about $444 billion. While Argentina has produced a top-level international basketball team, the number one sport is, without a doubt, soccer. Argentina's captain from its 1978 FIFA World Cup championship team: Daniel Passarella. The captain from its 1986 FIFA World Cup championship team: Diego Maradona.

Who are the top five scorers for Argentina's national team?
1. Messi (86)*
2. Gabriel Batistuta (56)
3. Sergio Aguero (41)
4. Hernan Crespo (35)
5. Diego Maradona (34)

Who won the Adidas Golden Ball (i.e., the MVP) at the 2014 FIFA World Cup? Answer: Messi.

For the best wine in the world, you'd go to California (specifically Sonoma and Napa Counties), France, Italy, Spain, Portugal, Germany, Australia, a lesser-known hub in Southern Illinois and Missouri, and, of course, Argentina and Chile. The latter two are known for very good wines.

A few wines from Argentina?
Felipe Staiti Vertigo Blend 2014
Catena Zapata Malbec Argentino 2015
Graffigna Reserve Pinot Grigio
Luigi Bosca Gala 2

However, for beer drinkers during the World Cup, a couple of the many beers fans can choose from in Argentina include Antares and Quilmes.

---

*   Still active, and this number will likely increase.

WHERE THE TEAM IS TODAY—TACTICS AND STRATEGIES

Argentina is always a nightmare for any team on the opposite side of the ball. Regardless of what era we're talking about, you can count on Argentina to have a stellar defense, good marking, good one-on-one defending, good team shape, and relentless pressure.

Offensively, Argentina tends to play up-tempo with individual talent that sets the standard of greatness worldwide, much like Brazil and Germany. The team's passing combinations are crisp, accurate, and exploit the opponent. As they say, "it's a game of inches," and with exemplary passing and dribbling, Argentina typically creates a higher frequency of quality scoring chances compared to other weaker squads around the world. As such, shots that come within inches of going over the goal line should increase as Argentina continues to assert pressure on its opponents. As Argentina strives for perfection with players that have an innate ability to deliver on that note in spades, this is a strong reason for why Messi, Otamendi, Di Maria, and Paredes will likely find themselves in the elimination rounds with a very strong chance to go deep in the tournament. Most of the players on the field are very versatile, and as Argentina thrives in its ability to come at teams from multiple angles—down the wings, through the middle, and across the field—their attack will be very dangerous.

One dormant factor that could hold Argentina back is temper. Argentina's players have a tendency to bark at a referee from time to time, meaning, quite often, especially if things aren't going according to plan. Very quickly a referee can turn into a scapegoat. As one player approaches a referee, demanding satisfaction, another will follow, and pretty soon the poor ref is swarmed. Call it a strategy. Call it a bad idea. The downside is that offending a referee might, in fact, account for calls going against Argentina at important intervals in the match. Nonetheless, the feisty, temperamental, and sometimes belligerent Argentinians are highly entertaining. In fact, for all its virtues and flaws, Argentina is must-see TV!

Tactics and strategies: Argentina will probably go with a 4-4-2, a 4-4-1-1, or a 4-2-3-1, as Messi is the focal point from an attacking midfield position. Whatever formation the coach may opt for, the key to success for Argentina comes in the form of individual talent blended with a strong eye for organizational team structure throughout the pitch.

Interestingly, at the 2010 FIFA World Cup, Argentina was accused by critics of utilizing a strategy called "soccer know-how" under the auspices of legendary player turned coach Maradona. Be that as it may, Argentina today is coming off the splendid 2021 Copa America championship, and the team is united like never before to put forth a multifaceted, structured, perfectly Argentine approach to the game, with perhaps a dab or two of "soccer know-how." With two World Cups under its belt, Argentina is a force to be reckoned with.

After Maradona passed away in 2020, this 2022 FIFA World Cup will be the first since his passing. Certainly, fans will be remembering all his brilliance and everything he did for the game as the tournament lingers on. And wouldn't it be nice for Argentina, in his honor, to reel in a third title. Maradona's World Cup journey will live on, ranging from the fouls he endured at the hands of Belgium in 1982 to South Korea in 1986, the eventual triumph at Azteca, the 1990 apostasy in Napoli, to his final attempt in 1994. As Maradona knew from personal experience: It ain't easy.

LIONEL SCALONI—A BRIEF COACHING PORTRAIT

Lionel Scaloni—born in 1978 in Rosario, Argentina—took over as Argentina's coach in 2018. As a 6'0" defensive wing-back in his day, Scaloni played for a handful of teams beginning with Newell's Old Boys in 1995 and ending with Atalanta in 2015. From 2003-06, he also played with Argentina. Eventually, after his playing days, he coached at Sevilla as an assistant, then Argentina, and now he's leading his home nation through what he hopes to be a historical championship run in Qatar. Winning the Copa America in 2021 was a good start. For fans, the next obvious step is the highest honor in the land: the FIFA World Cup.

In Qatar, Scaloni faces many challenges. One of the biggest perhaps is how to get the most out of Messi without placing too much pressure on the star to "carry the entire show" which is easier said than done. The balancing act here is getting the ball to Messi as often as possible while also including everyone else. That's certainly one way to look at it. A downside to the "get Messi the ball" approach is that chemistry with other players might get disrupted. Another avenue is to not intentionally focus on getting the ball to Messi, rather allow it to occur organically within the natural throws of possession. But then the downside here is that Messi might not be as involved in play. Oh boy, a coach's dilemma. No matter what happens—Messi sees too much of the ball or not enough—the media will criticize him. Scaloni's challenge will be to ride the waves of criticism while staying true to his plan.

The best attack plan is simple: Get the rest of the team to own possession à la Barcelona wherein Messi had his greatest years. With Barcelona, all players constantly touched the ball in a highly structured system that crowned all participants with a PhD in passing, and Messi thrived because the game was slowed down to a pace that he could operate from with complete mastery. Certainly, Argentina did well enough in South American qualifiers to get here. Yet it would be in Argentina's best interest to apply the approach of Barcelona so that Messi is in a place of comfort to best apply his magic.

Whatever the road traveled will be, without a championship trophy, Scaloni will have to face the critics, their endless backseat wisdom, and all their charm.

KEY PLAYERS AND THEIR CHARACTERISTICS

Messi said hold on a sec. After being pressured to retire following the 2018 FIFA World Cup loss in the final to Germany, there was a window of time in which fans couldn't tell whether he was done or not. The result was a brief froideur between him and his fervent followers, who, incidentally, expected perfection from his every move. Eventually, predictably, he was cajoled back into the squad. To the delight of fans everywhere, he was making that one last attempt at World Cup glory. In 2021, he got much closer with his first Copa America title—one that elicited a huge sigh of relief as teammates hoisted soccer's greatest talent in the air. Now it's back to the World Cup for possibly one last try. Wouldn't it be fitting if Qatar is the location for Messi and Argentina to regain the title, now the first World Cup tournament since the passing of Maradona? Messi—Argentina's answer to Maradona—has a quiet swagger. There's no dispute that he's one of the greatest to ever play, alongside many others like Cristiano Ronaldo, Neymar, and past greats such as Pele and Garrincha. It helps that he's won the Ballon d'Or on numerous occasions: 2009, 2010, 2011, 2012, 2015, 2019, and 2021.

Messi—who hails from Rosario, Argentina, and signed a contract with Barcelona on a napkin—will not wow you over with a flurry of step-overs. Rather, in a natural way, he wheels and deals, constantly aware of his surroundings; he very often turns away from trouble with the outside of his foot and scoots away from professional defenders with ease. It's not supposed to look so easy, yet he makes it appear so. In his early days, he had a burst of speed like no other. Nowadays he has less of a burst though he's still extremely quick and has the ability to navigate north to south with the best of them as he finds holes—and creates holes—in the defense. His instincts for maneuvering around defenders are innate. Add to this his exceptional vision and passing ability—often combining with one–twos—and he's always a danger around the box. Another added bonus is his ability to chip the ball with touch, precision, and an inner curve to its trajectory. So be it on the ground or in the air, Messi's passing is multifaceted and always dangerous. As for shooting, Messi has a very strong shot, and most often it's driven low with a bit of dip to its trajectory, a nightmare for goalkeepers.

Lautaro Martinez—born in 1997—plays a central role as Argentina's current prime striker alongside Messi. As Messi and fellow teammates provide creative support, 5'9" Martinez occupies the sole striker role up top as a clear and present scoring option. Though he doesn't just stand around. He has the ability to drop back deep for the ball, moving defenders around as he adds to the attack with passing, creativity, and a firm awareness of where his teammates are, what type of runs they might make, and where to deliver telling passes. Martinez adds value with link-up play, and he is more than willing to assist on goals just as much as he would like to score them. Thought of as one of the best strikers in the world, Martinez has tallied up over 55 goals at Inter Milan since 2018. Since joining Argentina in the same year, he's reached the 20-goal mark (as of 2022), and that number is expected to climb.

Leandro Paredes—a 5'11" defensive mid—made big news with his signing to PSG in 2019. Previously he had played with Boca Juniors, Chievo, Roma, Empoli, and Zenit Saint Petersburg. With PSG, he's risen to the top of his game, playing alongside legendary players. There's been some intrigue as well. According to *L'Equipe* (a French publication), allegedly around September 2020 a trio from PSG consisting of Paredes, Angel Di Maria, and the one and only Neymar took a jaunt to Ibiza— an island off the east coast of Spain—whereby COVID-19 was thought to be contracted. Sometimes strategy gets lost off the soccer field. Nonetheless, Paredes—who was born in 1994—has been one of Argentina's leading midfielders since 2017. He and midfield mate De Paul are crucial for their nation's success in Qatar.

Rodrigo De Paul, like Paredes, was born in 1994 and is a guiding force that Argentina is depending on for forward movement, defensive stops, and ball distribution throughout the pitch to set up dynamic opportunities for Messi, Di Maria, and Martinez. With club experience from Racing Club, Valencia, Udinese, and Atletico Madrid, De Paul joined Argentina in 2018 and has since acquired over 40 caps for his nation. Expect a lot of activity in the center of the field from De Paul and Paredes. Their partnership will be interesting to watch as Argentina pushes toward the final.

Angel Di Maria—born in 1988—still has the ability to charge forward at locomotive speed with the ball at his feet. Just try to keep up! It's his speed on the ball and cunning ability to see holes in the defense that make him such a formidable force. Despite his lanky build, the 5'11" Di Maria is a deadly attacker in the open field with skills that come naturally, as though the ball is innately connected to his touch. His club career has included stops with Rosario Central, Benfica, Real Madrid, Manchester United, and PSG. With Argentina, he made his first team debut in 2008, and he's made major contributions with over 20 goals scored.

Nicolas Otamendi is a no-nonsense defender. If you're coming at him with the ball, all bets are off. It's probably not going to end well for you. The 6'0" backline strong arm built like an iron wall has made a career off of hard tackles and taking no prisoners. Otamendi is an homage to tough guys. Born in 1988, Otamendi, now an established veteran, has suited up with Velez Sarsfield, Porto, Valencia, Atletico Mineiro, Manchester City, and Benfica. He played his first game for Argentina back in 2009. He's all business, and fans of Argentina are confident that he'll guide the team not only with toughness, but also experience and wisdom.

OVERALL PLAYER RATING

Lionel Messi: 10

Rodrigo De Paul: 9.9

Lautaro Martinez: 9.9

Angel Di Maria: 10

Leandro Paredes: 9.9

Nicolas Otamendi: 9.9

KEY PLAYER STATS
(Total career goals for their country)

	Games Played	Goals
Lionel Messi	162	86
Lautaro Martinez	38	20
Leandro Paredes	44	4
Rodrigo De Paul	41	2
Angel Di Maria	122	25
Nicolas Otamendi	91	4

WHAT TO WATCH FOR ON TV

Leading up to and during South American qualifiers for World Cup 2022, Argentina had many players to field, some of which included **goalkeepers** Franco Armani, Juan Agustín Musso, Emiliano Martínez, Agustín Federico Marchesín, Esteban Andrada, and Gerónimo Rulli; **defenders** Nicolás Tagliafico, Lucas Martínez Quarta, Juan Marcos Foyth, Gonzalo Ariel Montiel, Nahuel Molina, Marcos Acuña, Cristian Romero, Nicolás Otamendi, and Germán Pezzella; **midfielders** Rodrigo De Paul, Angel Di Maria, Exequiel Palacios, Alejandro Darío Gómez (AKA Papu), Guido Rodríguez, Giovani Lo Celso, Leandro Daniel Paredes, and Nicolás Domínguez; and **forwards** Lionel Messi, Ángel Correa, Julián Álvarez, Joaquín Correa, Paulo Dybala, Lautaro Martínez, Nicolás González, Lucas Alario, Lucas Ocampos, and Sergio Agüero.

Prior to landing in Qatar, Argentina made its way through South American qualifiers against Brazil, Uruguay, Ecuador, Colombia, Paraguay, Peru, Chile, Bolivia, and Venezuela.

Argentinians are averse to losing. It's both an endearing quality and the spark in the engine that pushes players to bum-rush a referee from time to time. As usual, it should be interesting to see how things play out as the team, which is more than capable of winning the whole tournament, rumbles through the field. Part of the reason Argentinians hate losing is because the team, regardless of the era, is always so good. The team is expected to win the World Cup every time, even in a down cycle. With huge expectations come feelings of hope and trepidation as fans know, deep down, that other equally qualified teams are vying for the same goal. In fact, in past tournaments, when Argentina has faced imminent defeat, that hope turns to dread. Soon after, hope is restored again as is the case with the World Cup cycle. People of Argentina have faced their fair share of World Cup disappointment. It can't be said enough how great Argentinian fans are for the game at large. If you've seen a sold-out River Plate vs. Boca Juniors match, you're struck with awe at the passion in the stands. When I was in Brazil in 1990 as a 14-year-old, the World Cup was underway in Italy as Careca and the Brazilians lost to magnificent Maradona and Argentina by a narrow 1-0 margin. The city in Brazil where I was staying turned eerily quiet. The fans of Argentina were celebrating on TV, quite vociferously, to which my host parent and a passionate Brazilian scoffed, "Latins!" To Argentinians, victory is beyond important. To say pride is part of the equation would be a vast understatement.

Yet, pride can only carry you so far when the last world championship was 1986, right?

Today, one could argue that Argentina—like Brazil—represents a blend of South American charm with the structured combination-passing approach of European club teams.

Yet fans of Argentina should wonder if a constant, relentless flow of an attack—that floods the goal like waves of an ocean crashing to shore—is more appropriate than a methodical, over-possession approach that served Messi so well during his tenure at Barcelona. When the game is slowed down to over-possession, it creates an interesting paradox in which dribbling becomes easier and players like Messi are more effective, versus the trading punches approach in which the flow of play is more frenetic, preventing a player to *calmly* select opportunities to dribble. If players are *calmly* selecting opportunities to dribble then it could be argued that they are *strategically* selecting opportunities to dribble, which obviously yields more success in the long run.

In essence, Argentina has opted for the trading punches approach. No doubt Argentina has constructive passing, but it throws players forward with the intent of crashing the goal with scoring chances. The players can't help themselves. They unleash a passionate attack. What happens is the team—full of superior players to that of most other teams around the world—typically goes straight for goal in an organized way (better known as "possession with purpose"). The idea is that Argentina's superbly talented players will just plain be better than opposition, possess the ball with dexterity, pounce with counterattacks, and drive in the goals.

It will be interesting to see how it plays out, as Argentina is certainly a tournament favorite.

URUGUAY
World Cup titles: 2 (1930, 1950)
Overall Team Rating: 7.7-8

A BRIEF TEAM HISTORY
The small country of Uruguay has a rich tradition of success in soccer. Uruguay was the first team to win the World Cup in 1930, setting the whole parade in motion. Let's take a brief look at the World Cup record of Uruguay.

1930: World Cup champions! Uruguay kicked things off as host nation and World Cup champs all in one! Historically, this amazing start has elevated Uruguay as soccer royalty, a badge of honor it still carries to this day.

1934: Uruguay didn't compete.

1938: And again, Uruguay didn't compete.

1950: World Cup champions! This was the year of the famous match against Brazil, in Brazil at the Maracana before an audience of close to 200,000! Uruguay stunned the crowd with a 2-1 win that went down in history as Uruguay's second World Cup title. In a game known as "the phantom of '50" Uruguay silenced the crowd with goals by Juan Alberto Schiaffino and Alcides Ghiggia. At that point in time, Italy had two World Cup titles, and Uruguay had two. Top of the world.

1954: Fourth place.

1958: Uruguay didn't qualify.

1962: Uruguay lost in the group stage.

1966: Uruguay got to the quarter-finals.

1970: Fourth place.

1974: Uruguay couldn't get past the group stage.

1978: Didn't qualify.

1982: Didn't qualify.

1986: Uruguay made it to the Round of 16.

1990: Uruguay made it to the Round of 16.

1994: Didn't qualify.

1998: Didn't qualify.

2002: Uruguay couldn't escape its group.

2006: Didn't qualify.

2010: Fourth place.

2014: Out in the Round of 16.

2018: Out in the quarter-finals.

SOUTH AMERICAN COMPETITIONS

Overall, Uruguay has done very well in the Copa America (previously known as the South American Championship). It has won a total of 15 times between 1916 and 2011. Uruguay won the Olympic gold medal for men's soccer in 1924 and 1928.

FACTS ABOUT THEIR COUNTRY

Uruguay is an extremely small country geographically yet large with heart and desire. At present, it has a population of approximately 3.5 million people and a GDP of around $62 billion.

Who are the top three scorers for Uruguay's national team?
1. Luis Suarez (68)*   **3.** Diego Forlan (36)
2. Edinson Cavani (58)**

A couple popular Uruguayan beers? Pilsen and Patricia will certainly make an appearance or two.

WHERE THE TEAM IS TODAY—TACTICS AND STRATEGIES

Individually, all the players are good. Uruguay has one of the best forwards in the world, perhaps *the* best forward (Luis Suarez, of course), yet there's a problem. As a team on offense, Uruguay hits a dead-end about 10 yards inside the half-line. It's not good. Dear Uruguay: Please fix whatever you're trying to do, or not do, or anything in-between because *flow* is not there. *Rhythm* is not there. *Creativity* is definitely not there. Uruguay is so painfully out of step with how good it could be that it hurts. There's potential there, but Uruguay lacks ingenuity. Where's another 1986 Enzo Francescoli? Where's another Diego Forlan, the FIFA World Cup Golden Ball winner from 2010? In the whole country, is there no one as remotely creative as Forlan? The Big U needs a retuning and now. Without a substantial change there are going to be major problems for Uruguay. This is a two-time World Cup champion, yet this team is uninspiring. The proof is in the 2022 World Cup qualifiers in which the Big U struggled mightily. A couple examples: October 10, 2021: Uruguay lost to Argentina by 3-0. October 14, 2021: Uruguay lost to Brazil by 4-1. That's a two-game total of 7-1. Not good! This doesn't

---

*   Still active, and this number will likely increase.

**   Still active, and this number will likely increase.

represent the entire spectrum of Uruguay's 2021 qualifiers, but it's very telling. Here's the thing, though. Uruguay's current ability creates a paradox. You'd think if a team is boring you might tune out and not watch. Wrong. Rather, the big U is so boring *you have to watch*! There's something there that makes it worth watching and worth trying to fix.

Will the Big U have moments of brilliance? Of course. Are the players athletic? Yes. Are the players built like one-story brick houses? Yes. Can the players move the ball around? Pretty much. But that's the thing. The players move the ball with such robotic motion that their play is dull. You probably can't expect much in the way of big World Cup results, and there is certainly room for improvement.

For now, let's look at **Tactics and strategies:** Uruguay will likely operate out of a 4-4-2 formation. It certainly has solid defenders. Is there a one-two punch toward goal? Sure. Cavani and Suarez.

Uruguay will lean heavily on the brilliant scoring capabilities of Suarez, one of the best in the business.

Uruguay's as close to a lost cause as a team can get this tournament while still being a middle-of-the-road squad that is better than most on the lower end of things. It's a national team desperately in need of artistic revival! No one should be surprised when Uruguay can't escape its group or perhaps loses in the Round of 16.

DIEGO ALONSO—A BRIEF COACHING PORTRAIT

Despite all the criticism hurled at Uruguay, there is hope in the form of its current coach, **Diego Alonso**. When Alonso took the job in 2021, it marked the close of Oscar Tabarez's long coaching tenure. Tabarez—a former defender—coached Uruguay from 2006-21. For a national team in the world of soccer, such an extended period as coach is unheard of. To say he was a veteran coach of Uruguay is a vast understatement. Without a doubt,

Tabarez established himself as an iconic coach of Uruguay. His approach with the Uruguay team followed in lockstep with traditional Uruguayan soccer values: strong defense, a flurry of counterattacks, with a few goal-scorers expected to carry the load. Now, with the introduction of Alonso, times are changing.

Alonso—born in 1975 in Uruguay—was a forward in his day, having played for the Uruguayan national team for seven games. He's coached a number of teams, including Bella Vista, Inter Miami, and in 2021, he assumed the role of head coach for his home nation. As the replacement for longtime Uruguayan coach, Tabarez, Alonso has a lot of expectations riding with this World Cup. For Uruguay, after years of less-than-exciting performances, Alonso has an opportunity to set the two-time World Cup champions back on top. For Uruguay fans, it's a longtime coming, and this is, without a doubt, a pivotal moment for the national team to reassert itself at the highest level. As coach, Alonso will be a key force. With his attack-minded approach, things are looking very interesting for the tiny South American nation. Uruguay might just turn things around and go from being a dull, defensive-minded squad to one that sparkles on offense.

KEY PLAYERS AND THEIR CHARACTERISTICS

Luis Suarez is a superstar forward you've seen with Liverpool, and the dynamic trio on Barcelona (Suarez-Messi-Neymar) where he slotted in an astounding 147 goals. Currently the scoring phenom is part of Atletico Madrid. The mild-mannered gentleman-about-town is cunning in the box with scoring ability like few others in the world. He seizes the ball with deft discernment, and his finishing touch is precise, to the point, and always dangerous for keepers. With only a yard or two of space inside the box, Suarez can make something out of nothing as he uses his body—including his wrist adorned with a protective strap—extremely well to hold off defenders to set up shots. He's aggressive, tenacious, full of vigor, and wants to win at all costs. He's the epitome of a gunslinger on the field—someone to watch closely throughout the tournament.

Federico Valverde—born in 1998 in Montevideo—is a midfielder with experience at Real Madrid where he joined in 2017. He's been relied upon heavily as he's played over 80 games for the Spanish mega-club. At 6'0", he's a younger talent that first debuted with Uruguay in 2017 (a big year for him). He's not going to impress anyone with scoring; as of October 2021, during the World Cup qualifiers, he had 35 caps with 3 goals. As his stats will likely increase, it's a good sign of his ability to score. Is he a big scorer? No, but on a team where the scoring is largely dominated by Cavani and Suarez, to get three goals is actually a plus. Watch for Valverde in midfield as he's more of a distributor, one who will do the work, intercept passes, get tackles, and light up the channels for optimal success with Cavani and Suarez. Prediction: You're looking at the future coach of Uruguay in Valverde.

Born in 1991 in Uruguay, **Matías Vecino Falero**—a 6'2" midfielder—joined Inter Milan, which was his biggest signing to date, in 2017. He made his debut for Uruguay back in 2016.

Rodrigo Bentancur—born in 1997—has club experience with Boca Juniors and Juventus as of 2017. The 6'2" midfielder first joined Uruguay in 2017. A quick note on Bentancur: not a big scorer. However, his contributions in midfield will enable more opportunities for the one-two punch of Cavani and Suarez.

Forward **Edinson Cavani**—born in 1987—is about 6'0" and stands out as one of Uruguay's leading scorers, right behind teammate Suarez. Cavani's had an interesting career climb that includes the likes of Danubio, Palermo, Napoli, Paris Saint-Germain, and Manchester United. Simply put, scoring essentially rests in the hands—or rather feet—of Suarez and Cavani.

OVERALL PLAYER RATING

Luis Suarez: 10   Rodrigo Bentancur: 9.2
Federico Valverde: 9.2   Edinson Cavani: 9
Matías Vecino Falero: 9.2

KEY PLAYER STATS
(Total career goals for their country)

	Games Played	Goals
Luis Suarez	132	68
Federico Valverde	42	4
Matías Vecino	60	4
Rodrigo Bentancur	49	1
Edinson Cavani	133	58

WHAT TO WATCH FOR ON TV

Essentially, as Uruguay sifts through its antediluvian pre-artistic revival period, a few key players at the disposal of coach Tabarez leading up to and during World Cup qualifiers for Qatar included **goalkeepers** Fernando Muslera, Martín Campaña, and Martín Silva; **defenders** José Giménez, Diego Godín, Giovanni González, Martín Cáceres, Ronald Araújo, Joaquín Piquerez, Sebastián Coates, and Matías Viña; **midfielders** Matías Vecino, Rodrigo Bentancur, Nahitan Nández, Gastón Pereiro, Lucas Torreira, Mauro Arambarri, Federico Valverde, Giorgian de Arrascaeta, Nicolás de la Cruz, and Brian Lozano; and **forwards** Luis Suarez, Jonathan Rodriguez, Maxi Gomez, Brian Rodriguez, Darwin Nunez, David Terans, Cristhian Stuani, Agustín Álvarez, Diego Rossi, and Edinson Cavani.

Prior to landing in Qatar, Uruguay had a tough journey through qualifiers in South America against Brazil, Argentina, Ecuador, Colombia, Paraguay, Peru, Chile, Bolivia, and Venezuela. Yet the gutsy approach of Uruguay, in all its resolve, came through.

For a team that lacks midfield ingenuity and positive offensive contributions from its defensive unit, any prospect of World Cup glory will be hard to come by. Still, keep an eye on **Diego Rossi**. He might be new to Uruguay's team, with his first appearance in 2022, but he did extremely well during his time with LAFC in MLS, during which he scored 48 goals. In the years to come, he should be a creative player for his nation with a knack for offensive contributions. As for Qatar 2022, Uruguay does have a significant one-two punch—Cavani and Suarez—that can keep things interesting. Will this be enough? Unfortunately, fans might not like the answer as Uruguay will likely struggle to reach the Round of 16. Should Cavani and Suarez provide enough muster to reach the second round, the chances of getting to the quarter-finals and beyond become bleak as the Big U will have to rely on its defensive prowess to keep scores low, and rely on penalty kicks to get by more talented teams. One would think that the coach and players are not thinking "penalty kicks" as an outright strategy, yet it might be their only hope. That's the current condition of Uruguay. When it's all said and done, on the way to the airport, Uruguayan players—and fans alike—will be waxing poetic about the missed chances, close calls, and all the ways it could've gone.

ECUADOR
World Cup titles: 0
Overall Team Rating: 7.7-8.3

A BRIEF TEAM HISTORY
Here's a quick glance at the World Cup record of Ecuador.
1930: Ecuador didn't compete.
1934: Didn't compete.
1938: Didn't compete.
1950: Didn't compete.
1954: Didn't compete.
1958: You guessed it, Ecuador didn't compete.
1962: Didn't qualify.

1966: Didn't qualify. (It goes like this for a while.)
1970: Didn't qualify.
1974: Didn't qualify.
1978: Didn't qualify.
1982: Didn't qualify.
1986: Didn't qualify.
1990: Didn't qualify.
1994: Didn't qualify.
1998: Didn't qualify.
2002: Ecuador finally qualified and couldn't escape its group.
2006: Ecuador made the Round of 16.
2010: Didn't qualify.
2014: Couldn't escape its group.
2018: Didn't qualify.

FACTS ABOUT THEIR COUNTRY

Ecuador—whose flag is yellow, blue, and red—is your quintessential tropical South American nation, one that resides next to neighbor Colombia on the northwestern corner of the continent. It has a population of around 17.7 million people and an estimated GDP of $106 billion.

The top three scorers of all time for Ecuador's national team are:
1. Enner Valencia (35)*   3. Eduardo Hurtado (26)
2. Agustin Delgado (31)

As for beer in Ecuador? You might find some Doggerlander, and Bandido Cuckoo Chocolate Stout!

WHERE THE TEAM IS TODAY—TACTICS AND STRATEGIES

Ecuador, not usually associated with World Cup greatness, is a vibrant team looking to change a few minds about its ability to succeed. What better place than Qatar! On course to achieving

---

* Still active, and this number will likely increase.

this dream-like scenario, Ecuador has a lot of work to do. However, if a team is going to make a stand in World Cup competition, it has to happen sometime, and there's no better time than now! **Tactics and strategies:** Ecuador will likely use a 4-3-3 (or perhaps a 4-4-2, which was also used leading up to the 2022 World Cup). Ecuador puts forth an aggressive attack that leans on the scoring exploits of forward star Enner Valencia (who leads his nation in goals).

On defense, some of Ecuador's issues include sloppy marking, one-on-one defending, team shape, and errors. These issues will certainly cause problems for the team. If it can quit these bad habits, it will have a lot less to worry about.

One the offensive side of things, Ecuador is not a "kill you with possession" type of team (the complete opposite of Spain). It will trade punches with opponents as it goes tit for tat in an all-out effort to create as many scoring chances as possible, which often turns out to be too many "hero passes" and crosses into the box on a wing and a prayer for a goal. Watch for Ecuador's counterattack as it will try to free up its players down the wings to take advantage of any scoring chances possible.

In essence, is Ecuador's strategy flawed? Likely. Will opposing teams look forward to Ecuador as an easy win? Also likely. Though, Ecuador has a lot to prove and has a talented group that fought its way through the ultra-competitive South American qualifiers.

GUSTAVO ALFARO—A BRIEF COACHING PORTRAIT

Gustavo Alfaro—born in 1962 in Argentina—has coached an assortment of teams including Quilmes, San Lorenzo, Rosario Central, and Boca Juniors. As of 2020, he took over the coaching responsibility of Ecuador, and, in the process, he's catapulted this often overlooked South American side into prime time. Is this merely a promotion tournament for Alfaro and Ecuador's players? That is, knowing full-well a championship is realistically out of reach, is everyone involved hoping to get promoted to a higher-paying club team? Unfortunately, in today's game, that's often the case. However, Alfaro got the team to this point, and, as far as he's concerned, a dark horse run in Qatar is definitely within the realm of possibilities.

KEY PLAYERS AND THEIR CHARACTERISTICS

Enner Valencia is the stud forward for Ecuador to watch. Born in 1989, the 5'9" striker extraordinaire has spread a pro career out in a variety of places, including appearances in Ecuador, Mexico, Turkey, as well as West Ham United and Everton. Back home in Ecuador, he holds the proverbial crown—sparkling with exotic South American jewels—as his nation's all-time leading scorer, and, at this point, no one seems to be catching him. As of Halloween 2021, he had scored 34 goals and is sure to make more. He's not shy of drama. He's brought himself up from a poor background to finally achieve success, but not without hitting some bumps along the way. Allegedly, in 2016, he crossed paths with the law in Ecuador for not paying child support, and in 2020 his sister was held hostage by a gang, eventually let go. One could argue that's par for the course for a soccer star these days. Regardless, Valencia is on a collision course with the top defenses in the world at the 2022 FIFA World Cup, certainly one of the biggest challenges of his life. To this point, Ecuador's track record with World Cups is dreadfully lacking. Will his time in Qatar be destined for an early exit? This might be unavoidable. Though, Valencia's quickness, speed, timing, instincts, technique, and hard shot are attributes he'll use to say otherwise.

Michael Estrada—born in 1996—is a 6'2" forward who should most likely accompany Enner Valencia up top on Ecuador's all-out assault in Qatar. The effectiveness of the all-out assault is another question, one that will be looming over Estrada and Valencia as the tournament progresses. Certainly, Ecuador is not a heavy favorite, yet fans back home will expect some kind of brilliance from their forward line. Estrada began his pro career with Macara in 2013. Since then, he's also suited up for El Nacional, Independiente del Valle, and Toluca. His first game for Ecuador was in 2017, and now, as a veteran for his nation, it's up to him. World Cup 2022 represents the biggest opportunity of his life to deliver a championship win or go home trying.

Gonzalo Plata—whose full name is Gonzalo Jordy Plata Jiménez—is a 5'10" winger who was born in 2000. Of the three main clubs in Portugal—Benfica, Porto, and Sporting CP—he's gained valuable experience with Sporting CP, especially. Prior to landing in Portugal, his professional experience began with Independiente del Valle in 2018. After joining Ecuador in 2019, he's done well with at least five goals as of fall 2021.

Moisés Isaac Caicedo Corozo, or as he's simply known, **Moises Caicedo**, is a center mid who despite being born in 2001 is full of experience at this level (15 games and counting) and ready for the big time. His pro career thus far has associated the 5'10" youth standout with Independiente del Valle, Brighton & Hove Albion, and Beerschot.

Sebas Mendez—whose full name is Jhegson Sebastián Méndez Carabalí—started at center mid vs. Brazil in the 2021 Copa America on June 27, 2021. Any time you start against Brazil, say, for a friendly, it's impressive. If you start as a center mid against Brazil in the Copa America, you must be doing something right. That was the case on June 27, 2021, as Mendez started at center mid alongside Moises Caicedo during the all-important Copa America and earned a 1-1 draw with the Samba Beat. Not bad for Mendez, who signed with Orlando City in 2019.

Carlos Gruezo—born in 1995 in Santo Domingo—spent a significant stretch with FC Dallas from 2016-19. The 5'7" midfielder first suited up for his national team in 2014 and since has collected over 30 games.

OVERALL PLAYER RATING

Enner Valencia: 9.1   Moises Caicedo: 8.9

Michael Estrada: 9   Sebas Mendez: 8.9

Gonzalo Plata: 8.9   Carlos Gruezo: 8.8

KEY PLAYER STATS

(Total career goals for their country)

	Games Played	Goals
Enner Valencia	72	35
Michael Estrada	34	8
Gonzalo Plata	28	5
Moises Caicedo	23	2
Sebas Mendez	30	0
Carlos Gruezo	44	1

WHAT TO WATCH FOR ON TV

Leading up to and during South American qualifiers for World Cup 2022, Ecuador had **goalkeepers** Alexander Dominguez and Hernan Galindez; **defenders** Andres Lopez, Christian Cruz, Robert Arboleda, Pervis Estupinan, Angelo Preciado, Xavier Arreaga, Felix Torres, Piero Hincapie, Diego Palacios, Mario Pineida, and Beder Caicedo; **midfielders** Jhonny Quinonez, Jose Carabali, Alexander Alvarado, Angel Mena, Carlos Gruezo, Sebas Mendez, Ayrton Preciado, Fernando Gaibor, Alan Franco, Moises Caicedo, Junior Sornoza, Christian Noboa, Juan Cazares, Renato Ibarra, and Gonzalo Plata; and **forwards** Enner Valencia, Michael Estrada, Walter Chala, Janner Corozo, Romario Ibarra, Leonardo Campana, and Fidel Martinez.

Ecuador navigated its way through qualifiers in South America against Brazil, Argentina, Uruguay, Colombia, Paraguay, Peru, Chile, Bolivia, and Venezuela. As of November 14, 2021, Ecuador was third place in qualifiers, not bad.

Ecuador—a beautiful, tropical, exotic nation—has a problem. When it makes the FIFA World Cup (a challenge in and of itself), it has been beset by early exit after early exit. How can promising Ecuador overcome this unavoidable reality?

Strong defense is a good start. Ecuador has athletic players who are quick, fast, physical, and aggressive. Tight marking could be an issue. Are defenders "reacting" or "anticipating" to situations? Hopefully, for Ecuador fans, it's not the former. Anytime players react to something on the field it's a recipe for disaster. Nations like Germany, Italy, France, and Brazil find success with experienced defenders that "anticipate" situations, which bodes well in the long run. Oftentimes, Ecuador—and other lower-ranked teams such as Australia and Saudi Arabia— will "react" to situations rather than "anticipate," and the results are defensive blunders. Simple fixes are always best.

A steady flow in the realm of offense is also what would best suit Ecuador, though this is easier said than done. Placing all its eggs in the goal-basket that is Enner Valencia will be detrimental as one player should never carry the entire load. Help from teammates with goals, obviously, will be of great importance. Counterattacks from Ecuador will be nonstop, as will "hero passes" into the box. Not the dreaded "hero pass" again! Unfortunately, that's the case here. When a team, such as Ecuador, lacks possession-based superiority, it will often get antsy and thrust many "hero passes" toward the box with a hope and a prayer. Typically, the best remedy for this situation is to improve the possession end of things, but it may be too late for this tournament. However, Ecuador has quality, up-tempo players, and it should make for exciting games. For all these reasons, Ecuador is a team to watch for!

THE TEAMS FROM NORTH AMERICA (3½)

UNITED STATES
World Cup titles: 0
Overall Team Rating: 9

A BRIEF TEAM HISTORY
Let's take a quick glance at the World Cup record of the United States.

1930: The United States placed third.

1934: The United Sates made the Round of 16.

1938: Didn't compete.

1950: The United States couldn't escape its group. However, it should be noted, the US defeated England 1-0 with a lineup that started a large number of talent from St. Louis, Missouri, including that of Harry Keough.

1954: Didn't qualify.

1958: Didn't qualify.

1962: Didn't qualify. (If you'd like, you can order takeout: It goes on for a while.)

1966: Didn't qualify.

1970: Didn't qualify.

1974: Didn't qualify.

1978: Didn't qualify.

1982: Didn't qualify.

1986: Didn't qualify.

1990: Couldn't escape its group. In CONCACAF qualifiers, Paul Caligiuri—a product of UCLA and later the star of

175

Pert shampoo commercials—scored the "shot heard round the world" in an epic must-win 1-0 defeat over Trinidad and Tobago in Trinidad. That lone goal—which was outstanding, a miraculous volley from deep—sent the US to the FIFA World Cup for the first time in a long time!

1994: The United States hosted and reached the Round of 16.

1998: Couldn't escape its group.

2002: The United States reached the quarter-finals.

2006: Couldn't escape its group.

2010: The United States made the Round of 16.

2014: The United States made the Round of 16.

2018: The United States didn't qualify.

CONCACAF COMPETITIONS

Within the realm of CONCACAF, the United States has done quite well in recent years. Within the CONCACAF Championship (held from 1963-89) and the Gold Cup (1991 to the present), the US has won the Gold Cup in 1991, 2002, 2005, 2007, 2013, 2017, and 2021.

FACTS ABOUT THEIR COUNTRY

The United States currently has a population of around 331 million people and a GDP of approximately $22.9 trillion.

Would you believe soccer is finally encroaching on football, basketball, and baseball? Believe it! It's happening. For years baseball was the number one sport in the US. Then, as the 1970s turned into the 80s, football and basketball slowly began a takeover. Since then, arguably, the popularity level in American sports would rank as:

1. Football

2. Basketball

3. Baseball

4. Soccer

This ranking would be one side of the coin. Soccer is gaining ground, but one can't disregard baseball and hockey. Arguably, the ranking could go as follows:

1. Football
2. Baseball
3. Basketball
4. Hockey
5. Soccer

Yet, soccer is knocking on the proverbial door as one of the most popular sports in America. A big reason soccer is growing so much is the FIFA World Cup. Basketball and hockey have respectable international tournaments, but the FIFA World Cup is the most popular tournament on earth. Soccer is really the top team sport in which "our country against yours" is elevated with such passion. The national pride that goes with soccer is unique, and this is a big reason why soccer has been knocking on the door of traditional sports in in the US. Fans are going crazy for it.

What's more, much of soccer's popularity in the US has gained momentum since about 2010. Also, the rise in popularity of Major League Soccer—the world's next Super League—has helped tremendously. Part of the reason is the international extravaganza of the whole thing. Case in point: the FIFA World Cup. Soccer is soon to take the place of baseball in America, and, someday it might just be number one.

Major League Soccer (MLS) was formed in 1996. Other pro leagues that have thrived include that of the Major Indoor Soccer League and North American Soccer League. The latter featured Pele during his last hurrah as a pro when he played for the New York Cosmos in the 70s.

For generations, NCAA college soccer in the US has represented a "pro league" when actual pro leagues were figuring things out. Who has the most championships of all time in NCAA Division 1 Men's Soccer?

1. Saint Louis University Billikens (10)
2. Indiana (8)
3. Virginia (7)

Who is the most capped player in USMNT history?
1. Cobi Jones (164)

Incidentally, Cobi Jones came out of nowhere. Would you believe he was a walk-on at UCLA? Well, it happened.

Who has the most goals in USMNT history? It's a tie.
1. Landon Donovan and Clint Dempsey (57)

Former FIFA World Cup champion Jürgen Klinsmann coached the USMNT from 2011-16.

Who are some of the fastest players in USMNT history?
1. Landon Donovan   **3.** Cobi Jones
2. Fernando Clavijo   **4.** Steve Cherundolo

US beers? Welcome to the land of beers! Here are a few classics the United States is known for:

Busch	Coors
Budweiser	Samuel Adams
Michelob	Sierra Nevada
Pabst Blue Ribbon	Blue Moon
Miller	

Busch Beer Bonus

Dating back to the beginning of soccer as we know it today (which would be the late 1800s and early 1900s), St. Louis, Missouri, was known as the headquarters of soccer in America.* One of the giants of beer has been Anheuser-Busch, founded in St. Louis in the 1800s. From the 1970s to the early 2000s, it sponsored Busch Soccer Club, which was known as one of the best club teams in North America.

---

*   My latest book, This Is Our CITY, examines the revival of St. Louis soccer in the US. Available in fall 2022.

The Busch family—via Budweiser—had sponsored international soccer events for generations. After many, many years, this St. Louis company had become essentially a worldwide company. To this day, you'll still see Budweiser advertisement during international soccer events. Interestingly, as this 2022 FIFA World Cup is underway, St. Louis City SC will be getting ready for its inaugural MLS season in 2023, joining the ranks of LA Galaxy, Portland Timbers, Seattle Sounders, New England Revolution, Atlanta United FC, and the many teams of Major League Soccer! MLS, as popular as ever, has been home to a few FIFA World Cup champions, including Branco, Lothar Matthaus, Youri Djorkaeff, Denilson, Kleberson, Kaka, Alessandro Nesta, Henry, Pirlo, David Villa, and Bastian Schweinsteiger!

WHERE THE TEAM IS TODAY—TACTICS AND STRATEGIES

Since the 1990s, the USMNT has faced an interesting dilemma. It will do very well in its own backyard—CONCACAF—but when it comes to the FIFA World Cup, things fall apart. Certainly, there have been successful moments—a big win over Algeria in 2010 in South Africa, for example—yet more often than not, the US has earned an early exit. What's more, the US is continually unable to tame its final athletic frontier: winning a men's World Cup! By and large, the US has dominated every other sport as it leads all nations in Olympic gold medals. Yet the men's team has not won a World Cup, whereas the US women have done quite well (with four World Cup championships: 1991, 1999, 2015, 2019). The USMNT has not reached the semi-finals (in the modern era), much less a championship. With this in mind, tactics and strategies seem more important than ever.

Yet, since the 1970s, the USMNT has fielded incredibly talented players ranging from Pat McBride, Al Trost, Ty Keough, Steve Pecher (the hard-tackling Mr. Red Card), Steve Trittschuh, Paul Caligiuri, Tab Ramos, Mike Sorber, Preki, Joe-Max Moore,

Landon Donovan, Clint Dempsey, Steve Ralston, and Brad Davis who have pushed American soccer in the right direction. What's more, coaches have done what they can to move mountains for success. Such coaches include Lothar Osiander, Bob Gansler, John Kowalski, Bora Milutinovic, Steve Sampson, Bruce Arena, Bob Bradley, Jurgen Klinsmann, Bruce Arena (Part II), Dave Sarachan, and most recently Gregg Berhalter.

Considering the previous efforts from talented players and coaches, what went wrong? Why hasn't the USMNT reached a FIFA World Cup championship? The answer may surprise you. In large part, past teams struggled at the World Cup level because, for generations, the US didn't have a viable pro outdoor league. MLS only formed in 1996! That's a very recent undertaking!* The arrival of MLS gave players valuable exposure to a viable professional outdoor league. With the implementation of MLS, it has taken a few years for an incremental shift in the "flow" on the field, but that has occurred (a bit like continental drift), and today the team is looking more and more like a mix between Germany, Spain, and France. Therefore, thanks to MLS and a larger amount of US talent taking to European clubs, the USMNT has benefitted greatly.

As such, the international soccer community has cause for concern. Berhalter is keen to taking advantage of this current situation. There is no better time than now to seize the moment and make a huge splash in Qatar! The millions of US fans that are taking to bars, celebrating each game like it's 1999, are expecting huge results!

Tactics and strategies: The US will most likely utilize a 4-3-3 as Berhalter has found confidence in midfielders Musah, Adams, and McKennie, with forward threats from Pulisic, Weah, Aaronson, Pepi, and Ferreira during qualifiers in 2021-22.

---

*   Many pro teams from Europe date back to the late 1800s.

Defensively, with Dest providing a wealth of experience from Barcelona, the athletic backline is focused on keeping team shape in place to best deflect opposition forces from entering the danger zone; with aerial prowess, the backline is looking good in terms of defending against corners and set-pieces. One area of concern will be defending against wily counterattacks that may penetrate the US's backline as it recovers focus from attacks of its own. Petty mistakes around the box, that arise from lack of discipline, will also have to be addressed if the US wants to keep in the game and progress in Qatar.

Offensively, can the US keep a good flow going in possession? That's a serious question the team must address in order to keep things moving in a healthy direction on the field throughout the duration of the tournament. However, it's not just a "good flow" in possession, but a "progressive flow." This is key. The team needs "progressive flow" in possession.

There's always a temptation to play free-flowing soccer. Every team around the world has this urge. Essentially, free-flowing soccer is fool's gold; it is merely "trading punches" with opponents. If the US falls prey to trading punches with opponents, it might just see itself sitting on a plane for an early departure out of the Middle East. Rather, if possession can remain strong, the US has a chance to keep opponents off the ball, thus increasing scoring opportunities. Furthermore, if the US gets bogged down in its own end as a result of an opponent dominating possession, will Musah, Aaronson, Pulisic, Adams and others be able to string together successful counterattacks? This will be key as the USMNT moves forward.

When it's all said and done, for better or worse, this little experiment rests in the hands of the coach. If Berhalter wins, he'll be a hero. If things go wrong, he'll have a lot of explaining to do. The nature of coaching!

GREGG BERHALTER—A BRIEF COACHING PORTRAIT

Gregg Berhalter—Mr. Always-With-a-Water Bottle—has a big task ahead. US fans have grown by the millions, and these fans want results. By results we're talking about a presence in the semi-finals of a FIFA World Cup and even the final itself. Americans don't like to lose at sports. There's a storm of frustration brewing, as patience is wearing thin. After all, as the United States has dominated sports around the world for generations (*the* Olympic gold medal leader!), Berhalter faces the last athletic frontier of American sports: men's soccer! Once the US wins a FIFA World Cup, which will happen someday, it can claim complete world dominance. There's a slight problem: Despite having the talent to win a World Cup every year, some believe the problem has to do with the guidance—this is called "welcome to the brutal world of blame the coach." Enter the most recent US punching bag—pardon—coach: Gregg Berhalter.

Once upon a time, Berhalter was a defender for the USMNT (1994-2006). Born in 1973 in New Jersey, Berhalter's pro career took him to Crystal Palace, TSV 1860 Munich, and LA Galaxy. After coaching Columbus Crew from 2013-18, he took over the USMNT in 2018. Leading up to Qatar, he's entertained a very large pool of players for the USMNT. He helped to finesse the talent as the team qualified out of the "Octagonal" that featured Mexico, Canada, Panama, Costa Rica, Jamaica, Honduras, and El Salvador. In 2021, combined with the veteran leadership of outside mid Paul Arriola, Berhalter and the USMNT—which many referred to as a "B" or "C" team—won the coveted Gold Cup with a 1-0 victory in the final over Mexico. It was a great achievement, and Berhalter looks to carry this momentum to Qatar.

KEY PLAYERS AND THEIR CHARACTERISTICS

Christian Pulisic—a UEFA Champions League champion with Chelsea—operates as the engine for the USMNT, providing that much-needed drive with dashing runs from midfield, vision, one–twos, and the innate ability to constantly test defenses with quickness and explosive speed. It's as if Landon Donovan and Clint Dempsey were combined into one player. Pulisic has arrived, and he's intent on making his mark in World Cup 2022. If ever there were a single player to lead the US into the semi-finals of a FIFA World Cup, it just might be him. Around 2010, Brazilians began reluctantly murmuring that the US isn't an easy game anymore. Pulisic is a big reason why.

Timothy Weah—an attacking player typically found on the right wing—has a very good first touch. It seems every time he has the ball, he's dangerous. With his quickness, change of pace, and eye for goal, he's a player opponents should watch out for. His father, George Weah, won the Ballon d'Or in 1995 when he played for A.C. Milan, and in 2018 he became the President of Liberia. Timothy, who has experience playing for Paris Saint-Germain, Celtic, and Lille, joined the USMNT in 2018. He's gained over 20 caps so far.

Juventus: He was sent home for breaking COVID protocol. USMNT: He was sent home for breaking COVID protocol. That's a lot of breaches in protocol. **Weston McKennie**, the bad boy of Qatar? Well, let's just say Luis Suarez has some competition. Somewhere along the way, McKennie went all in on a pretty daring Kwame fade circa 1990, and that's not all. He's also ready to take over Qatar. McKennie, who has been playing in Europe and for a while lived in Germany as a youth, is hoping to combine with teammates to do just that: achieve high-end results.

Tyler Adams—who is originally from Wappinger, New York—will provide valuable service to his teammates in midfield throughout the tournament. Adams—born in 1999, about 5'8" tall—has experience overseas with RB Leipzig where he's played in over 70 games. Not a big scorer, Adams will provide positive reinforcement in defense, break-up plays, and possession-oriented passing on offense. Since Adams made his debut for the USMNT in 2017, he's acquired over 25 caps. As a guy who "moves" like a soccer player, he's got good technique, vision, and passing ability. Perhaps most valuable is his high work-rate.

Sergiño Dest—at about 5'7"—is just plain good. How did he join Barcelona? Maybe because he was born in Netherlands— that's a good start, anyway. Have you seen him play? If you haven't yet, just know that he is a perfect archetype for Barca in that, as an outside defender, he's technically gifted, calm, smart, and loves combination passing. At long last, the USMNT has a member who also plays for Barcelona! For US soccer fans, it's rather odd to hear that out loud. Times are changing for the USMNT, and having Dest on the field is a step—or two or three—in the right direction.

Walker Zimmerman—born in 1993 in Georgia—is phenomenal at center defense not just because he's a sound defender or because he's good in the air, but because of his ability to possess the ball well with a high level of technical ability. If only he and Tim Ream were paired up—regularly— as the two center backs, but that's a story for another day! Zimmerman—6'3"—has the presence, focus, and poise to lead the USMNT deep into the tournament, and fans should be relieved that he's back there, ending the attack for opposition and starting the attack for the US.

Brenden Aaronson—born in 2000 in New Jersey—has a sneaky way of causing danger with opposing defenses. As an attacking mid, he comes across innocent enough, but when it's least expected, he pounces on opportunities with skill, technique, vision, and know-how. He's a subtle force to be reckoned with, and he almost always creates havoc for other teams, typically finding himself in very good positions for scoring chances. His club experience has placed him with Bethlehem Steel, Philadelphia Union, and Red Bull Salzburg. Quite recently, in fact, in 2020, he got called up to the USMNT. He's a play creator, and other coaches should be weary of his every move.

BONUS Where's Nagbe?

One glaring concern is the absence of NCAA champion, Hermann Trophy* winner, three-time MLS Cup champion, MLS All-Star, 2017 Gold Cup champion, 2017 Gold Cup Best XI, and experienced USMNT midfielder **Darlington Nagbe**! Many (meaning, all) smart soccer fans have noticed his absence. Now, one player won't win or lose a World Cup. This is especially the case when the player in question is Nagbe, a possession-minded midfielder, vs. Messi, a one-man show that can change a game on his own. However, it also could be successfully argued that Nagbe is the best pure midfielder the USMNT has ever had. And he's not on the World Cup roster! He wasn't even on the qualification roster! In fact, when Berhalter took over as coach in 2018, Nagbe seemed to mysteriously disappear from the national team altogether. Some have said Nagbe isn't good on defense. But then, the same could be said about Modric, Iniesta, Xavi, Ronaldinho, and Platini. Berhalter gallivants around claiming he has the best team on the field, but can this be true without Nagbe?

A similar situation has happened before when Taylor Twellman won the 2005 MLS MVP award, yet he was mysteriously excluded from the US roster for the 2006 FIFA World Cup; in that tournament the US couldn't escape its group and finished 25th overall.

At Berhalter's disposal, there are a lot of talented US players available to man the team. However, Nagbe is in a different category. Again, he's only one player. Yet, he's very talented. It will be interesting to see how World Cup 2022 goes without him.

---

*   An elite award given annually to the best collegiate soccer player in the United States. A handful of previous winners include Jordan Morris, Claudio Reyna, Alexi Lalas, and Tony Meola.

OVERALL PLAYER RATING

Christian Pulisic: 9.7   Sergiño Dest: 9.4
Timothy Weah: 9.1   Walker Zimmerman: 9.3
Weston McKennie: 8.9   Brenden Aaronson: 8.9
Tyler Adams: 8.9

KEY PLAYER STATS

(Total career goals for their country)

	Games Played	Goals
Christian Pulisic	51	21
Timothy Weah	25	3
Weston McKennie	35	9
Tyler Adams	30	1
Sergiño Dest	17	2
Walker Zimmerman	31	3
Brenden Aaronson	22	6

WHAT TO WATCH FOR ON TV

Leading up to and during North American qualifiers for World Cup 2022, the United States had a number of intriguing players such as **goalkeepers** Zack Steffen, Matt Turner, Sean Johnson, Ethan Horvath, and Brad Guzan; **defenders** Tim Ream, DeAndre Yedlin, Walker Zimmerman, Antonee Robinson, James Sands, Chris Richards, Mark McKenzie, Sam Vines, Reggie Cannon, Miles Robinson, Shaquell Kwame "Shaq" Moore, Sergiño Dest, John Brooks, George Bello, Cameron Carter-Vickers, Matt Miazga, Joe Scally and Aaron Long; **midfielders** Tyler Adams, Yunus Musah, Cristian Roldan, Gianluca Busio, Sebastian Lletget, Kellyn Acosta, Weston McKennie, Jackson Yueill, Julian Green, Djordje Mihailovic, Malik Tillman, Luca de la Torre, and Paul Arriola; and **forwards** Christian Pulisic, Ricardo Pepi, Brenden Aaronson, Jesús Ferreira, Timothy Weah, Gyasi Zardes, Haji Wright, Matthew Hoppe, Josh Sargent, Jordan Pefok, Giovanni Reyna, Daryl Dike, Nicholas Gioacchini,

Jonathan Lewis, Rubio Rubín, Tyler Boyd, Jozy Altidore, and Jordan Morris.

The Americans pretty much sat atop the group, lingering around second and fourth place throughout the qualifiers against CONCACAF rivals Mexico, Costa Rica, Canada, Panama, Honduras, Jamaica, and El Salvador, though it wasn't exactly smooth sailing. In the beginning of the qualifiers, there were a lot of concerns that the team might get left behind as they struggled against Canada, Panama, Costa Rica, and even to some extent, Jamaica. Mexico was there, too, reminding CONCACAF it was in charge (for the most part, anyway).

There was talk about **Josh Sargent**, that his role likely should've been more prominent during qualifiers. Was he utilized properly? Questions remain. Sargent—a 6'1" forward from St. Louis with polished technique and scoring touch—has stood out as an American overseas success story with Werder Bremen and Norwich City. There should have been combinations up top with Sargent, Christian Pulisic, Ricardo Pepi, Brenden Aaronson, Jesús Ferreira, and Timothy Weah. Yet, you can only have so many players on the field at once.

Another force to be reckoned with was **Matthew Hoppe**. He stood out significantly in the 2021 CONCACAF Gold Cup with a game-winning goal against Jamaica in the quarter-finals, along with impressive runs down the wing.

And what about the Dike factor? **Daryl Dike**—a 6'2" brickhouse at around 225 pounds—proved in the 2021 CONCACAF Gold Cup that you either really like his game or you really don't! He had moments of showmanship and moments when an errant pass was just a bit outside. Yet his presence created a lot of hype, to be sure.

This all leads one to wonder, who are the right players? How can the right players elevate the team to elite international status? Who are the wrong players? Are there too many wrong players in the lineup? So what is the right lineup? Well, that's the role of a coach. The strength of the situation is that the US *has many players to choose from*! Always a good thing! In part, this only adds to the allure and mystery of the USMNT.

The United States might very well be the most interesting team in the 2022 FIFA World Cup. Why? As stated, it's the best sports nation in the world except for men's soccer! The World Cup championship for the men is America's last athletic frontier! American soccer will completely be there when it wins the World Cup. The thing is, no one can quite agree on how the men can win the World Cup. "Set-pieces are the key." "Set-pieces are important, but the team's overall plan should not completely rely on set-pieces." "This player, that player." And so on. Then, inevitably, the team returns empty-handed. Berhalter wants to change that; he wants the team to return with medals and not a pat on the back!

If he remains injury free, keep an eye out for **Giovanni Reyna**, the son of Claudio Reyna. Giovanni has proven to be an exceptional player that the USMNT is looking to utilize for optimal success. He has a creative spark and is crafty on the ball, an offensive element that should serve the USMNT well in Qatar if he's availableA front line with Pulisic, Aaronson, Ferreira, Weah, and Reyna is very dangerous, and other teams will have a lot of trouble dealing with it!

Expect strong defense, quick counterattacks, vibrant attacks, optimism on set-pieces, surging runs down the lines from midfielders, and an offense that, largely speaking, will do well if Pulisic does well. He's the focal point of the team. So if he can get the ball often, and get into a flow, good things will result for others—particularly the forwards and midfielders that can line up shots from around the top of the box. Furthermore, with Pulisic charging down the center of the field, many fouls should result which will bring about a number of free-kick opportunities just outside the box. Should a few go in, here and there, the US will be in good shape.

This team Berhalter has constructed is very new to fans. Gone are the old names that lingered for so long, such as Michael Bradley. Enter a new group that has a lot to prove in the 2022 FIFA World Cup. This isn't the backyard of CONCACAF, where the US often plays against teams such as El Salvador, Bermuda, and Martinique. The World Cup is a whole different level. Pressure is mounting on Berhalter. The team has potential to win the whole World Cup, but fans around the world expect the US to lose, so it turns into a question of how badly will the US lose? So badly that Berhalter is immediately fired or not so badly in that he keeps his job for a year or two? It will be very interesting to see how his formula pans out in Qatar against the best of the world. With expectations so high, this is a "make it or break it moment" for Berhalter.

MEXICO
World Cup titles: 0
Overall Team Rating: 9.5

A BRIEF TEAM HISTORY
Let's take a brief look at the World Cup record of Mexico.
1930: Mexico couldn't escape its group.
1934: Didn't qualify.
1938: Didn't compete.
1950: Couldn't escape its group.
1954: Couldn't escape its group.
1958: Couldn't escape its group.
1962: Couldn't escape its group.
1966: Couldn't escape its group.
1970: Mexico hosted and reached the quarter-finals.
1974: Didn't qualify.
1978: Couldn't escape its group.
1982: Didn't qualify.
1986: Reached the quarter-finals.

1990: Didn't compete.
1994: Made the Round of 16. (Enter the Round of 16 curse.)
1998: Made the Round of 16.
2002: Made the Round of 16.
2006: Made the Round of 16.
2010: Made the Round of 16.
2014: Made the Round of 16.
2018: Made the Round of 16.

CONCACAF COMPETITIONS

Within the realm of CONCACAF, Mexico has traditionally been the leader. It has won multiple championships in the CONCACAF Championship (held from 1963-1989), and the Gold Cup (1991 to the present), including 1965, 1971, 1977, 1993, 1996, 1998, 2003, 2009, 2011, 2015, and 2019. As of 2017, Mexico placed fourth in the Confederations Cup in Russia.

FACTS ABOUT THEIR COUNTRY

Mexico—an attractive vacation destination—has a population of around 126 million people and a GDP of about $1.3 trillion.

Mexico hosted the FIFA World Cup in 1970 and 1986. It will co-host in 2026 with the United States and Canada!

Who is the most capped player on Mexico's national team?
1. Claudio Suarez (177)

Very soon, after this publication, Andrés Guardado should likely surpass Suarez. Guardado should keep going, gaining more caps.

Who are the top scorers in the history of Mexico's national team?

1. Javier "Chicharito" Hernandez (52)*	**2.** Jared Borgetti (46)
	3. Cuauhtemoc Blanco (38)

---

* Still active, and this number will likely increase.

A popular beer in Mexico? You guessed it: Corona is a go-to for thousands of fans. Corona and a lime twist? Now we're talking! And don't forget Tecate, Modelo, Dos Equis, and Pacifico.

WHERE THE TEAM IS TODAY—TACTICS AND STRATEGIES

In a distant galaxy, long-long ago, circa 2012, Mexico was thought to have had one of its best teams ever that included the likes of Guardado, Chicharito, Marquez, and Giovani dos Santos. As we sit, 10 years later, Mexico is hoping to topple that bunch with another legendary group that features Jesus "Tecatito" Corona, Héctor Herrera, Edson Álvarez, Orbelín Pineda, Raúl Jiménez, and Hirving Lozano.

Tactics and strategies: Mexico will likely field a 4-3-3 or a 3-5-2. Though more often than not, Mexico has been using a 4-3-3; so the 3-5-2, which was used, albeit briefly in 2021, comes off as more of a makeshift formation. Perhaps the coach wanted to tinker. Regardless, expect a 4-3-3. In general, tinkering with formations isn't good. If that ends up being the case with Mexico during World Cup 2022, then you just might be seeing another early exit for El Tri in the Round of 16. And the last thing Mexico fans want is for the team to, yet again, leave another World Cup prematurely. They want a real-world champion! So how to get there? Well, the stage is set, and despite utter despair looming around every Qatari corner, Mexico is hoping to eradicate its Round of 16 curse—which has followed the team every World Cup since 1998—with a launch into the quarter-finals, and perhaps beyond.

More than ever before, this team is passing the ball in elite fashion, with combinations flourishing all over the field. Recently, Héctor Herrera, Edson Álvarez, and Andrés Guardado have been brilliant in this regard. Jesus "Tecatito" Corona is off the charts dangerous, and Lozano is fast like nobody's business, with the ability to test defenses left and right. Also of note, in past years, Mexico suffered from the "trading punches" syndrome that so many squads around the world fall prey to. In the past 15 years or so, Mexico has upped its game into a highly organized possession-friendly side. Watch out for this as El Tri is a dynamo of a passing unit and will use this to its advantage. The team has quickness and speed, with many scoring options and depth on the bench. All in all, Mexico is a major threat in Qatar.

GERARDO MARTINO—A BRIEF COACHING PORTRAIT
Gerardo Martino—born 1962 in Argentina—is a phenomenal coach. Period. Most coaches are former players, and it's one thing to run drills, but it's another thing to coach like Brian Clough— one of the all-time great coaches—would. Martino is like Clough. Martino is a conductor, one that orchestrates the players based on their technique, chemistry, flow, and direction as a team. He conducts his players around the field according to a grand musical score, like how Michio Kaku suggests everything is governed by "music!" Melody and harmony. Martino also has a special sense of what makes a good player. This, in part, is his genius. Combine the good players in just the right way, with attention to detail, a little magic, and you've got Martino's grand symphony.

Martino has had a fascinating career path. As an attacking midfielder, he played professionally approximately 15 years off and on with Newell's Old Boys and one game for Argentina in 1991. He has coached a lot of high-quality teams, including Paraguay, Newell's Old Boys, Barcelona, Argentina, Atlanta United, and as of 2019, Mexico. He was the coach who led Atlanta United to the 2018 MLS Cup championship. His experience as attacking mid means his sense of the game is sensational, as shown by his teams finding the right way to attack. As of December 2, 2021, his assistant coaches were all Argentinian, adding a little South American spice to Mexico's menu of coaches.

In 2007 Martino was named South American Coach of the Year, and he was Coach of the Year for MLS in 2018. As good as he is, coaches don't last long in Mexico, and the pressure is on.

KEY PLAYERS AND THEIR CHARACTERISTICS

Jesus "Tecatito" Corona—born in 1993—has perhaps the best nickname in the tournament: Tecatito! Get used to it; he's a showman! Tecatito is found on the right wing where he can razzle-dazzle defenders, and he is one of the best. But if you're Mexico, you might ask whether you should play him in a central position so he can go at defenses from a different angle? If yes, he can operate out of the middle, going toward the top of the box, with a multitude of options, which, given his gifted creative ability, might just lead to more scoring chances for Mexico. Yet Tecatito will more than likely be out wide. Bottom line: He's a creative pulse, and when he's on the field good things tend to happen.

Héctor Herrera—the man with a plan—has a brilliant ability to string together passes with gifted touch, vision, and placement. Sometimes he blends in, and his play can pass by quickly, yet he sets up teammates in a very subtle—yet genius—way. As a playmaker, he's a team organizer and one of the best in North America. Born in 1990, Herrera has gained valuable insight from Pachuca, Porto, and Atletico Madrid. He debuted with Mexico in 2012, currently with over 95 caps. For aficionados, he's a player to watch. In ways that aren't quantified by stats, he's constantly doing the *little things* for team success.

Edson Álvarez—born in 1997 and is about 6'2"—operates as a defensive mid for El Tri. He's basically an instigator—always in the middle, creating drama, riling up opponents. He has club experience from America and Ajax, the Dutch mega-team known for its passing. This experience will carry over well as Álvarez combines with Herrera and others to scramble opponents with dashing passes. Álvarez joined Mexico in 2017, and he's gathered over 55 caps.

Andrés Guardado—born in 1986—might be getting older for a player yet he still has a unique quality. Like few others in the tournament, he's a versatile midfielder with an undefinable quality to get things done. He has an innate ability that always seems to be a threat. He sweeps around the field, ready at a moment's notice to unleash his dangerous left foot, always aware of teammates and keen to set up good passes for them. He's darty, smart, instinctual, well coached, and on the cusp of greatness at every moment. The 5'7" super mid has club experience with Atlas, Deportivo La Coruna, Valencia, Bayer Leverkusen, PSV, and Betis. He joined Mexico for the first time in 2005. Currently he has over 170 caps. This should be his last World Cup hurrah, and he'll likely come off the bench for valuable support. He's an all-time great for El Tri.

Orbelín Pineda—born in 1996—has a thin 5'8" frame, but that doesn't stop him from being a threat around larger defenders. He's crafty, sly, deceptive, cunning, quick, and confident. As such, he's most dangerous when he gets into spaces between defenders where he wreaks havoc with a dribble or pass. For years, he's been a fixture in Liga MX, having played with Queretaro and Guadalajara. In 2019, he signed with powerhouse Cruz Azul. Pineda's first game for Mexico was in 2016. Now a veteran, he has over 45 games under his belt.

Raúl Jiménez—born in 1991—has carved a place for himself as one of Mexico's biggest threats. He's graced the field with the clubs America, Atletico Madrid, Benfica, and Wolverhampton Wanderers. Having joined the national team in 2013, the 6'3" forward has amassed over 25 goals and is after more. He's reliable with hold-up play, as he presents a good target for teammates to utilize in and around the box for possession. He has strength to hold off foes, aerial ability, and versatility as a forward. It's tough to follow in the footsteps of great Mexican forwards like Hugo Sanchez, El Matador, and Chicharito, but Jimenez is holding his own.

Hirving Lozano is just plain fast! His pace is breathtaking. He has the unteachable ability to soar down the line past defenders in pursuit of goal with blazing wheels. There are a few fast players in this tournament—Mbappé, Buchanan, Davies, and Sterling—that are world-class fast, and Lozano is at the top of the list. Lozano's talents have been quickly gobbled up by Pachuca, PSV, and Napoli. Since 2016, he's been with Mexico, surpassed 55 caps, and hit the 15-goal mark. He's a must-see talent in Qatar!

OVERALL PLAYER RATING

Jesus Corona: 9.7   Orbelín Pineda: 9.4

Héctor Herrera: 9.7   Raúl Jiménez: 9.1

Edson Álvarez: 9.1   Hirving Lozano: 9.7

Andrés Guardado: 9.7

KEY PLAYER STATS

(Total career goals for their country)

	Games Played	Goals
Jesus Corona	71	10
Héctor Herrera	100	10
Edson Álvarez	58	3
Andrés Guardado	175	28
Orbelín Pineda	48	6
Raúl Jiménez	97	30
Hirving Lozano	58	15

WHAT TO WATCH FOR ON TV

Leading up to and during North American qualifiers for World Cup 2022, Mexico had a number of intriguing players such as **goalkeepers** Guillermo Ochoa, Alfredo Talavera, Rodolfo Cota, Jonathan Orozco, and Hugo González; **defenders** Néstor Araujo, Julio César Domínguez, Johan Vásquez, Jorge Eduardo Sánchez, Osvaldo Rodríguez, Jesús Gallardo, Luis Alfonso Rodríguez, Héctor Moreno, César Montes, Carlos Salcedo, Gerardo Arteaga, Miguel Layún, and Diego Reyes; **midfielders** Héctor Herrera, Edson Álvarez, Andrés Guardado, Luis Romo, Carlos

Alberto Rodríguez, Orbelín Pineda, Sebastián Córdova, Roberto Alvarado, Uriel Antuna, Jonathan dos Santos, Rodolfo Pizarro, Érick Gutiérrez, Diego Lainez, Érick Aguirre, and Jesus Manuel Corona; and **forwards** Raúl Jiménez, Rogelio Funes Mori, Henry Martín, Hirving Lozano, Alexis Vega, Alan Pulido, José Juan Macías, and Javier Hernández (AKA "Chicharito").

Mexico was a clear leader as it navigated through qualifiers against CONCACAF foes Costa Rica, United States, Canada, Panama, Honduras, Jamaica, and El Salvador.

Here's part of the problem with Mexico: There's so much talent, it's hard to list it all! In addition, it's certainly hard for the coaching staff to put all of it on the field at once because the rules of soccer—as everyone knows—only allows for 10 field players, which is a shame because Mexico has a deep roster.

A few players outside of the Key Players to keep an eye on are Uriel Antuna, Jonathan dos Santos, Rogelio Funes, Alexis Vega, Alan Pulido, Héctor Moreno, Luis Alfonso Rodríguez, and Néstor Araujo.

One of these days Mexico is sure to crack through the Round of 16 (!) and enter the quarter-finals. This team certainly has the potential to achieve that and more. It is loaded with offensive firepower, with chemistry to boot. Possession is good, creativity follows.

A few areas of concern, however, will lie in its ability—or really inability—to hold on to leads, avoid sloppy errors on defense, counterattacks, and defending corner kicks. Another important issue lies in Mexico's inability to deal with adversity. Often, if down a goal or two, and things look bleak, players lose focus, tempers flair, and things begin to unravel. You compound this with the Round of 16 curse—accompanied by unthinkable pressure from millions of fans back home—and "Houston, we have a problem." If Mexico accepts that things aren't meant to go perfectly, it can bounce back with confidence. If Mexico can tighten up on defense for the duration of a game (easier said than done), then it can expect big results.

Of course, in goal, you have the great **Guillermo Ochoa**. Nothing against him, he's a great keeper, but Mexico needs to be known for more than short goalkeepers with bright outfits (Jorge Campos—5'6"—who was quite good), or one with funny hair and more for its field players.

As usual, a lot is riding on this FIFA World Cup: pride, the breaking of a curse, an elusive World Cup championship, and the honor of being one of the world's best soccer-playing nations, which is where Mexicans feel they belong.

CANADA
World Cup titles: 0
Overall Team Rating: 8.3

A BRIEF TEAM HISTORY
Let's take a quick glance at Canada's World Cup record. It's pretty quick. If you're concerned you might read this section and miss the last quarter of the Maple Leafs game…you won't.

1930: Canada didn't compete.
1934: Didn't compete.
1938: Didn't compete.
1950: Didn't compete.
1954: Didn't compete.
1958: Didn't qualify.
1962: Didn't compete.
1966: Didn't compete.
1970: Didn't qualify.
1974: Didn't qualify.
1978: Didn't qualify.
1982: Didn't qualify.
1986: Qualified for the World Cup and couldn't escape its group.
1990: Didn't qualify.
1994: Didn't qualify.
1998: Didn't qualify.

2002: Didn't qualify.
2006: Didn't qualify.
2010: Didn't qualify.
2014: Didn't qualify.
2018: Didn't qualify.
Well, that about sums it up.

CONCACAF COMPETITIONS

As for the CONCACAF Championship (held from 1963-1989), and the Gold Cup (1991 to the present), Canada walked away with first place in 1985 and 2000! In the 1985 run, Dale Mitchell had four goals. In 2000, Carlo Corazzin got four goals.

FACTS ABOUT THEIR COUNTRY

Canada has a population of about 38 million, and its GDP is around $2 trillion. One of the coldest places on earth, Canada has traditionally been associated with hockey, the fine art of curling, and the highly competitive world of ice fishing. Yet soccer is also extremely popular. The Vancouver Whitecaps, for example, have been very popular, largely to people in the area, dating back to the 70s. Not to be outdone, Toronto FC has a following that borders on madness.

Who are the leading scorers for Canada's national team?

1. Cyle Larin (24)*   **2.** Dwayne De Rosario (22)

Watch out for Jonathan David. He soon might take the lead with goals! Branko Segota—born in 1961 in Yugoslavia—won multiple championships in the MISL as a versatile striker and played for Canada's national team from 1980-88.

---

*   Still active and this number will likely increase.

A few awesome beers from Canada?

Propeller London Style Porter	Alexander Keith's India Pale Ale
Denison's Weissbier	Maudite
Beau's Lug-Tread Lagered Ale	La Fin du Monde
	Molson Canadian
St-Ambroise Pumpkin Ale	

Trivia: What is the oldest brewery in Canada?
Answer: Molson Brewery (1786).

Trivia: What movie featured fictional brothers Bob and Doug McKenzie, hockey, and brewery, and, of course, beer?
Answer: *Strange Brew*.

WHERE THE TEAM IS TODAY—TACTICS AND STRATEGIES

Canada has some soul-searching to do. After all, this is its second FIFA World Cup appearance ever. What is their purpose here? To win the whole thing? (Good luck!) To get promotions for individual players? (Ahem!) If, indeed, the dormant strategy is to propel individual players to higher clubs, then Canada is in trouble. When a team collectively sees a tournament as an opportunity for personal advancement, then the team suffers. Unfortunately, a miraculous World Cup championship in only its second appearance ever seems unlikely.

Still, Canada's not bad. Though it's not great, either. In fact, Canada is *full of speed* and might just catch a few overconfident sides off-guard. A few of Canada's speedsters include Alphonso Davies, Tajon Buchanan, and Richie Laryea. Watch out for them as they can break a game wide open in a heartbeat!

Tactics and strategies: Canada was seen using a 3-4-2-1, 4-4-2, 3-5-2, and 4-2-3-1 during the 2022 World Cup qualifiers in CONCACAF. Where do we start? Usually, it's ill-advised to spin out multiple formations in a short period of time. In 2021, this was the case for Canada during its World Cup qualification campaign. The flipside to this critique is that, somehow, on December 4, 2021, Canada found itself sitting in first place during qualifiers. At that time, it went like this:

1. Canada
2. United States
3. Mexico
4. Panama
5. Costa Rica
6. Jamaica
7. El Salvador
8. Honduras

Since Canada hasn't had an overflow of success over the years, this should be (and likely is) counted as a victory for its soccer program. For a nation that has constantly grappled with its preordained destiny as the fifth- or sixth-ranked team in CONCACAF, always behind Mexico, the United States, Costa Rica, Honduras, and perhaps the mighty Jamaicans, it's a good feeling for the Canadians to sit in the number one spot, for the time being anyway!

A big strategy for Canada in Qatar is to keep the qualification momentum going strong! Can this be done? Certainly! It's very possible! In doing so it will utilize the wings often with the speed of Davies and Buchanan while trying to isolate Canadian scoring sensation, Cyle Larin.

As was the case in the 1986 FIFA World Cup, Canada gave France—Platini, Giresse, and Tigana—fits with strong resistance. Though Canada will need to rely on much more than strong resistance in Qatar if it wants to break through as an international threat. It will have to own its possession game with confidence, much as Iceland—a fellow underdog from a northern latitude—has done in recent times. Owning possession will establish an open avenue for Canada to fight back against traditional powers. If Canada sits back and allows more experienced teams to define possession, then it's in trouble. It needs to stand its ground, own possession, and utilize its remarkable speed when possible.

Canada will need to arrive in Qatar early, get used to breathing the air, get valuable training sessions in, and get into a groove quickly before games begin. In terms of depth, it will have to keep the bench actively ready both physically with touches on the ball and psychologically as the pressure of the grand stage might be daunting for a nation not used to being there. Also, if the Canadians can tighten up errors on defense, things should move in a positive direction.

JOHN HERDMAN—A BRIEF COACHING PORTRAIT
John Herdman—born in 1975 in England—hasn't exactly coached Real Madrid, Liverpool, or Bayern Munich, which would make him a genuine underdog leading an underdog. Prior to landing the position as Canada's skipper, Herdman coached the women's national teams of New Zealand (2006-11) and Canada (2011-18). As coach of Canada in unchartered World Cup territory, Herdman will have to think outside the box a bit. All in all, he's passionate about the team, and sometimes that moves mountains. Canadian fans feel like their time is due. Herdman just might be the guy to bring this grand Canadian soccer World Cup championship fantasy to fruition.

KEY PLAYERS AND THEIR CHARACTERISTICS
Alphonso Davies—born in 2000—played with Vancouver Whitecaps from 2016-18 before signing with Bayern Munich in 2018. A *Canadian* signed with Bayern Munich? That's right. Though he was born in Ghana (after his parents fled Liberia), Davies eventually attained citizenship in Canada where he flourished as a young player, and with Bayern Munich he's been deployed, largely, as an outside back. He's versatile and can play outside back, outside mid, and forward. His speed is noteworthy as he and teammate Buchanan are two of the three fastest in North America (the other, arguably, is Lozano from Mexico). Davies made his first appearance with Canada's varsity team in 2017 and has since surpassed 30 caps and met the 10-goal mark.

Cyle Larin—born in 1995—has made a name for himself in the record books as Canada's all-time leading scorer. He and phenom Dwayne De Rosario were tied for the lead in late 2021 with 22 goals each. Since then, Larin has exceeded that tally, and more goals are likely around the corner. At around 6'2", Larin has worked his way through a few soccer channels, including that of American soccer. He was once a member of the UConn Huskies; then in 2015-17, he played in MLS for Orlando City. As for Canada, his first game with the national team was in 2014; he's since gathered over 50 games, with over 20 goals. He'll be a major target up top for Canada as Davies and Buchanan work off him from the sides.

Jonathan David—born in 2000—is a 5'11" forward, and he's intent on leaving Qatar with a goal or two. He should be up top with Larin, wreaking havoc for defenses. His club path has taken him to Gent (where he attained 30 goals) followed by a signing with Lille in 2020 (where he's done well). He has a few years to play yet, and he's in the mix for Canada's all-time scoring list.

Tajon Buchanan will take you for a fast ride! This guy can move! Arguably, if injury free, he's the fastest player in World Cup 2022. He's definitely the fastest in CONCACAF. He and Davies blew past opponents in qualifiers and are hoping to blaze a trail in Qatar as well. Familiar particularly to New England Revolution fans, Buchanan—who should be 23 years old during the World Cup—is very new to Canada's national team as he first suited up in 2021.

Richie Laryea—born in 1995—has some quickness and speed to help out the team during the tournament. Feisty and ready for action, he could prove pivotal as a midfielder and outside back as Canada seeks to enter the Round of 16, and who knows from there. He's taken a step or two within the realm of American soccer, having suited up with Akron Zips and Orlando City. As of 2019, he became a regular with Toronto FC, and in that same year, he debuted with Canada's national team.

Jonathan Osorio—born in 1992—is a gifted 5'10" midfielder with experience from SC Toronto and Toronto FC. With the latter he's acquired over 245 games, with over 35 goals. He joined Canada in 2013 and has over 50 caps.

OVERALL PLAYER RATING

Alphonso Davies: 9	Tajon Buchanan: 8.5
Cyle Larin: 8.7	Richie Laryea: 8.7
Jonathan David: 8.7	Jonathan Osorio: 8.8

KEY PLAYER STATS
(Total career goals for their country)

	Games Played	Goals
Alphonso Davies	32	12
Cyle Larin	52	24
Jonathan David	32	21
Tajon Buchanan	24	4
Richie Laryea	30	1
Jonathan Osorio	55	7

WHAT TO WATCH FOR ON TV

Leading up to and during North American qualifiers for World Cup 2022, Canada had a number of intriguing players such as **goalkeepers** Milan Borjan, Maxime Crépeau, Dayne St. Clair, and Jayson Leutwiler; **defenders** Alistair Johnston, Samuel Adekugbe, Kamal Miller, Steven Vitória, Doneil Henry, Richie Laryea, Derek Cornelius, Zachary Brault-Guillard, Scott Fitzgerald Kennedy, Ashtone Morgan, and Marcus Godinho; **midfielders** Samuel Piette, Stephen Eustáquio, David Wotherspoon, Jonathan Osorio, Atiba Hutchinson, Mark-Anthony Kaye, Junior Hoilett, Liam Fraser, Russell Teibert, and Scott Arfield; and **forwards** Alphonso Davies, Lucas Cavallini, Tajon Buchanan, Cyle Larin, Jonathan David, Liam Millar, Charles-Andreas Brym, Tesho Akindele, Theo Corbeanu, and Tosaint Ricketts.

Canada essentially fought its way through the 2022 World Cup qualifiers against CONCACAF rivals Mexico, United States, Costa Rica, Panama, Honduras, Jamaica, and El Salvador.

Speed is the name of the game for Canada! At present, arguably the three fastest players in CONCACAF are 1) Tajon Buchanan (Canada), 2) Hirving Lozano (Mexico), and 3) Alphonso Davies (Canada). People certainly praise Davies for his speed. He has an interesting boost around the outside of the box, and he seems to coast past defenders whereas Buchanan and Mexico's Lozano come across as straight-up track stars. Richie Laryea isn't too slow either. It's a team that has speed in abundance, and if Canada gets anywhere this World Cup, a lot of it will have to do with this extreme ability.

Lucas Cavallini—born in 1992—is a 5'11" striker that made a move to the Vancouver Whitecaps in 2020 where he's done well with a handful of goals. Since 2012, he's earned over 15 goals for Canada, which is a leader for the team. In Qatar, he could prove interesting as a substitute.

When it comes to the history of Canadian soccer, it's not so much that Canada *was* unknown in the world of soccer, it's that it *still is* unknown in the world of soccer. This is something the Canadian bunch in Qatar wants to adjust, and it's a team that wants to emphatically let the world know that it belongs with the elite on the world stage.

Overall Player Rating: Keep in mind, we're comparing all talent to the greats, such as Pelé, Maradona, Platini, and Ronaldinho as the highest standard. Still, Canadian players are without a doubt talented within the ranks of international soccer and certainly for CONCACAF.

The fact that Canada has a presence in Qatar represents an opportunity of a lifetime. It has a chance to prove everyone[*] wrong in the 2022 FIFA World Cup.

---

[*] Millions of naysayers that do not believe in Canada and think it will place dead last in its World Cup group.

Canada—the underdog of all underdogs—has a tough group of players that have focus and determination. It's a team of hustle that exploits the flanks with hard work, speed, daring, and confidence. It will be very interesting to see how things play out in Qatar!

COSTA RICA
World Cup titles: 0
Overall Team Rating: 8.1

A BRIEF TEAM HISTORY
Let's take a quick glance at the World Cup record of Costa Rica.
1930: Costa Rica didn't compete.
1934: Didn't compete.
1938: Didn't compete.
1950: Didn't compete.
1954: Didn't compete.
1958: Didn't qualify.
1962: Didn't qualify.
1966: Didn't qualify.
1970: Didn't qualify.
1974: Didn't qualify.
1978: Didn't qualify.
1982: Didn't qualify.
1986: Didn't qualify.
1990: Made the Round of 16.
1994: Didn't qualify.
1998: Didn't qualify.
2002: Couldn't escape its group.
2006: Couldn't escape its group.
2010: Didn't qualify.
2014: Made the quarter-finals.
2018: Couldn't escape its group.

CONCACAF COMPETITIONS

Costa Rica's inner-CONCACAF journey has been a completely different story than their World Cup tribulations. Looking back at history, Costa Rica has been one of the best teams in Central America. Prior to the huge push from the United States as of the 1980s and 90s, Costa Rica and Mexico essentially dominated what is now CONCACAF.

For the CCCF Championship—a specific tournament for Central American and Caribbean countries—Costa Rica became champions in 1941, 1946, 1948, 1953, 1955, 1960, and 1961.

For the CONCACAF Championship, held from 1963-1989 (known as the CONCACAF Gold Cup as of 1991), Costa Rica took home first place in 1963, 1969, and 1989.

The Copa Centroamericana—a smaller tournament for Central American Football Union teams—has been a stage for Costa Rica to remind Central America it's the boss, as it has earned numerous first-place finishes from the 1990s through 2014.

FACTS ABOUT THEIR COUNTRY

Costa Rica—waving flags of red, white, and blue—is a small Central American country nestled in-between Nicaragua and Panama. It's a tropical vacation destination known for good food and coffee. Currently Costa Rica has a population of about 5 million people and a GDP of around $65 billion. Who has the most goals for Costa Rica's national team?
1. Rolando Fonseca (47)

In 2015, Costa Rica chose New Balance for its uniforms. Beer from Costa Rica? Bora should make a few rounds!

WHERE THE TEAM IS TODAY—TACTICS AND STRATEGIES

Costa Rica always has competition from Honduras and Panama for the title of "the best team in Central America," yet you can usually put your money on Costa Rica for results. Ruin a parade for Panama? Call in Costa Rica! Ruin a national celebration for Honduras? Call in Costa Rica! The big team on the Central America block would be Costa Rica.

Once you get out of the tiny neighborhood of Central America, and that of CONCACAF as well, there's a major problem that Costa Rica will face yet again at the World Cup level in Qatar where it will become a small fish in a big pond.

How can Costa Rica strategize for this dilemma? Good question! While attaining the title "World Cup champion" might seem far out of reach, the means to get there include using veterans Bryan Ruiz, Joel Campbell, and Celso Borges, all of whom possess craft and guile. In previous years, a big part of Costa Rica's charm has been the creative one-two punch of Ruiz and Campbell, two of North America's best talents. However, despite their obvious gifts on the ball, both are getting older in soccer years and can't carry the weight of the squad much longer. In fact, this should likely be their last World Cup journey. Still, Costa Rica fans are depending on one last surge from their bag of tricks in hopes of a miraculous history-making run in 2022. Costa Rica fans take the national team quite seriously, as they know Ruiz and Campbell can catch anyone off-guard. In addition, with the highly respected goalkeeping talent of Keylor Navas, along with the midfield wisdom of Celso Borges, some fans think there's hope.

Tactics and strategies: Watch out for a 4-2-3-1 or a 5-3-2. Ruiz, if healthy, should be in the center of the attack acting as a creative mid, which serves him best. Additionally, Campbell, if healthy, should be nearby with his spark ready at a moment's notice. With attacking options such as Moya, Venegas, Fuller, Tejeda, and Borges, Costa Rica presents a well-rounded attack that must be taken seriously.

Nice execution around goal for Costa Rica is paramount. It can get to that point with relentless possession. Possession from Costa Rica is pretty good—but not great—and this will be critical should the team expect to move forward in Qatar. As a lower-middle-of-the-road side, Costa Rica will have to depend on set-pieces for a little luck here and there, while at the same time it needs to tighten up on defensive errors so that Navas doesn't have to make 54 saves a game! If the Costa Ricans can clamp down on defense and produce turnovers, then a sparkling counterattack might just be its best ally.

LUIS FERNANDO SUAREZ—A BRIEF COACHING PORTRAIT

Luis Fernando Suárez—full name Luis Fernando Suárez Guzmán—has previously coached a number of teams, including Ecuador (2004-07) and Honduras (2011-14). In 2021, not long before the 2022 World Cup, he took over Costa Rica. Born in 1959 in Colombia, he brings South American pizazz to the product on the field. As such, Costa Rica has flair, athleticism, a little razzle dazzle, good passing combinations, an eye for strong defense, and good counterattacks down the lines. The challenge is great for a miraculous championship run, yet Luis Fernando Suárez has optimism on his side, as well as the luxury of low expectations. Still though, can he guide Costa Rica to higher ground? It's possible, and the path to future World Cup success for Costa Rica has a lot to do with the direction he takes this team.

KEY PLAYERS AND THEIR CHARACTERISTICS

Joel Campbell is not quite the player he was a few years ago, yet he's still a talent. Around five to six years ago, he was arguably the best player in CONCACAF. At that time, Costa Rica was a much more potent force than it is today. Campbell has played with a number of clubs like Arsenal, Lorient, Betis, and Sporting CP. He started playing with Costa Rica in 2011, with over 20 goals to his name. He's a crafty player. He can hurt opponents with dribbling, smart passes, and good instincts around goal.

Bryan Ruiz, like Campbell, has been a go-to player for Costa Rica for years. Ruiz also seems to move the ball in the right way; something always seems to be brewing when he's around. Who says no one watches Costa Rica? Various clubs have taken notice. Over time, Ruiz has played for some good ones, such as Gent, Twente, Fulham, PSV, and Sporting CP. He's older in soccer years, and this will most likely be his last opportunity at World Cup glory. He's the captain, the veteran. He first played for Costa Rica in 2005. He's acquired more than 140 appearances, with over 25 goals. He is a crafty midfielder. He and Campbell will easily go down as two of the best to ever play for Costa Rica.

Celso Borges—born in 1988—is a 6'2" midfielder who has played a staggering amount of games for Costa Rica. Since 2008, he's been in the books for over 145 appearances. He's also scored over 20 goals.

Yeltsin Tejeda—born in 1992—plays defensive mid for Costa Rica and has done so since 2011 whereby he's surpassed 60 caps. He's not much of a goal-scorer, but he'll keep a tidy ship.

Johan Venegas is a versatile talent as both a winger and forward. The 6'0" impact player had somewhat of an impact with the Montreal Impact from 2015-16, a sojourn that included 32 games and two goals. He took marching orders from there over to Minnesota United where he gathered up 22 games and two goals. His luck later improved when, during 2018-20, with Costa Rican club Saprissa, he accumulated 112 games, with 43 goals. Now we're talking. He since moved on to a Costa Rican club most people can't pronounce: Alajuelense, founded in 1919. Its nickname, by the way, is La Liga—much better! He signed with "La Liga" in 2021 where he's done very well. As for Costa Rica's national team, count him in for some goals. Since his arrival in 2014, he's scored over 10.

Kendall Waston—born in 1988—is a 6'5" center defender who has played with Saprissa, Vancouver Whitecaps (where he scored 14 goals), and FC Cincinnati. Having first played for Costa Rica in 2013, he is considered a veteran. Since 2013, he's gathered over 55 caps and a handful of goals.

Keylor Navas—born in 1986—is one of the best keepers worldwide; he has seen time with Saprissa, Levante, Real Madrid, and Paris Saint-Germain. Among many honors, he was given the Best Goalkeeper Award in the 2009 CONCACAF Gold Cup; he also won the 2014 and 2017 CONCACAF Men's Player of the Year. He's guarded the net for his nation since 2008, with over 100 caps. It's going to be a struggle for Costa Rica, but with the 6'1" Navas in goal, there's hope.

OVERALL PLAYER RATING

Joel Campbell: 9.3   Johan Venegas: 8.3
Bryan Ruiz: 9.3   Kendall Waston: 7.4
Celso Borges: 8.9   Keylor Navas: 9.9
Yeltsin Tejeda: 8.5

KEY PLAYER STATS
(Total career goals for their country)

	Games Played	Goals
Joel Campbell	117	25
Bryan Ruiz	144	29
Celso Borges	153	27
Yeltsin Tejeda	68	0
Johan Venegas	79	11
Kendall Waston	61	7
Keylor Navas	107	0

WHAT TO WATCH FOR ON TV
Leading up to and during North American qualifiers for World Cup 2022, Costa Rica had a number of intriguing players such as **goalkeepers** Keylor Navas, Leonel Moreira, and Aarón Cruz; **defenders** Ricardo Blanco, Keysher Fuller, Óscar Duarte, Bryan Oviedo, Francisco Calvo, Kendall Waston, Rónald Matarrita, Cristian Gamboa, Giancarlo González, Ian Smith,

Waylon Francis, and Joseph Mora; **midfielders** Celso Borges, Yeltsin Tejeda, Allan Cruz, Randall Leal, Jimmy Marín, Luis Díaz, David Guzmán, Ariel Lassiter, Elías Aguilar, Osvaldo Rodríguez, and Marvin Angulo; and **forwards** Bryan Ruiz, Johan Venegas, Joel Campbell, José Guillermo Ortiz, Jonathan Moya, Marco Ureña, Mayron George, and Deyver Vega.

Throughout the 2022 World Cup qualifiers, Costa Rica faced off against CONCACAF rivals Mexico, United States, Canada, Panama, Honduras, Jamaica, and El Salvador. Though, it wasn't exactly smooth sailing. In the beginning of the qualifiers there were a lot of concerns that the team might get left behind. Certainly, for a time, there was a struggle as Canada, Panama, and even to a lesser extent, Jamaica, were putting up good fights. Not to mention Mexico was there, reminding CONCACAF it was in charge.

Is it time to start taking Costa Rica seriously? Within the confines of a World Cup, it's a complicated answer. Yes, in that Costa Rica has talented players who can make a difference. No, in that Costa Rica has players and teams that (in past years) haven't done much.

Though Costa Rica might be a contender for the cup, it will have a hard time getting there, but that's part of the beauty of it. Costa Rica can be a team that causes fits for Germany, France, Brazil, and Argentina. If it can turn a few counters into goals, that would be great; if it can knock in a corner kick or two, that would be wonderful; if it can pull off an upset or two, that's exactly what the tiny country from Central America needs in order to define its place in World Cup 2022.

As a team, it has a knack to connect passes with forward movement. As a smaller nation, it shouldn't be completely dismissed, even if its chances of winning the whole thing are next to none. Dull, boring games with Costa Rica? Not a chance. It's a team to watch whether it walks away triumphantly or not.

THE TEAMS FROM AFRICA (5)

A quick note on African competitions:
Africa Cup of Nations
First tournament: 1957.
(The Africa Cup of Nations, AKA the African Cup of Nations, might also be referred to as the Africa Nations Cup, AKA the African Nations Cup. Herein, it's referred to as the Africa Cup of Nations.)

African Nations Championship
First tournament: 2009.
This is a different tournament from the Africa Cup of Nations.

MOROCCO
World Cup titles: 0
Overall Team Rating: 8

A BRIEF TEAM HISTORY
A brief look at the World Cup record of Morocco.
1930: Morocco—with ties to France—didn't compete.
1934: Morocco—with ties to France—didn't compete.
1938: Morocco—with ties to France—didn't compete.
1950: Morocco—with ties to France—didn't compete.
1954: Morocco—with ties to France—didn't compete.
1958: Didn't compete.
1962: Didn't qualify.

1966: Didn't compete.
1970: Morocco couldn't escape its group.
1974: Didn't qualify.
1978: Didn't qualify.
1982: Didn't qualify.
1986: Made the Round of 16.
1990: Didn't qualify.
1994: Couldn't escape its group.
1998: Couldn't escape its group.
2002: Didn't qualify.
2006: Didn't qualify.
2010: Didn't qualify.
2014: Didn't qualify.
2018: Morocco couldn't escape its group.

AFRICAN AND OTHER COMPETITIONS

Morocco won the Africa Cup of Nations in 1976, hosted by Ethiopia that year. In addition, Morocco won the FIFA Arab Cup in 2012. In recent years, Morocco has won the African Nations Championship in 2018 and 2020.

FACTS ABOUT THEIR COUNTRY

Morocco is perched on the northwest corner of Africa with a connection to Spain and Europe. For many years, Morocco has been known as a land of mystery that is home to Casablanca, coast-side casinos, and a very intriguing archaeological site of Volubilis. The current population of Morocco is approximately 37 million people, and it has an estimated GDP of $122 billion. As of 2019, Morocco has been sporting Puma jerseys.

Who is the top scorer in the history of Morocco's national team?
1. Ahmed Faras (36)

You might stumble across these beers in Morocco:

Pelforth Ambree	33 Export
Castel Beer	Flag Speciale
Beaufort Lager	Casablanca Lager

WHERE THE TEAM IS TODAY—TACTICS AND STRATEGIES

Morocco has talented players, yet, as a unit, it's a team (and program) trying to make a difference during a FIFA World Cup. Despite some sparkling goals in the FIFA World Cup 1986, Morocco has struggled to get into World Cups, and once there it has struggled to advance. The 2022 FIFA World Cup is an open opportunity for its veterans and younger players to have a go at the grand prize.

Tactics and strategies: Morocco will probably go with a 4-3-3. However, keep an eye out for other formations. The quickness Morocco has on defense is a sturdy backdrop for any formation it fields. In the grand scheme of things, formations don't matter if you're listening to someone like Brian Clough; it's how the players play in a given formation that matters. Defensively, Morocco also brings a lot of confidence from its players having a wealth of Euro club experience. This is certainly a luxury. During possession, defenders tend to take positions out wide, as the wings are utilized often in attack and during transition.

Offensively, Morocco will unleash a counterattack that has energy and eyes for goal. The passing is swift, as Morocco tries to include as many players as possible. The lineup has depth, yet it lacks a true superstar. This might be a hindrance as Morocco moves forward. Goals, or lack thereof, will be a telling issue for the team. One might expect quality play from Morocco, while at the same time, a low-scoring affair might be the end result. To counteract this, Morocco will bring forth a steady, relentless attack, one that includes numbers up front, has motion, energy, and zest for goal.

VAHID HALILHODZIC—A BRIEF COACHING PORTRAIT

Vahid Halilhodžić—born in 1952 in Yugoslavia—had a successful career as a 6'0" forward with Nantes (where he scored 93 goals), Paris Saint-Germain, and the Yugoslavian national team (where he had 15 caps and 8 goals from 1976-85). In his coaching life, he's led Lille, Rennes, Paris Saint-Germain, Ivory Coast, Algeria, Japan, and Nantes. He started with Morocco in 2019. His biggest challenge with Morocco will be to find a way into the Round of 16, with an eye for the quarter-finals. Easier said than done as he's working with and against Morocco's history in the FIFA World Cup.

KEY PLAYERS AND THEIR CHARACTERISTICS

Youssef En-Nesyri—born in 1997—is currently a leading scorer for Morocco, a dazzling 6'2" forward who has played with a few clubs, including Malaga, Leganes, and Sevilla. With the latter, he's put in over 20 goals. As for Morocco, his first appearance was in 2016, and he's scored over 10 goals for his nation. A player on the move, Youssef should be a vital component of Morocco's success in Qatar.

Ayoub El Kaabi—born in 1993 in Casablanca—stands around 6'0" and is a forward who has played with Wydad AC and Hatayspor. With Morocco, since 2018, he's reached 15 caps and a handful of goals. He'll be seeking more opportunities to place the ball in the back of the net.

Adel Taarabt—born in 1989 in Fez, Morocco—has traveled through elite soccer-circles at Lens, Tottenham Hotspur, Queens Park Rangers, Fulham, A.C. Milan, Benfica, and Genoa. As a versatile midfielder, the 5'10" Adel has seen significant action with Morocco since 2009, with over 25 caps and a few goals to date.

Sofyan Amrabat—born in 1996—has skill and wisdom picked up from Utrecht, Feyenoord, Club Brugge, and Fiorentina. As a 6'0" midfielder, he's represented Morocco over 35 times since 2017. He's not a big scorer, though. Yet, what he embodies is a fortress of Moroccan stone. Formidable, durable, dependable. He's part of a Moroccan front that's determined to make advances at the World Cup level.

If you're looking for a reliable defender, look no further than **Romain Saïss**. The team captain has an opportunity to make a stand in World Cup 2022. As a 6'2" defender with years of experience under his belt with Wolverhampton Wanderers (dating back to 2016), not to mention over 170 matches where he chiseled his game in the action-packed theater that is the EPL, he intends on stepping off the plane in Qatar with the intent of winning a championship.

Steadiness, experience, speed, and quickness is what you'll get with right-back **Achraf Hakimi**. Despite being a young player (born in 1998), the 5'11" defender has some 10 years of youth experience at Real Madrid. He also has a stellar background at the senior level with clubs Real Madrid, Borussia Dortmund, Inter Milan, and Paris Saint-Germain. In 2016, he took the field with Morocco and has gained over 50 caps. He's a top player for Morocco fans to depend on.

OVERALL PLAYER RATING

Youssef En-Nesyri: 9.2   Sofyan Amrabat: 8.9
Ayoub El Kaabi: 8.9   Romain Saïss: 9.1
Adel Taarabt: 8.9   Achraf Hakimi: 9.2

KEY PLAYER STATS
(Total career goals for their country)

	Games Played	Goals
Youssef En-Nesyri	48	14
Ayoub El Kaabi	23	8
Adel Taarabt	30	4
Sofyan Amrabat	36	0
Romain Saïss	63	1
Achraf Hakimi	51	8

WHAT TO WATCH FOR ON TV

Leading up to and during African qualifiers for World Cup 2022, Morocco had a talented group that included **goalkeepers** Yassine Bounou, Anas Zniti, Ahmed Reda Tagnaouti, and Munir Mohamedi; **defenders** Achraf Hakimi, Adam Masina, Nayef Aguerd, Romain Saïss, Sofian Chakla, Souffian El Karouani, Jawad El Yamiq, Sofiane Alakouch, Samy Mmaee, Achraf Lazaar, Zouhair Feddal, Issam Chebake, and Nabil Dirar; **midfielders** Imran Louza, Fayçal Fajr, Ilias Chair, Aymen Barkok, Sofyan Amrabat, Selim Amallah, Adel Taarabt, Yahya Jabrane, and Oussama Tannane; and **forwards** Ayoub El Kaabi, Sofiane Boufal, Munir El Haddadi, Achraf Bencharki, Youssef En-Nesyri, Ryan Mmaee, Zakaria Aboukhlal, Soufiane Rahimi, Hakim Ziyech, and Youssef El-Arabi.

Morocco did very well throughout the 2022 World Cup qualifiers in Africa in Group I that included Guinea-Bissau, Guinea, and Sudan.

The nuance Morocco has is interlaced with a large amount of players that exude Euro-club polish that has been gleaned over time. Morocco will turn Europe's club team training tactics—which feature structured passing—against all teams it faces in the World Cup. This will begin with its competition in Group F against Belgium, Canada, and Croatia. Morocco's current approach is similar to that of Brazil; Brazil is a team that has so many players with European club experience that it has lost some of its classic Jogo Bonito style. Morocco certainly isn't at the level of Brazil, yet Moroccan players are exuding a structured passing approach that exemplifies European clubs. Morocco will blend its fluid, counterattacking, approach with structured European passing combinations. As such, this team will be a threat in World Cup 2022.

Moroccans are calm and skillful and possess eruptive energy on offense. It's a team with passion that has the ability to strike fast and hard. One thing that might hold Morocco back is the inability to completely own a game. It tends to be a "trading punches" side that can't hit as hard as some of the other powerhouse teams.

Can Morocco remain steady enough throughout the group stage to advance further? This will be tough. The group stage, perhaps, is the most exciting part of the World Cup as "everyone has a chance." If Morocco finds itself down a goal or two, which is very possible, will it have enough resolve to stay calm and fight back? Often, teams like Morocco with little to lose (other than a whole lot of pride) get caught up in the identity of being a team with "low expectations" and play down to that level. If Morocco can master the art of "steady," things could change in its favor, big time. It will be interesting to see if Morocco can hold its own, face adversity, and get past the group stage, perhaps into the quarter-finals—depending on how things land in the Round of 16.

Although Tunisia is a strong dark horse choice out of Africa, don't take your eyes off Morocco! This team brings a vibrant attack and is full of talented players that can surprise opponents with flashes of brilliance at any moment!

SENEGAL
World Cup titles: 0
Overall Team Rating: 8

A BRIEF TEAM HISTORY
A brief look at the World Cup record of Senegal.
1930: Senegal didn't compete.
1934: Didn't compete.
1938: Didn't compete.
1950: Didn't compete.
1954: Didn't compete.
1958: Didn't compete.
1962: Didn't compete.

1966: Didn't compete.
1970: Didn't qualify.
1974: Didn't qualify.
1978: Didn't qualify.
1982: Didn't qualify.
1986: Didn't qualify.
1990: Didn't compete.
1994: Didn't qualify.
1998: Didn't qualify.
2002: Senegal made the quarter-finals.
2006: Didn't qualify.
2010: Didn't qualify.
2014: Didn't qualify.
2018: Senegal couldn't escape its group.

FACTS ABOUT THEIR COUNTRY

Senegal's present population is around 15.8 million people, with an estimated GDP of $28 billion. It's a small country in West Africa that neighbors Mauritania, Mali, the Gambia, and Guinea-Bissau. Who is the all-time leading scorer in Senegal's history?
1. Sadio Mané (33)*

If you're in Senegal, you might come across a popular beer known as 33 Export. Excited fans are sure to line them up during matches!

WHERE THE TEAM IS TODAY—TACTICS AND STRATEGIES

One might assume that a team with a scant World Cup history would only be happy just to be at the table, but Senegal is in the peculiar position of being a team eager to reach the final of a World Cup. This has to happen sometime, right, and why not now? After all, Senegal shocked a lot of fans with its quarter-

---

*   Still active, and this number will likely increase.

finals appearance in 2002. So it stands to reason that Senegal is ready to make another move in Qatar.

Tactics and strategies: Senegal's formation will likely be a 4-3-3.

Defensively, Senegal has speed, aggressiveness, and experienced hands with time in Europe to add some polish. If Senegal can capitalize on turnovers with quick, efficient counters, then perhaps it can put a few powerhouse squads on thin ice. However, Senegal will need to stay alert on set-pieces, not overcommit, and watch for petty errors around its box.

Offensively, Senegal has moments of brilliance coupled with fumbled attempts at goal. This means one thing: As a team unit, it needs to concentrate on steadiness. With steadiness comes patience. If Senegal can remain patient, work the two-man game, and get all positions involved, then good things are around the corner. With only two previous World Cup appearances, Senegal is looking for a rhythm. Goals will help. Winning cures all ills in big tournaments. With a keen eye on possession, patience, combination passing, and smart dribbling, Senegal should find more quality shots on goal, which will increase its chances to score.

A few players that will keep hope alive include Sadio Mané, Idrissa Gueye, Cheikhou Kouyaté, Kalidou Koulibaly, Famara Diédhiou, and Ismaïla Sarr. It's a team looking for that quintessential, groundbreaking World Cup achievement. This would be a semi-finals appearance, which is where no African team has been before, and a championship game appearance. The latter would be great. One step at a time. The 2002 FIFA World Cup was great, as Senegal reached the quarters. With a little time to reflect, Senegal is hoping history will repeat itself.

ALIOU CISSE—A BRIEF COACHING PORTRAIT

Aliou Cissé—born in 1976 in Senegal—was a midfielder and defender as a player. He appeared with Lille, Paris Saint-Germain, Montpellier, Birmingham City, Portsmouth, Sedan, and Nimes.

He also gathered up 35 caps for Senegal (1999-2005). In 2015, a decade after he ended his playing career with Senegal, he took over as coach; as such, he's had a few years under his watch now, enough time to implement his vision. Back in the World Cup, his grand design is halfway there. The next step would be to take it to the limit and shock the world with a championship. As one of the tournament's underdogs, his team of ultra-talented players might be the special generation Senegal's been waiting on.

KEY PLAYERS AND THEIR CHARACTERISTICS

Sadio Mané—approximately 5'9"—is currently Senegal's premiere forward with over 30 goals. He's the force necessary to put his team over the top. With him making runs around goal, there's hope for fans in Senegal. Throughout his club career—with stops at Metz, Red Bull Salzburg, Southampton, and Liverpool—he's put the ball into the net. Notably, with Liverpool, where he signed in 2016, he's played in over 190 games, with over 85 goals. With Senegal, he's been a regular since 2012. His scoring prowess will be front and center for a nation hungry for World Cup success.

Idrissa Gueye—born in 1989—is a 5'9" defensive midfield stud that's played with some of Europe's finest sides: Lille, Aston Villa, Everton, and PSG. He made his first appearance with Senegal in 2011. He's now sitting on over 90 caps. His veteran experience will come in handy should Senegal want to have success in Qatar.

Cheikhou Kouyaté gets a lot of playing time at club level: with Anderlecht (2008-14), 153 games; with West Ham United (2014-18), 129 games; with Crystal Palace, where he signed in 2018, over 125 games and counting. Then there's Senegal. With his national team he's played in over 80 matches since 2012. He's clearly durable; he's a force at midfield and defense. But is he worn out? Could he be a step behind elite opponents? Little injuries might be nagging him along the way, yet he should also make a difference for Senegal on its quest for World Cup glory.

Kalidou Koulibaly—Senegal's captain—leads from defense as he plays center-back. At 6'2", he'll be a guiding force on the backline, with the responsibility of breaking up plays and setting the pace for possession. His club career thus far has been fruitful, with stops at Metz, Genk, and Napoli. With Napoli, he's played in more than 235 games since 2014, with just over 10 goals. In 1991, he was born in France and eventually played for the French U20 squad but then switched over to Senegal's senior national team for his debut back in 2015.

Famara Diédhiou—born in 1992—is a 6'4" striker who has seen time with a few clubs, yet his lengthiest appearance so far has been with Bristol City: 154 games and 46 goals.

Ismaïla Sarr—born in 1998—is a 6'1" winger who has been seen with Metz, Rennes, and Watford, where, at each step of the way, his goal tally incrementally increased. In addition, with Senegal, Sarr has scored a handful of goals since his debut in 2016.

OVERALL PLAYER RATING

Sadio Mané: 9.3

Idrissa Gueye: 8.9

Cheikhou Kouyaté: 8.9

Kalidou Koulibaly: 8.9

Famara Diédhiou: 8.4

Ismaïla Sarr: 8.8

KEY PLAYER STATS

(Total career goals for their country)

	Games Played	Goals
Sadio Mané	91	33
Idrissa Gueye	94	7
Cheikhou Kouyaté	82	4
Kalidou Koulibaly	62	0
Famara Diédhiou	24	10
Ismaïla Sarr	47	10

WHAT TO WATCH FOR ON TV

Leading up to and during African qualifiers for World Cup 2022, Senegal had a formidable group that included **goalkeepers** Édouard Mendy and Alfred Gomis; **defenders** Saliou Ciss, Kalidou Koulibaly, Pape Abou Cissé, Bouna Sarr, Ibrahima Mbaye, Abdou Diallo, Fodé Ballo-Touré, Lamine Gassama, and Youssouf Sabaly; **midfielders** Idrissa Gueye, Nampalys Mendy, Cheikhou Kouyaté, Moustapha Name, Pape Matar Sarr, Mamadou Loum, Joseph Lopy, Pape Cheikh Diop, and Cheikh N'Doye; and **forwards** Boulaye Dia, Sadio Mané, Habib Diallo, Krépin Diatta, Ismaïla Sarr, Famara Diédhiou, Keita Baldé, Sada Thioub, Mbaye Diagne, and Abdallah Sima.

Senegal navigated through the 2022 World Cup qualifiers in Africa in Group H that included Namibia, Congo, and Togo.

In Qatar, Senegal will bring gusto, passion, and high-performance value to each game. In so far as winning the whole World Cup, Senegal has a lot of work to do. It's a team that shouldn't be taken lightly. With Sadio Mané in good form, things are possible. It's got what it takes to upset a France, Belgium, or Argentina. The players are fierce and ready for action. It's a matter of whether they "can remain steady" throughout the trials and tribulations of a high-pressure World Cup atmosphere. If they can pull that off, then watch out, because Senegal has a presence.

As was correctly predicted by yours truly in the 2018 FIFA World Cup, Senegal did not escape its group. This time around things might be different. One might quantify Senegal as a "protégé" of Nigeria, so to speak. Obviously, Senegal and Nigeria are competitors but Senegal comes across as a "less dangerous Nigeria." One might say Senegal's a little of Nigeria meets Cameroon meets Ghana, with a touch of Benin. All in all, Senegal could—and should—take advantage of its underdog status.

TUNISIA
World Cup titles: 0
Overall Team Rating: 8.1

A BRIEF TEAM HISTORY
A brief look at the World Cup record of Tunisia.
1930: Tunisia didn't compete.
1934: Didn't compete.
1938: Didn't compete.
1950: Didn't compete.
1954: Didn't compete.
1958: Didn't compete.
1962: Didn't qualify.
1966: Didn't compete.
1970: Didn't qualify.
1974: Didn't qualify.
1978: Tunisia couldn't escape its group.
1982: Didn't qualify.
1986: Didn't qualify.
1990: Didn't qualify.
1994: Didn't qualify.
1998: Couldn't escape its group.
2002: Couldn't escape its group.
2006: Couldn't escape its group.
2010: Didn't qualify.
2014: Didn't qualify.
2018: Tunisia couldn't escape its group.

AFRICAN AND OTHER COMPETITIONS
Tunisia walked away, defiantly, as champions of the Africa Cup of Nations in 2004. Tunisia won the FIFA Arab Cup in 1963. In 2022, Tunisia won the Kirin Cup Soccer, a tournament hosted in Japan.

FACTS ABOUT THEIR COUNTRY

Tunisia's population is around 11.7 million people, with an estimated GDP of $44 billion. Tunisia's national team has quite the entourage: Head Coach, Assistant Coach, Goalkeeper Coach, Sporting Director, Team Administrator, a Physiotherapist (why not!), a Fitness Coach, the Team Doctor, someone regarding Osteopath, a Nutritionist, a Video Analyst, Team Manager, a Media Officer, and, finally, an Officer for Security.

Who has the most caps for Tunisia?
1. Radhi Jaidi (105)

Who is the all-time leader in goals for Tunisia?
1. Issam Jemâa (36)

Beer in Tunisia? Try Celtia and Berber! Fans will likely have some available during games!

WHERE THE TEAM IS TODAY—TACTICS AND STRATEGIES

Where would Tunisia be without strategy? Its entourage, which is well put together, well thought out, thorough, and well orchestrated, is a sign of its commitment to excellence. This carries over to its style of play. Strategy is the name of the game for Tunisia; it's a team that is very refined, skillful, crafty, creative (to an extent; we're not talking about Brazil here), technical, thoughtful, and full of short-passing combinations.

Tactics and strategies: With respect to Tunisia, look for a 4-3-3.

Defensively, Tunisia has a way of swarming the ball with numbers and a press like a group of sharks homing in on prey. It's a team that tends to push numbers back on defense, while sending up a few in transition—common yet worth mentioning. Perhaps Tunisia lacks significant nuance in its team shape from time to time; subtle, but it could use improvement.

Offensively, Tunisia confounds opponents with sharp, passing combinations. Players are crafty, and it's a team effort. However, there's no true superstar presence. This presents an issue for Tunisia moving forward. A remedy for this potential disaster is what Tunisia does best, as if by default: It brings together a sound team effort. In a way, it's a little like Netherlands in the 70s without Cruyff; the remaining Dutch phenoms had to pick up the slack with every player contributing (which is what Netherlands was already doing, yet maybe it increased in the absence of Cruyff), and, lo and behold, Netherlands got results! Tunisia, in its own way, needs to do the same.

In the long run of this World Cup, that is, outside of group play, Tunisia faces a challenge. If, by some chance, the Eagles of Carthage escape its group, you should take notice. The idea of staying united with a strong eye for passing, possession, and owning the ball is what will help create an auspicious ending for the North African magicians. At some point, Tunisia, easily considered a less-prestigious national team, has to step up and demand respect with results. Though, it won't be easy.

JALEL KADRI—A BRIEF COACHING PORTRAIT

Jalel Kadri—born in 1971 in Tunisia—took over the head coaching job in 2022. Obviously there has been very little time to adjust as coach and prepare for the World Cup, and perhaps Coach Kadri is not really afforded a fair opportunity to get his team ready with such a limited amount of time! Luckily, he was the assistant coach for Tunisia from 2021-22. So he's not jumping on board without any prep time whatsoever. Still, taking over a team in the same year as the World Cup is a tough task for any coach. Kadri certainly has the opportunity and challenge of a lifetime. A few previous coaches of Tunisia include Mondher Kebaier (2019-22), and one of the greats from French soccer, Alain Giresse (2018-19). Tunisia is a very crafty team. It's a team that is hungry for World Cup success. As conductor, will now be wanting to make the most of his opportunity. Perhaps he's not a household name, but he's coached few club teams from Tunisia and Saudi Arabia, such as AS Kasserine (Tunisia) and Damac FC (Saudi Arabia). Being in the 2022 FIFA World Cup is extremely exciting. The next step, of course, would be to take his crafty, skillful group of players and lead them into the championship match in Qatar! Kadri is not just playing the role of underdog coach, he's got a team and millions of fans back home that are regarded as massive World Cup underdogs. In essence, Tunisia winning the 2022 FIFA World Cup would be like Hickory winning the Indiana High School State Championship in *Hoosiers*, which would make Kadri Gene Hackman. Anything's possible, but it's going to be a struggle!

KEY PLAYERS AND THEIR CHARACTERISTICS

Hannibal Mejbri—born in 2003 in France—is a young player that you might have seen with Manchester United. The 6'0" midfielder joined one of England's most dominant clubs in 2021, after spending some time in its youth ranks. What's more, he appeared with France's U16 and U17 national teams before joining Tunisia's senior national team in 2021. He is a young player to keep an eye on.

Ferjani Sassi—born in 1992 in Tunisia—has played with a few clubs, including Metz, ES Tunis, Al Nassr, and Zamalek (where he played in over 100 games). Since 2013, he's become a veteran performer with Tunisia. The 6'1" midfielder will be called upon for strong minutes, distribution, organization, and guidance.

Youssef Msakni fills out Tunisia's roster as a versatile 5'10" forward who can also play on the wing. He's put up significant numbers with Tunisia's Esperance Tunis (104 games, 37 goals) and Qatar's very own Al-Duhail (119 games, 73 goals). As for Tunisia, he's been around since 2010, with over 15 goals.

Wahbi Khazri—born in 1991 in France—is a 6'0" attacking mid and forward who is making a push for Tunisia's all-time scoring record with over 20 goals so far. His club career has taken him to Bastia, Bordeaux, Sunderland, Rennes, and Saint-Etienne. With the latter, he's done quite well having scored over 30 goals since 2018. After brief experiences with Tunisia U20 and France U21, Khazri opted for Tunisia's senior national side, where he's performed since 2013. In 2018, he was named Tunisian Footballer of the Year.

The 5'8" attacking mid **Naïm Sliti**—who was born in France—has significant experience from the French clubs Sedan, Red Star, Lille, Dijon, and Saudi Arabia's Al-Ettifaq. Sliti is one to watch, as he's tallied 65-plus caps, with over 10 goals for Tunisia.

OVERALL PLAYER RATING

Hannibal Mejbri: 8.9   Wahbi Khazri: 9.1
Ferjani Sassi: 8.9   Naïm Sliti: 8.9
Youssef Msakni: 8.9

KEY PLAYER STATS

(Total career goals for their country)

	Games Played	Goals
Hannibal Mejbri	16	0
Ferjani Sassi	76	6
Youssef Msakni	85	17
Wahbi Khazri	69	24
Naïm Sliti	67	13

WHAT TO WATCH FOR ON TV

Leading up to and during African qualifiers for World Cup 2022, Tunisia had a skillful group that included **goalkeepers** Farouk Ben Mustapha, Mouez Hassen, and Aymen Dahmen; **defenders**

Bilel Ifa, Montassar Talbi, Yassine Meriah, Aymen Abdennour, Ali Maâloul, Mohamed Dräger, Hamza Mathlouthi, and Mohamed Ali Yacoubi; **midfielders** Ghailene Chaalali, Hannibal Mejbri, Ferjani Sassi, Mohamed Ali Ben Romdhane, Yassine Chikhaoui, Saad Bguir, Anis Ben Slimane, Wahbi Khazri, and Mohamed Amine Ben Amor; and **forwards** Youssef Msakni, Fakhreddine Ben Youssef, Seifeddine Jaziri, Naïm Sliti, and Firas Chaouat.

Tunisia navigated through the 2022 World Cup qualifiers in Africa in Group B that included Zambia, Equatorial Guinea, and Mauritania.

In Qatar, the Eagles of Carthage—a very cool nickname—will be up against it, to say the least! It's a team with little World Cup experience, not much in the results column at the World Cup level, and it's a small nation that rests in the backwater of international soccer conversations. While people are talking about Neymar's multi-million-dollar shoe deal with Puma, they are not juxtaposing that with Hannibal Mejbri's recent news with Manchester United. Not to mention, the outside left-back talents of **Ali Maâloul**, who throws in many persuasive fake kicks on offense, might go unnoticed. It shouldn't! This is a solid team that placed second in the 2021 FIFA Arab Cup. Unfortunately for Tunisia, it will get lost in the shuffle of World Cup conversations.

In many respects, Tunisia is "off the grid" as a team when it comes to World Cup glory. This won't stop the nucleus of Wahbi Khazri (if he's available), Hannibal Mejbri, Ferjani Sassi, Youssef Msakni, Naïm Sliti, and Mohamed Ali Ben Romdhane from focusing on skillful play toward a heavy underdog triumph in Qatar. This group doesn't exploit the wings quite as much as others. It's a team that focuses on ingenuity, short passing, and team unity. Despite being a lower-ranked side, it's one to watch for in Qatar.

GHANA
World Cup titles: 0
Overall Team Rating: 8

A BRIEF TEAM HISTORY
Let's take a quick glance at the World Cup record of Ghana.
1930: Ghana didn't compete.
1934: Didn't compete.
1938: Didn't compete.
1950: Didn't compete.
1954: Didn't compete.
1958: Didn't compete.
1962: Didn't qualify.
1966: Didn't compete.
1970: Didn't qualify.
1974: Didn't qualify.
1978: Didn't qualify.
1982: Didn't compete.
1986: Didn't qualify.
1990: Didn't qualify.
1994: Didn't qualify.
1998: Didn't qualify.
2002: Didn't qualify.
2006: Made the Round of 16.
2010: Made the quarter-finals.
2014: Couldn't escape its group.
2018: Ghana didn't qualify.

AFRICAN AND OTHER COMPETITIONS
Ghana won the Africa Cup of Nations in 1963, 1965, 1978, and 1982.

FACTS ABOUT THEIR COUNTRY

In West Africa you'll find Accra, the seaside capital of Ghana. Ghana's population is about 31 million people, with an estimated GDP of $73.5 billion.

Who is the leading scorer in the history of Ghana's national team?
1. Asamoah Gyan (51)

A few beers you're likely to find in Ghana? Keep an eye out for:

Stone Strong Lager	Club Premium Lager
Club Shandy	Star Lager

WHERE THE TEAM IS TODAY—TACTICS AND STRATEGIES

Led in the past by Ghana's scoring sensation Asamoah Gyan, a movement of confidence has arisen in this small West African nation. There's something about Ghana that produces talented soccer players. In fact, for a while, the USMNT had the creative services of Freddy Adu, who originally was born in Ghana before landing on the East Coast of the United States and eventually began a longstanding merry-go-ride with different clubs around the globe. Pro clubs have taken notice of Ghana's creative pool of gamers and turn to Ghana as a source of talent. West Africa has been a hotbed of soccer, including Cameroon, Nigeria, and Liberia.

Today's national team from Ghana represents a group that has seen the world of international soccer through the eyes of a number of clubs. The result is a refined group that is edging closer and closer to the ultimate goal of reaching the semi-finals of a FIFA World Cup—a place no African team has ventured before. Of course, this isn't the only goal in mind. Ghana wants a strong performance, and, in doing so, it wants to further show the world how talented it is at the highest level. Another goal, of course, would be to win the World Cup. Yet, first off, given its World Cup record, Ghana needs to concentrate its efforts on escaping its group and getting past the Round of 16.

Tactics and strategies: Expect a 4-2-3-1 from Ghana, a formation it has been seen with leading up to this World Cup.

Defensively, with four defenders, Ghana can assert its strength on opposing attacks with depth—four backs. The balancing act of the three mids up top help with rhythm and flow once possession is achieved. Petty mistakes need to be eradicated, as much as possible for Ghana to pursue success in Qatar as they lead to turnovers, set-pieces, and shots on goal—which is what Ghana doesn't want!

Offensively, with production from André Ayew, Jordan Ayew, Caleb Ekuban, Mubarak Wakaso, Thomas Partey, and Jonathan Mensah, if all players—forwards, mids, and defenders—add to the attack, then Ghana can navigate through the tournament with more quality chances on goal, which is the idea.

Ghana will use its athleticism, speed, quickness, and eagerness to flow into the attack from multiple positions to its advantage. And, by and large, it should be exciting soccer for millions of fans around the world!

OTTO ADDO—A BRIEF COACHING PORTRAIT

Otto Addo—born in 1975 in West Germany—played as a midfielder back in the day for Hannover 96, Borussia Dortmund, and Mainz 05. As of 2022, he became coach of Ghana, right on the doorstep of World Cup 2022! As a former player for Ghana's national team, he seems to have come full circle. It's a pivotal moment for the Black Stars, as this could be a groundbreaking World Cup that sets a precedent for all future competitions. If, indeed, Ghana can make history with a surge into the semi-finals, and perhaps a World Cup championship, the whole history of world soccer will be altered forever. And Addo will be right in the middle of it!

KEY PLAYERS AND THEIR CHARACTERISTICS

André Ayew—born in 1989 in France—will grab your attention as Ghana's 5'9" scoring stud who wheels and deals especially well from the wing. From 2007-15, he scored 44 goals for Marseille. With two stints at Swansea City, he put in over 40 goals. He's played with Ghana since 2007 with over 20 goals.

Jordan Ayew—born in 1991 in France—is a versatile 6'0" forward and midfielder who has caught the attention of fans at Marseille, Lorient, Aston Villa, Swansea City, and Crystal Palace. All the same, Ghana fans are familiar with his talent as he's scored over 15 goals for Ghana since 2010.

Mubarak Wakaso—born in 1990 in Ghana—is a talented 5'7" midfielder who distributes the ball for Ghana and should be instrumental for the team in Qatar. He's suited up for Villarreal, Espanyol, Alaves, and Shenzhen.

Thomas Partey sets the tone of the party in midfield where the 6'1" sensation has turned a few heads at Atletico Madrid (2015-20), with over 130 games and 12 goals, followed by a move in 2020 to Arsenal, where he's played in over 35 games. He's a veteran with Ghana since his debut in 2016. Since then, he's acquired 35-plus caps and over 10 goals.

You'll get a strong defensive effort out of the 6'2" **Jonathan Mensah**. He signed with Columbus Crew in 2017 and has added up over 140 games for the Ohio-based super team. Mensah has a long history with Ghana, dating back to his first game in 2009 whereby he's played in over 65 games.

OVERALL PLAYER RATING

André Ayew: 9

Jordan Ayew: 9

Mubarak Wakaso: 8.7

Thomas Partey: 9

Jonathan Mensah: 8.8

233

KEY PLAYER STATS
(Total career goals for their country)

	Games Played	Goals
André Ayew	107	23
Jordan Ayew	81	19
Mubarak Wakaso	70	13
Thomas Partey	40	13
Jonathan Mensah	69	1

WHAT TO WATCH FOR ON TV

Leading up to and during African qualifiers for World Cup 2022, Ghana had a determined group that included **goalkeepers** Joe Wollacott, Lawrence Ati-Zigi, Richard Ofori, and Razak Abalora; **defenders** Andrew Yiadom, Joseph Aidoo, Baba Rahman, Daniel Amartey, Alexander Djiku, Nicholas Opoku, Gideon Mensah, Kasim Adams Nuhu, and Jonathan Mensah; **midfielders** André Ayew, Mubarak Wakaso, Samuel Owusu, Mohammed Kudus, Iddrisu Baba, Kamaldeen Sulemana, Thomas Partey, Alfred Duncan, Jeffrey Schlupp, and Afriyie Acquah; and **forwards** Jordan Ayew, Daniel-Kofi Kyereh, Caleb Ekuban, Richmond Boakye, Joel Fameyeh, and Emmanuel Boateng.

Ghana navigated through the 2022 World Cup qualifiers in Africa in Group G that included South Africa, Ethiopia, and Zimbabwe.

In Qatar, you'll see a small country from West Africa intent on bringing a lot of heat to the field. Ghana—nicknamed the Black Stars—will be led, in part, by the flowing talents of André Ayew, Jordan Ayew, Mubarak Wakaso, Thomas Partey, and Jonathan Mensah. This is a team who is very eager to make a stand. Given the experience and savvy of said players, this Ghanaian side could be very dangerous for opponents in Qatar as opponents clash in bitter on-field battles for World Cup supremacy. Ghana, in recent years, has had the ability, confidence, and swagger to do some real damage. It's a team *not* to be taken lightly. It's ready to set up shop in its corner of Qatar, to assume dominion. Be ready for a few upsets in the 2022 FIFA World Cup. If and when such upsets occur, Ghana is a frontrunner to reap the rewards!

CAMEROON
World Cup titles: 0
Overall Team Rating: 8.4

A BRIEF TEAM HISTORY
Let's take a quick glance at the World Cup record of Cameroon.
1930: Cameroon didn't compete.
1934: Didn't compete.
1938: Didn't compete.
1950: Didn't compete.
1954: Didn't compete.
1958: Didn't compete.
1962: Didn't compete.
1966: Didn't compete.
1970: Didn't qualify.
1974: Didn't qualify.
1978: Didn't qualify.
1982: Couldn't escape its group.
1986: Didn't qualify.
1990: Made the quarter-finals.
1994: Couldn't escape its group.
1998: Couldn't escape its group.
2002: Couldn't escape its group.
2006: Didn't qualify.
2010: Couldn't escape its group.
2014: Couldn't escape its group.
2018: Cameroon didn't qualify.

AFRICAN AND OTHER COMPETITIONS
Cameroon won the Africa Cup of Nations in 1984, 1988, 2000, 2002, and 2017.

FACTS ABOUT THEIR COUNTRY
If you were to find yourself in the West African nation of Cameroon and wanted to visit the capital city, you'd go to Yaounde. Walking through its streets, you'd probably overhear the nation's common language of French, followed by English. Other languages include Cameroonian Pidgin English, Fula, and Ewondo. Currently, Cameroon's population is around 26.5 million people, with an estimated GDP of $44.8 billion.

Who is Cameroon's most capped player?
1. Rigobert Song (137)

Who has scored the most goals in the history of Cameroon's national team?

1. Samuel Eto'o (56)   **2.** Roger Milla (43)

Beer you might stumble across in Cameroon?
Mutzig   Beaufort
Harp Premium   Castel Beer
33 Export

WHERE THE TEAM IS TODAY—TACTICS AND STRATEGIES
The mighty Cameroon! How can one forget the magical run of the Indomitable Lions in the 1990 FIFA World Cup? First with the astounding defeat over world-champion, Argentina, by a leaping header that led to a 1-0 shocker in Milan (with cards left and right; two ejections for Cameroon), which was followed

by Roger Milla* hysteria, and eventually ended with a chill-induced heartbreaker in the quarter-finals against dream-crushers England—send your letters of dissatisfaction to one Gary Lineker! Since then, honestly, Cameroon hasn't exactly captured the same fervor in a World Cup, yet fans have wanted to revisit that magical time in 1990. As if by transposing time, people want that dashing team—Roger Milla, N'Kono, N'Dip, Tataw, Kunde, Massing, Ebwelle, Mbouh, Andre Kana-Biyik, M'Fede, Francois Omam-Biyik, Pagal, and Makanaky—to jump into the TV and take flight once again! Well, it hasn't happened, yet. There was the Cameroon era of Samuel Eto'o (1997-2014), with plenty of sparkle, but it wasn't the same. Just maybe, this time around things will be different. Maybe it'll be special once again.

Tactics and strategies: Cameroon has been seen in recent times with a 4-3-3. It's a formation that should benefit the team as four defenders will help balance out Cameroon's back line. The three mids and three forwards will create a swarming formation of defense that can cover more of the field with marking.

Offensively, Cameroon will be able to launch significant numbers into the attacking third. With its formidable quickness and speed, it's a team that can exploit the wings and get overlapping runs into play with great results. With many players joining the attack, Cameroon is a side that will keep opponents in precarious positions.

If Cameroon can jump out to a lead, will it keep the tempo going and look for more goals? Or will it relent, and hold on to possession for the duration of a match? Good questions.

On the flipside, if Cameroon goes down a goal and finds itself in a bind, will it capitulate by losing focus? Will it rush forward like a well-organized pickup team searching for gold, and be content with half-chances on goal? Or will it hold on to possession and

---

*   Roger "old man" Milla that is. At the time, his age was uncertain. It was thought to be around 40. Yet he was performing like one of the best players in the tournament.

systematically dismantle the other side with the idea of creating quality shots on goal? At this point, one thing is pretty clear: Expect a lot of free-flowing soccer from the exciting Cameroonians.

RIGOBERT SONG—A BRIEF COACHING PORTRAIT

Rigobert Song—born in 1976 in Cameroon—was a defender who played with Metz and Liverpool. He played extensively for Cameroon's national team (1993-2010). In 2022, he assumed the position of head coach for his nation's national team. Now the challenge is within sight: Take Cameroon where the 1990 squad almost got—the semi-finals and perhaps the final of a World Cup. Qatar could be the stage for Cameroon to make history and achieve soccer royalty. Rigobert Song, with all his experience, is the guy Cameroon fans are investing their hopes and dreams in. As the 2022 FIFA World Cup unfolds, fans will see firsthand whether his guidance will pay off at the highest level. For a nation that is eager to stake its claim on the World Cup stage, if things don't go very well, it will be interesting to see if this is the last whistle he blows for Cameroonian practice jerseys.

KEY PLAYERS AND THEIR CHARACTERISTICS

The 6'0" forward **Vincent Aboubakar**, who is known for scoring a goal or two, is likely to generate a wee bit of excitement on the field. On the club scene, he netted 16 goals with Lorient, and with Porto he notched in 36. As of 2021, he joined Al-Nassr (the prime time of Saudi Arabia) where he's hoping to continue his scoring ways. As for Cameroon, he's a team leader with over 30 goals and counting.

Christian Bassogog—born in 1995 in Cameroon—has versatility as a 5'8" forward and wing who has seen time with Cameroon since 2016 where he's since gained over 40 caps, with a handful of goals.

Eric Maxim Choupo-Moting—born in 1989 in West Germany—keeps the on-field party going as a 6'3" forward who has sported the Mainz 05, Schalke 04, Stoke City, Paris Saint-Germain, and super club Bayern Munich jerseys. He played for the U19 and U21 national teams of Germany before joining the senior team of Cameroon. Since 2010, he's represented the Indomitable Lions more than 65 times, with over 15 goals.

Karl Toko Ekambi—born in 1992 in France—will get things going as a 6'0" forward with time spent at Sochaux, Angers, Villarreal, and Lyon. Since 2015, he's regularly been seen with Cameroon, with 50 caps and counting.

André-Frank Zambo Anguissa—born in 1995 in Cameroon—plays defensive midfield for Cameroon with an extensive club background that has taken him to Marseille, Fulham, Villarreal, and Napoli. In 2017, he first appeared with Cameroon and has gathered over 40 caps so far.

OVERALL PLAYER RATING

Vincent Aboubakar: 9

Christian Bassogog: 8.8

Eric Maxim Choupo-Moting: 9.2

Karl Toko Ekambi: 8.7

André-Frank Zambo Anguissa: 8.8

KEY PLAYER STATS
(Total career goals for their country)

	Games Played	Goals
Vincent Aboubakar	87	33
Christian Bassogog	42	7
E. Choupo-Moting	68	18
Karl Toko Ekambi	50	12
André Anguissa	42	5

WHAT TO WATCH FOR ON TV

Leading up to and during African qualifiers for World Cup 2022, Cameroon had a formidable group that included **goalkeepers** Simon Omossola, Devis Epassy, André Onana, and Fabrice

Ondoa; **defenders** Nouhou Tolo, Michael Ngadeu-Ngadjui, Olivier Mbaizo, Collins Fai, Jérôme Onguéné, Harold Moukoudi, Joyskim Dawa, Jonathan Ngwem, and Serge Leuko; **midfielders** André-Frank Zambo Anguissa, James Léa Siliki, Samuel Gouet, Pierre Kunde, Martin Hongla, and Arnaud Djoum; and **forwards** Moumi Ngamaleu, Karl Toko Ekambi, Stéphane Bahoken, Vincent Aboubakar, Christian Bassogog, Eric Maxim Choupo-Moting, Ignatius Ganago, Léandre Tawamba, Clinton N'Jie, and Serge Tabekou.

Cameroon navigated through the 2022 World Cup qualifiers in Africa in Group D that included Ivory Coast, Malawi, and Mozambique.

In Qatar, the Indomitable Lions will have to be extra cautious of poachers on set-pieces. This may be the team's undoing. Sloppy defense is the likely cause of set-pieces. Cameroon must also be aware of this.

Controlling the tempo of each game will be of great importance. Watch for Cameroon in this regard. If it can keep control of the ball while taking its opponent off the ball for long stints of time, then, and only then, will Cameroon have a chance. If this does not happen, which is likely the case, then you'll see Cameroon tumble into a rabbit hole of "trading punches" with the opposition, and this is never a good thing.

One thing that Cameroon is good at is connecting passes to forward moving players. If this team can create a good rhythm on the move, that is, *moving forward*, then perhaps a few goals will follow, and so will a trip to the Round of 16. But don't get too excited. Without a firm possession-oriented attack, one that *flows across the field and back*, Cameroon will get caught in no-man's land, isolating attacking players. A good remedy for this dilemma is to use the two-man game as often as possible.

In short, if the two-man game (which produces good chemistry between teammates) is used properly, then good things should happen. If Cameroon does not use the two-man game and keeps passing to someone new (which often does not produce chemistry between teammates), then expect a fun but frustrating result from the Indomitable Lions.

Despite having the ultra-talented play of Vincent Aboubakar, Christian Bassogog, Eric Maxim Choupo-Moting, Karl Toko Ekambi, and André-Frank Zambo Anguissa, if Cameroon decides to completely commit to free-flowing soccer, then you're bound to see exciting games, but rest assured, Cameroon won't be seen for long! If Cameroon commits fully to "trading punches," then it might as well purchase an early flight back to Yaounde, where players can hear criticism in French, English, Cameroonian Pidgin English, Fula, and Ewondo.

All the same, Cameroon has a way of tantalizing millions of viewers each tournament with the possibility of pulling off the upset of all upsets, a fairy-tale story: A World Cup championship!

The thing is, Cameroon is obviously a threat, but to what extent? Make no mistake, Cameroon is ready to compete. This is a good team, with exceptional players in certain positions, yet Cameroon will endure a significant struggle in Qatar. Success should likely come in the form of an appearance in the Round of 16, maybe the quarter-finals. First things first: Escaping the group stage!

Don't forget that the legacy of Cameroon rests in the 1990 team led by Roger Milla, the ageless wonder who very well could've won that whole tournament! South Korea in 2002 had a similar underdog story; it, too, was a team that could've won the whole thing. So when we think of Cameroon in this 2022 World Cup, it's hard to escape the fairy-tale notion of yet another gifted group of players that might have what it takes to do the unthinkable. But will this team be the one to make World Cup history? As a lower middle-of-the-pack team, Cameroon will provide a lot of excitement, hope, and, who knows, maybe a miraculous run.

THE TEAMS FROM ASIA (4½)

Asia typically is allowed 4½ teams by FIFA. As host nation, Qatar automatically qualified. So for this 2022 World Cup, Asia placed 6 teams.

AUSTRALIA

World Cup titles: 0
Overall Team Rating: 8.7

A BRIEF TEAM HISTORY

Let's take a quick glance at the World Cup record of Australia.

1930: Australia didn't compete.
1934: Didn't compete.
1938: Didn't compete.
1950: Didn't compete.
1954: Didn't compete.
1958: Didn't compete.
1962: Didn't compete.
1966: Didn't qualify.
1970: Didn't qualify.
1974: Couldn't escape its group.
1978: Didn't qualify.
1982: Didn't qualify.
1986: Didn't qualify.
1990: Didn't qualify.
1994: Didn't qualify.

1998: Didn't qualify.
2002: Didn't qualify.
2006: Made the Round of 16.
2010: Couldn't escape its group.
2014: Couldn't escape its group.
2018: Australia couldn't escape its group.

ASIAN COMPETITIONS

Australia won the AFC Asian Cup in 2015 and the OFC* Nations Cup in 1980, 1996, 2000, and 2004.

FACTS ABOUT THEIR COUNTRY

Australia, an exotic vacation destination, home of Sydney, Melbourne, Perth, the late-great Steve Irwin ("The Crocodile Hunter"), and home to memories of the decadent Australian rules football culture of the 1990s. Australia seems to have it all. Notwithstanding the dystopian world trodden upon by Mel Gibson in *Mad Max*, it's a wonderful place, though jetlag is often associated with a visit Down Under. Currently, Australia has around 25.9 million people and a GDP of about $1.6 trillion.

In 2000, Australia hosted the Olympics. The Australian Open is a major tournament for pro tennis. The "black sports bra for men" factor! The "black sports bra for men" is in vogue with players around the world, many of whom are from Australia. As to why is somewhat of a mystery!

Who has the most caps for Australia?

1. Mark Schwarzer (109)   **2.** Tim Cahill (108)

Who has the most goals in the history of Australia's national team?
1. Tim Cahill (50)

---

*   Oceania Football Confederation.

Some awesome beer you might stumble upon in Australia?
Moon Dog Craft Brewery   Foster's
Wildflower Gold   Tooheys
Six String Brewing Company   Coopers

WHERE THE TEAM IS TODAY—TACTICS AND STRATEGIES

Australia is a very interesting team in that it has good organization, team shape, and player technique. As a group, the players cause turnovers and are methodical on offense. Overall, Australia is "organizationally athletic" on the field. With its smart "professional training ground" possession soccer, it's a team that can hang with anyone in the world. Yet, Australia can't seem to get over the hump. For starters, it lacks creativity. Australia is certainly creative in the sense that it can produce possession-oriented soccer, but here's the thing, it still needs that creative pulse. Another glaring issue: Australia lacks dribbling threats! Furthermore, there are no big-time scoring threats. Over the years, Australia has maintained an offensive mindset that kind of dumps all the scoring responsibility on one man: the number nine forward. And guess what? With Tim Cahill—Australia's all-time leading scorer—that was a pretty good option. When you look at the scoresheet, you realize that, yes, Australia does have scoring threats from different options— Mathew Leckie, Awer Mabil, Jamie Maclaren, Mitchell Duke, Martin Boyle, Adam Taggart, Harry Souttar, Jackson Irvine, Tom Rogic, and Aaron Mooy—but the scoring is mostly under 10 goals per individual. This is a pressing issue. There isn't a heavy-hitting (more than 25 goals) threat in the lineup. A team can't build for long-term success with that approach. Scoring from multiple threats is a key component of the game that Australia is lacking. Australia needs to find more productivity from all angles, which it's more than capable of.

Australia is not a traditional soccer powerhouse. It's a program relatively new to "being this good." The Aussies have some serious game, and it's a program that can only continue to improve.

Australia's in that class of teams that include Saudi Arabia, Mexico, the United States, Cameroon, and South Korea. At any moment, one of these teams can have what it takes to catapult into the final of a World Cup. Even if each of the aforementioned teams has a World Cup record that might not suggest an upcoming quick leap to the final of a World Cup, these programs are still right on the cusp of greatness.

Tactics and strategies: On route to World Cup glory, Australia will likely go with a 4-2-3-1, a 4-3-3, or a 4-3-1-2 (which is basically the same as a 4-3-3). These are formations Australia used during World Cup qualifiers to good effect. The World Cup is another story. The 4-2-3-1 is popular these days, and it should suit Australia well as it provides depth on defense with a strong balance from midfield to the forward lines. If used appropriately, Australia could be very dangerous with the 4-2-3-1. The 4-3-3 should also serve Australia's interests as it allows for defensive pressure to be applied on most sections of the field, which could play to Australia's advantage in terms of turnovers. All in all, Australia will provide a complete effort on both sides of the ball.

Defensively, Australia has strength in aerial battles, and you'll get strong tackles all around. Contact is a prerequisite to make the squad. Look for it. It'll be there. This is a tough, take no prisoners, side. It's one looking for a fight, a challenge, and a chance to prove it belongs with the best. One would imagine, given the Aussie mindset, that players aren't sitting in the locker room hoping for the weakest opponent. Rather, this team is more than likely *wanting* to play against the best in order to prove *it is the best*.

Offensively, look for similar patterns in passing sequences to that of parent-nation England. Call it EPL Light. With a touch of Spain, Australia moves the ball forward with smart possession, and many short passes followed by shifting the point of attack from wing to wing. One challenge ahead is that Australia might, and likely will, face a "now what" situation. That is, when the ball is successfully switched, now what? At this point, it's wise to hasten the short-passing schemes immediately, establish dominance over possession, and move the ball toward goal. In this "now what" conundrum, the lack of creative dribbling will hinder Australia's progress. What cures this? Goals. But, if you're Australia, how do you get more goals? Better creative dribbling to enhance the creative flow. It's a catch-22. Despite this setback, Australia makes up for it with a strong effort from kickoff to the last whistle.

GRAHAM ARNOLD—A BRIEF COACHING PORTRAIT
Graham Arnold—born in 1963 in Australia—has the luxury of viewing the game from a forward's point of view. In his day, he was a striker who suited up with Sydney United, Sanfrecce Hiroshima, and Northern Spirit (Australia); he also joined the Australian national team (1985-97) for 54 games, with an impressive 19 goals to show for it. As of 2018, he's taken the honor of leading Australia into a new realm of success. The 2022 FIFA World Cup will be an uphill battle, but it's one that will define his distinguished career.

KEY PLAYERS AND THEIR CHARACTERISTICS
Mathew Leckie—born in 1991—stands out as the leading scorer for Australia's current team. As a versatile 5'11" forward and winger, he has tallied up experience with German sides Borussia Monchengladbach, FSV Frankfurt, FC Ingolstadt 04, Hertha BSC, and Australian dynamo Melbourne City. As a veteran with Australia, his first game was in 2012, and he's gained over 10 goals. A lot will be riding on his shoulders as Australia seeks an entry into the Round of 16 and perhaps further.

    Tom Rogic—born in 1992—is about 6'2" and has become known as a midfielder for Celtic (since 2013) where he's played in over 175 games, with over 30 goals. As a trusted veteran with Australia, his first national team game dates back to 2012. He has since gained 50 caps and shows no signs of stopping. Additionally, he's knocked in around 10 goals to date.

Aaron Mooy—born in 1990—is a hardworking 5'9" midfielder who has time spent at Huddersfield Town, Brighton & Hove Albion, and Shanghai Port. With Australia, he first appeared for the senior national team in 2012. He's a veteran presence with over 50 caps and a few goals to boot.

A winger and forward who has seen time with Australia since 2018 would be **Martin Boyle**. The 5'8" talent can give a full effort from end to end. He has played over 185 games for Hibernian (Scotland), with over 45 goals. During Asian qualifiers for World Cup 2022, he was called upon as a starter for some important matches against Japan and Saudi Arabia.

Ajdin Hrustic—born in 1996—provides a creative touch as a 5'11" attacking mid who's seen time with Dutch club Groningen and Eintracht Frankfurt in Germany. He's not an out-and-out scorer but has the ability to apply a finishing touch here and there. Look for distribution from his feet as Australia marches through competition with a well-orchestrated passing scheme.

Adam Taggart—born in 1993—originally comes from Perth (far-removed from the sophisticated coffee houses of Sydney and Melbourne), way out in Western Australia. With 6'0" Taggart, Australia has a forward threat that's tallied up several goals during his time with Perth Glory (Australia), Newcastle Jets (Australia), Brisbane Roar (Australia), Suwon Samsung Bluewings (South Korea), and Cerezo Osaka (Japan). He's represented Australia's senior national team since 2012 with over five goals to date.

Jackson Irvine—born in 1993 in Melbourne—can be found at midfield for Australia. The 6'2" talent has played with Hull City (England), Hibernian (Scotland), and FC St. Pauli (Germany). He debuted with Australia in 2013 and has exceeded 45 games with over five goals.

Mitchell Duke—born in 1991—will give you strong minutes as a forward and winger. In 2021, he started playing with Fagiano Okayama in Japan. He's been around with the Australian national team for a minute as his first game was back in 2013. As of December 28, 2021, he was among team leaders with seven goals. On the road to Qatar, he got an important goal during Asian qualifiers in a 1-1 tie against China on November 16, 2021, a game in which he started as center forward.

OVERALL PLAYER RATING

Mathew Leckie: 9.1   Ajdin Hrustic: 9

Tom Rogic: 9.1   Adam Taggart: 8.9

Aaron Mooy: 8.9   Jackson Irvine: 9

Martin Boyle: 8.9   Mitchell Duke: 8.9

KEY PLAYER STATS

(Total career goals for their country)

	Games Played	Goals
Mathew Leckie	71	13
Tom Rogic	53	10
Aaron Mooy	52	7
Martin Boyle	18	5
Ajdin Hrustic	19	3
Adam Taggart	16	6
Jackson Irvine	48	7
Mitchell Duke	20	7

WHAT TO WATCH FOR ON TV

Leading up to and during Asian qualifiers for World Cup 2022, Australia had a focused team with many options that included **goalkeepers** Mathew Ryan, Daniel Vukovic, and Andrew Redmayne; **defenders** Trent Sainsbury, Aziz Behich, Miloš Degenek, Bailey Wright, Ryan McGowan, Rhyan Grant, Fran

Karačić, Harry Souttar, and Bradley Smith; **midfielders** Jackson Irvine, Ajdin Hrustic, James Jeggo, Riley McGree, Kenny Dougall, Tom Rogic, Aaron Mooy, and James Holland; and **forwards** Mathew Leckie, Awer Mabil, Nikita Rukavytsya, Jamie Maclaren, Mitchell Duke, Martin Boyle, Andrew Nabbout, Christopher Ikonomidis, Adam Taggart, Daniel Arzani, Brandon Borrello, and Apostolos Giannou.

Australia navigated through the 2022 World Cup qualifiers in Asia in Group B that included Japan, Saudi Arabia, Oman, Vietnam, and China. There are plenty of solid options for Australia, such as James Jeggo, Awer Mabil, Trent Sainsbury, Aziz Behich, Rhyan Grant, and Harry Souttar. These players offer balance and stability. The effort will be team first. This isn't a flashy team that hogs the ball. Rather, Australia puts forth a unified team effort. Along with the players mentioned above, a forward to watch out for is **Jamie Maclaren**, one of the team's leading scorers. Within a roster of many talented players, Maclaren is certainly a threat for Australia, one that other teams should keep an eye on. Providing comfort in front of the net is a reliable keeper, **Mathew Ryan**, who received a superstar nod this tournament.

In Qatar, watch out for a unit that operates as one. This is a strength of Australia. Will Australia be able to depose France, Germany, or perhaps Brazil? Probably not. But it's possible. It's why we watch. Australia is that team. It's a hop, skip, and a jump away from Switzerland taking down Spain 1-0 in World Cup 2010. If Australia can muster up the courage to be so bold, which it's more than capable of, then what's next? Will it be able to continue the trend and take down another Goliath?

As one of Asia's top programs, Australia is now entering its fifth World Cup in a row. In 2006, Australia made the Round of 16, a good result for the most part. However, in 2010, 2014, and 2018 it couldn't escape its group. Will Qatar in 2022 be any different? Despite Australia's confidence, athletic prowess, national pride (which it has in abundance), and a go-get-em attitude, this is a lower ranked team in this World Cup. The Aussies are in desperate need of a breakthrough moment at the World Cup level. It's a nation that has drastically improved its soccer program over the last 20 to 30 years. The buildup with possession is overwhelmingly impressive, yet, without a viable creative pulse, Australia will be left behind. Nonetheless, Australia is marching forward. It wants to prove all doubters wrong. Australia needs to get out of its group stage rut to achieve World Cup success. A Round of 16 place for the Socceroos? The pressure's on.

IRAN
World Cup titles: 0
Overall Team Rating: 8

A BRIEF TEAM HISTORY
Let's take a quick glance at the World Cup record of Iran.
1930: Iran didn't compete.
1934: Didn't compete.
1938: Didn't compete.
1950: Didn't compete.
1954: Didn't compete.
1958: Didn't compete.
1962: Didn't compete.
1966: Didn't compete.
1970: Didn't compete.
1974: Didn't qualify.
1978: Iran couldn't escape its group.
1982: Didn't compete.
1986: Didn't compete.
1990: Didn't qualify.
1994: Didn't qualify.
1998: Couldn't escape its group.

2002: Didn't qualify.
2006: Couldn't escape its group.
2010: Didn't qualify.
2014: Couldn't escape its group.
2018: Iran couldn't escape its group, yet again.

ASIAN COMPETITIONS

Iran has traditionally been one of the top teams in Asia, having won the AFC Asian Cup in 1968, 1972, and 1976. Iran won the Asian Games in 1974, 1990, and 1998, and it won the West Asian Football Federation Championship (WAFF) in 2000, 2004, 2007, and 2008.

FACTS ABOUT THEIR COUNTRY

The modern-day capital of Iran is Tehran. In the ancient world, Iran was known as Persia. Today, Iran's population is about 83 million people, and it has a GDP of around $611 billion.

Who has the most caps for Iran's national team?
1. Javad Nekounam (151)

Who is the all-time leading scorer for Iran's national team?
1. Ali Daei (109)

Iran's jersey suppliers have bounced around a bit. It's been an interesting journey. From 1978 onward, Iran has used Adidas, Puma, Amini, Shekari, Puma, Shekari, Daei Sport (an Iranian company founded by a former player, Ali Daei), Puma, Merooj (an Iranian company founded by Dr. Majid Saedifar), Daei Sport, Legea, Uhlsport, Givova (founded in Italy in 2008), Adidas, Uhlsport, and Merooj. In a sports world dominated by Nike, it's cool to see Uhlsport making an appearance!

As for beer in Iran? For the most part, because of religious and cultural beliefs, Iran has banned alcohol. A piece from *Al*

Jazeera Media Network points out, "Producing, selling, and consuming alcohol is strictly forbidden in Iran—with some exceptions for religious minorities—and those caught with it face the punishment of flogging."[13] *ABC News* adds, "Trading and drinking alcohol is illegal in Iran, and those seeking alcoholic drinks often rely on a chain of black market dealers without knowing where and how the drinks are produced. The dealers themselves are often not sure of the source of the alcohol."[14] Currently, fans might be enjoying something of a non-alcoholic nature instead.

WHERE THE TEAM IS TODAY—TACTICS AND STRATEGIES

Iran—otherwise known as Team Melli—faces a challenge ahead. First of all, Team Melli has never escaped its World Cup group. Ever. Gone are the midfield services of **Masoud Shojaei**—who stopped playing for Iran's national team in 2019. As a dribbler, he was skillful, deceptive, and tricky; a midfielder that often wound up on the ground because the other team had no option but to foul him.

Iran must pick up the pieces where he left them. Past Iranian teams have never exuded overwhelming amounts of creativity in their play, either. If Iran can tap into a creative vibe, one that yields more quality scoring chances, then it might have a leg up.

Next up on its list of challenges is the group stage—more specifically, the teams Iran will face in the group stage. Those teams are England, the United States, and Wales. Also, Iran is dealing with an overall team *psychology,* a sort of mental hurdle caused by its inability to ever escape its World Cup group. Though it can sound a bit hyperbolic, a team's mental state plays a real role in game performance. Like Mexico's "Round of 16 curse," Iran seems to have the "group stage curse." Can the team collectively surmount this obstacle and fight its way through the group stage into the Round of 16?

This is where Sardar Azmoun, Mehdi Taremi, Karim Ansarifard, Alireza Jahanbakhsh, and Ehsan Hajsafi come into the picture. This group carries the weight of fans' hopes for World Cup success.

Tactics and strategies: Essentially, Iran employs a 4-4-2 which allows the team's inner aggression to unleash on defense, with two forwards keeping opposition defenders under duress. With the balance of four mids and four defenders lined up behind the forwards, a game performance can unfold, like a lotus flower, as Iran attempts to regain possession of the ball.

Offensively, Iran pushes forward like a tidal wave as it tries to catch opponents off-guard with a flurry of attacks down the wings, bodies in and around the box, with physical play to usurp space around the goal for absolute on-field domination. Iran has on its side quickness, speed, and aggressive attacking players who play each moment as if it were their last. Expect crosses into the box, hero passes toward goal, and a quick tempo. Do not expect any form of over-possession (like you see with Spain). Iran is a team that trades punches, which, in part, is why you'll probably not see Team Melli in the Round of 16. It's not the most patient side in the world, but there's always hope.

DRAGAN SKOCIC—A BRIEF COACHING PORTRAIT

Dragan Skočić—born in 1968—has a rather interesting coaching history that includes stops with Al Nassr (Saudi Arabia), Rijeka (Croatia), Malavan (Iran), Foolad (Iran), and Sanat Naft (Iran). Given his experience with Iranian clubs, it was only logical that he ended up as the coach of Iran's national team. He accepted this position in 2020. However the 2022 FIFA World Cup pans out, Dragan is at the top of his career. Still, Iran has never escaped its group in World Cup action, so asking Dragan to pull a rabbit out of his hat is asking a bit much. At this moment in Iran's soccer-playing history, reaching the Round of 16 would be spectacular for Dragan.

KEY PLAYERS AND THEIR CHARACTERISTICS

Sardar Azmoun—born in 1995—is a 6'1" goal-hungry forward who joined Zenit Saint Petersburg in 2019 and has scored more than 50 times since. (Impressive!) From there, he made a move to Bayer Leverkusen. He is the game-changer for Iran. He is thought of by some as an Iranian Messi. He has a creative side coupled with good acceleration, and he's good in the air. Ali Daei, Iran's all-time scorer (109), laid down the groundwork for the next great scorers. Azmoun—who, at this point, has over 35 goals for Iran—has taken the lead as he follows in Daei's footsteps on his quest for more goals and the ultimate prize, a World Cup appearance in the Round of 16! After a brief retirement from the national team, which allegedly occurred thanks to overwhelming criticism from fans that caused family issues, Azmoun is back. With Azmoun playing at the top of his game, Iran could surprise us all.

Mehdi Taremi is a dangerous 6'2" forward, perhaps Iran's second-best threat. In 2020, he signed up with Porto where he's had success with over 35 goals. He's been an extremely solid performer with Iran's national team since 2015. He's gone over 55 caps, with over 25 goals. Alongside Azmoun, Taremi brings punching power to the team.

Karim Ansarifard—born in 1990—is a 6'1" forward who played with Nottingham Forest in 2018-19. He's yet another offensive threat in Iran's potent attack. He positions well in the box, finishes well, and he can distribute to teammates (a plus). Karim is a gamer. He can put the ball in the back of the net. Above all, Iran is hoping to cash in on his scoring prowess. So far for his country, he's scored over 25 goals.

Alireza Jahanbakhsh—born in 1993—is a versatile 5'11" attacking mid who can help Iran in lots of ways, including on the wing. He's played with a few teams including Brighton & Hove Albion and Feyenoord. Since 2013, he's turned into a veteran force with Iran, having acquired 60-plus caps and over 10 goals.

Ehsan Hajsafi—the team captain—has versatility as an outside left-back, and he'll be expected to guide the squad with wisdom, calm, and focus. Born in 1990, the 5'10" veteran has been seen with Olympiacos (Greece), Tractor (Iran), Sepahan (Iran), and AEK Athens (Greece). A few assets include his speed, strong shot from outside the box, and accuracy on free kicks. For his national team, he's a mega-performer. So far, he's played in over 115 games. He might just be getting started! The record for Iranian caps earned is 151. Keep an eye out for him taking that title someday!

OVERALL PLAYER RATING

Sardar Azmoun: 9.1   Alireza Jahanbakhsh: 8.6

Mehdi Taremi: 9   Ehsan Hajsafi: 8.9

Karim Ansarifard: 9

KEY PLAYER STATS

(Total career goals for their country)

	Games Played	Goals
Sardar Azmoun	63	40
Mehdi Taremi	58	27
Karim Ansarifard	92	29
Alireza Jahanbakhsh	62	13
Ehsan Hajsafi	119	7

WHAT TO WATCH FOR ON TV

Leading up to and during Asian qualifiers for World Cup 2022, Iran had a good team that included **goalkeepers** Alireza Beiranvand, Hossein Hosseini, Hamed Lak, and Mohammad Rashid Mazaheri; **defenders** Sadegh Moharrami, Ehsan Hajsafi, Shojae Khalilzadeh, Milad Mohammadi, Omid Noorafkan, Mohammad Hossein Kanani Zadegan, Majid Hosseini, and Morteza Pouraliganji; **midfielders** Saeid Ezatolahi, Ahmad

Nourollahi, Vahid Amiri, Saman Ghoddos, Mehdi Torabi, Ali Gholizadeh, Milad Sarlak, Alireza Jahanbakhsh, Kamal Kamyabinia, Omid Ebrahimi, and Ali Karimi; and **forwards** Allahyar Sayyadmanesh, Karim Ansarifard, Sardar Azmoun, Kaveh Rezaei, Mehdi Ghayedi, and Mehdi Taremi.

Iran navigated through the 2022 World Cup qualifiers in Asia in Group A that included South Korea, United Arab Emirates, Syria, Lebanon, and Iraq.

Like a cobra backed into a corner, Iran is ready to unleash a venomous attack. It's a team that follows its instincts to score. Always a tough opponent, Iran gets after it, with speed, aggression, and strength. It's an all-out battle to the end with Team Melli.

From Cyrus the Great to the Shah Mohammad Reza Pahlavi, this team is entering the realm of history. As the ball rolls forward, so too does the destiny of this soccer program. These players are entrenched in a nation that has roots dating back to ancient times. Where soccer reigns supreme as a sport in modern Iran, strategies for big tournaments, such as this World Cup, abound. After all, the soccer pitch is like a battlefield of pride. For millions of Iranian fans, the prospect of usurping the title from the typical kings— Brazil, Germany, and France—is very tantalizing.

Interestingly, part of Iran's challenge has to do with a simple, albeit subtle, nuance. If it gets an early lead, it doesn't have much of a chance to stay in the competition. That is, Iran's possession game is limited. So as a team that essentially thinks "forward, score now," Iran's going to have a hard time keeping a lead as it continues to trade punches with opponents. This back-and-forth does not suit Iran's needs, but it will most likely live and die by this choice.

Should you tune out? Absolutely not! Iran should be a lot of fun to watch. Not to mention, the ongoing saga of whether they will reach the Round of 16 should make Iran one of the more interesting teams to follow in the opening group stage during World Cup 2022. This is a team with a lot to prove, and we could be hearing more from them down the road.

JAPAN
World Cup titles: 0
Overall Team Rating: 9.3

A BRIEF TEAM HISTORY
Let's take a quick glance at the World Cup record of Japan.
1930: Japan didn't compete.
1934: Didn't compete.
1938: Didn't compete.
1950: Didn't compete.
1954: Didn't qualify.
1958: Didn't compete.
1962: Didn't qualify.
1966: Didn't compete.
1970: Didn't qualify.
1974: Didn't qualify.
1978: Didn't qualify.
1982: Didn't qualify.
1986: Didn't qualify.
1990: Didn't qualify.
1994: Didn't qualify.
1998: Couldn't escape its group.
2002: Made the Round of 16. In 2002, Japan also co-hosted with
    South Korea.
2006: Couldn't escape its group.
2010: Made the Round of 16.
2014: Couldn't escape its group.
2018: Japan made the Round of 16.

ASIAN COMPETITIONS

Japan won the AFC Asian Cup—which dates back to 1956—in 1992, 2000, 2004, and 2011. Right now, this makes Japan the leader.

FACTS ABOUT THEIR COUNTRY

Japan currently has a population of around 125 million people, and a GDP of about $5.3 trillion. A moment in history: National Foundation Day honors the year 660 BC, which, by the way, recognizes the first Japanese emperor, Emperor Jimmu. Japan's largest win? It was against the Philippines in 1967. The score was 15-0. Who is the top scorer in the history of Japan's national team?
1. Kunishige Kamamoto (75)*

What beer are you likely to find in Japan?
Kirin   Asahi Super Dry
Sapporo

The oldest brand of beer in Japan? Sapporo is Japan's oldest, dating to 1876!

WHERE THE TEAM IS TODAY—TACTICS AND STRATEGIES

Japan is a consummate World Cup underperformer. Japan either can't escape its group or makes it no further than the Round of 16. With that said, of all the Asian teams that could likely step forward (very soon) and win a FIFA World Cup, it's Japan.

During World Cup qualifiers on March 30, 2021, Japan decimated Mongolia 14-0! Atta way! No Mercy! Mercy is for the weak! "What is the problem, Mr. Lawrence?"**

---

* There was a discrepancy as to Kunishige Kamamoto's goal tally for Japan. As of December 24, 2021, Wikipedia's team page for "Japan national football team" listed him at 75 total goals, while the personal page of "Kunishige Kamamoto" listed him at 80 goals for his nation.

** If you're under the age of 20, it's advised that you rent The Karate Kid (1984).

It is within Japan's athletic DNA to someday take the World Cup by storm with skill, organization, speed, power, possession, strong defense, and class. While right now its chances aren't super great, it's only a matter of time before Japan figures it out. The national team has benefited greatly from the J.League, founded in 1992. If not for the J.League we might not—and probably *would* not—be talking about Japan in this light. The J.League has proven monumental for the growth of Japan's national team. The exposure of many legendary players[*] coming through, setting an example, has rubbed off on Japan's up-and-coming international stars in positive ways. Furthermore, it has given home-grown players a chance to compete in a viable league. Hence, the J.League has proven essential for Japan's growth as a soccer-playing nation. Japan's national team in the 1980s was a far cry from what it is today. You can thank the J.League for that.

Tactics and strategies: Japan will probably go with a 4-3-3, maybe a 4-2-3-1.

Defensively, Japan is very capable of sitting back patiently, waiting to pounce on its opponent. Supported by good team shape, Japan's highly trained, athletically gifted stars unleash a fury of pressure at a moment's notice. Japan's defense is smart, strong, tough, fearless, relentless, and physical. A weakness which has presented in the past few decades would be its inability to eliminate errors around its goal, display confidence for lengthy periods, and keep ownership of the ball during possession. It's no secret that Japan's defenders are quite capable of possessing the ball; however, one area of improvement would be to step up the possession to the competent level of artistry of Spain. After all, defenders have the most touches throughout a game. This is

---

[*]   Zico, Jorjinho, Dunga, Leonardo, Diego Forlan, Hulk, Pierre Littbarski, Gary Lineker, Michael Laudrup, Hristo Stoichkov, and Lukas Podolski, to name a few.

why skillful defenders matter! Why teams with skillful defenders that possess the ball with *artistic ownership* thrive! Artistry on defense is very important. Japan has it, but not to the extent of Spain, France, or other powerhouses. Addressing this issue on defense could potentially make Japan unstoppable.

Offensively, Japan blends the stylings of the Netherlands meets Spain with an East Asian touch of technique and sportsmanship. It's a thoughtful approach, one that includes smart passes, combinations, some critical dribbling in isolated situations, and surges toward goal that resemble a coach's Xs and Os. Japan's offense is methodical, precise, and organized.

Once improvements are made to defensive schemes, things will flow harmoniously for Japan. Japan has everything it takes to be elite. It's really just a matter of time. At this point, though, Japan's biggest opponent might be itself.

HAJIME MORIYASU—A BRIEF COACHING PORTRAIT

The Blue Samurai are led by **Hajime Moriyasu**. Born in 1968 in Japan, Moriyasu played midfield for Sanfrecce Hiroshima, Kyoto Sanga FC, Vegalta Sendai, and 35 games for the Japanese national team from 1992-96. As coach, he's led Sanfrecce Hiroshima and Japan U23, and in 2018 he took over Japan's senior national side, where he remains today. With his sights fully set on the 2022 FIFA World Cup in Qatar, Moriyasu has an opportunity to prove Japan's worth on the biggest stage. It shouldn't be easy, considering Japan's disappointing World Cup record to date. While most aren't expecting Japan to be appearing in the final match, Moriyasu and his players are motivated to bring their best.

KEY PLAYERS AND THEIR CHARACTERISTICS

No one said defensive mid was easy! You run a lot, you get dirty with tackles, you carry the load, you grind it out. Fit and ready for it all would be **Wataru Endo**. Born in 1993, he takes up the mantle of defensive mid, where he's usually centrally based. Call it "defensive mid," call it "team organizer," he has a huge responsibility to organize the flow of possession from defenders to forwards and bring it all home. Without his guiding hand, things will unravel. His experience from VfB Stuttgart should help in this regard. In 2015, he first stepped up with Japan's senior national team. Since that point, he's gathered over 40 caps, with a few goals for good measure.

Yuya Osako—born in 1990—rests as Japan's current top goal machine with over 20 and counting. As a 6'0" forward, he adds depth to Japan's roster as a lethal scoring threat, assist man, and play developer. In the past, he's played for 1860 Munich, 1. FC Koln, and Werder Bremen, and as of 2021 he suited up for Vissel Kobe. He first played on Japan's senior side in 2013, so he is a veteran with over 55 appearances.

Takumi Minamino balances out the attack for Japan as a major scoring threat alongside Osako. At 5'9", Minamino is a well-rounded attacking mid and winger who wreaks havoc for opponents from all angles with speed, technique, vision, and positional awareness. In Europe, he's played for Red Bull Salzburg, Liverpool, and Southampton. For Japan's senior national team, he's turned into a veteran, having first played in 2015, and has 40-plus games under his belt and over 15 goals.

Genki Haraguchi—born in 1991—has been a big presence with Japan over the years with over 70 caps and 10-plus goals. It's yet to be seen what impact he might have in 2022. While he's only in his early-30s, players at this point face a likelier possibility of suffering injuries.

Junya Ito—born in 1993—provides spark at outside mid and right-back. At 5'9", he's put up big minutes for Genk, with over 20 goals. With Japan, he's shot past 35 games played while currently hovering around the 10-goal mark.

OVERALL PLAYER RATING

Wataru Endo: 9   Genki Haraguchi: 9.1

Yuya Osako: 9.4   Junya Ito: 9.1

Takumi Minamino: 9.4

KEY PLAYER STATS

(Total career goals for their country)

	Games Played	Goals
Wataru Endo	41	2
Yuya Osako	57	25
Takumi Minamino	42	17
Genki Haraguchi	73	11
Junya Ito	36	9

WHAT TO WATCH FOR ON TV

Leading up to and during Asian qualifiers for World Cup 2022, Japan had a promising group that included **goalkeepers** Eiji Kawashima, Shūichi Gonda, Daniel Schmidt, Kosuke Nakamura, and Shusaku Nishikawa; **defenders** Miki Yamane, Shogo Taniguchi, Ko Itakura, Yuto Nagatomo, Takehiro Tomiyasu, Hiroki Sakai, Yuta Nakayama, Maya Yoshida, Sei Muroya, Naomichi Ueda, Gen Shōji, Sho Sasaki, and Shinnosuke Hatanaka; **midfielders** Wataru Endo, Gaku Shibasaki, Genki Haraguchi, Daichi Kamada, Takumi Minamino, Junya Ito, Ao Tanaka, Ritsu Dōan, Hidemasa Morita, Koji Miyoshi, Takefusa Kubo, Kento Hashimoto, and Hayao Kawabe; and **forwards** Kyogo Furuhashi, Yuya Osako, Takuma Asano, Ayase Ueda, Daizen Maeda, and Ado Onaiwu.

Japan navigated through the 2022 World Cup qualifiers in Asia in Group B that included Australia, Saudi Arabia, Oman, Vietnam, and China.

Japan faces a struggle in Qatar. Japan, like the United States, is not a traditional soccer power. Japan, like the United States, is a leader at the Olympics. Japan, like the United States, has a lot of pride when it comes to sports, yet it can't quite get over the FIFA World Cup hurdle for men's soccer. Japan, like the United States, should be (very soon) a world power in soccer. Currently Japan is right on the cusp of greatness. As such, it has something to prove. But Japan seems to be in a rut. Since its first World Cup appearance in 1998, Japan hasn't been able to achieve much success. 2002, 2010, and 2018 represent Japan's best World Cup results so far—the Round of 16, and that's it! Still, it's a team yearning for something greater. Given Japan's stature with athletics in general, pressure is high. This tension and drama is what makes the sport so entertaining! And this will make Japan an exciting team to watch.

Similar to the United States, who introduced MLS back in 1996, Japan entered the realm of modern professional soccer with the J.League in 1992. Pro outdoor leagues are correlated with the success of a nation's national team. With this late start regarding a reliable pro outdoor league, Japan has made great strides with its national team, and the urgency to produce big results on the World Cup stage is more prevalent now than ever before. As a national team that shows gritty promise, Japan needs that breakthrough moment.

Japan's roster is a cool group, patient on the surface. The team knows how good it is. Yuya Osako, Takumi Minamino, Junya Ito, and Wataru Endo will affirm Japan belongs on this elite stage. They will bring technically sound possession, creative play, vibrant attacks, and fierce defense.

Japan has many achievements, but wouldn't it be nice to finally add the Jules Rimet Trophy to its national treasure? The immaculate, million-dollar high-tech stadiums of Qatar provide the backdrop. Millions of Japan fans—enjoying Kirin, Sapporo, Asahi Super Dry, and the world's finest sushi—will be surveying each moment, discussing the possibilities as the 2022 FIFA World Cup carries on. As the group stage unfolds, it will be very clear if Japan is ready to take this World Cup and triumphantly raise the prized trophy.

SAUDI ARABIA
World Cup titles: 0
Overall Team Rating: 9.2

A BRIEF TEAM HISTORY
Let's take a quick glance at the World Cup record of Saudi Arabia.

1930: Saudi Arabia didn't compete.
1934: Didn't compete.
1938: Didn't compete.
1950: Didn't compete.
1954: Didn't compete.
1958: Didn't compete.
1962: Didn't compete.
1966: Didn't compete.
1970: Didn't compete.
1974: Didn't compete.
1978: Didn't qualify.
1982: Didn't qualify.
1986: Didn't qualify.
1990: Didn't qualify.
1994: Made the Round of 16.
1998: Couldn't escape its group.
2002: Couldn't escape its group.
2006: Couldn't escape its group.
2010: Didn't qualify.
2014: Didn't qualify.
2018: Saudi Arabia couldn't escape its group.

ASIAN COMPETITIONS
Saudi Arabia has won the AFC Asian Cup in 1984, 1988, and 1996. It won the Arabian Gulf Cup in 1994, 2002, and 2003-04. Saudi Arabia also won the FIFA Arab Cup in 1998 and 2002.

FACTS ABOUT THEIR COUNTRY
Saudi Arabia has a population of about 34 million people and a GDP of around $779 billion. Who has the most caps for Saudi Arabia?
1. Mohamed Al-Deayea (178)

Who are the top scorers in the history of Saudi Arabia's national team?
1. Majed Abdullah (72)   **2.** Sami Al-Jaber (46)

There might not be much beer drinking in Saudi Arabia. On behalf of *BBC News*, Mario Cacciottolo wrote: "The issue of drinking alcohol in Saudi Arabia has come sharply into focus once again after a British man was caught with homemade wine."[15] This can't be good. "Karl Andree, 74, was arrested by Saudi religious police and has spent more than a year in prison—it had been reported that he was also facing 360 lashes but it has since emerged that he was going to be spared flogging because of his age and ill-health."[16] Oy vey. Different part of the world. "Alcohol is prohibited in Saudi Arabia and the Foreign Office warns Britons not to flout these rules—but how easy is it to get your hands on booze out there, despite this strict ban?"[17] Cacciottolo added: "Tony, a 49-year-old Briton, has worked around much of Saudi Arabia as a business consultant, and lived there for almost five years. He is currently out of the country but plans to return.

He says those living on the compounds populated by Westerners have access to mainly homemade wine and beer, as well as 'a spirit known as Sidique, which is basically neat distilled alcohol.'"[18] Essentially, beer isn't quite as readily available as it is in England, Australia, and Brazil.

WHERE THE TEAM IS TODAY—TACTICS AND STRATEGIES
The Green Falcons, the champion of the FIFA Arab Cup in 1998 and 2002, are demanding respect as a soccer-playing nation.

From the viewpoint of Saudi Arabia, its time is now. But here's the problem with that. True, Saudi Arabia is a talented team, one that should be very dangerous in this 2022 FIFA World Cup. But, Saudi Arabia's FIFA World Cup record is lousy. Its best showing so far was a Round of 16 appearance back in 1994, where it met the end of the road by way of a 3-1 loss to Sweden. So in terms of "big-time World Cup performances," Saudi Arabia is still in the hunt. As the Saudis are not a favorite in 2022, it's still a team that can be dangerous to its opponents.

Tactics and strategies: Expect to see Saudi Arabia in a 4-2-3-1.

Defensively, the Saudis need to be aware of counterattacks, tight marking, over-committing on the ball, and lunging in on tackles. Essentially, simple defensive errors could prevent Saudi Arabia from the tournament of its life.

Offensively, the Saudis use overlapping runs down the line well; this creates energy and movement, and it looks good, on paper anyway. Though, Saudi Arabia might suffer in the department of possession soccer. If it can't establish frequency with the two-man game, and short passing combinations that strategically take the ball away from the other side, then Saudi Arabia will not dominate possession. This will be an issue for the Saudis.

On the plus side, Saudi Arabia has an exciting approach. A major boost for the team should come in the forms of Fahad Al-Muwallad, Salem Al-Dawsari, Saleh Al-Shehri, Yasser Al-Shahrani, Abdullah Al-Hamdan, Firas Al-Buraikan, and Salman Al-Faraj.

When it comes to club soccer, a lot of credit should be given to Saudi Arabia. Its national team roster is full of home-grown talent! It's like the olden days of a World Cup whereby the national teams mainly consisted of individuals that played professionally in their respective countries. An obvious argument against this tactic would be in lieu of Saudi players gaining substantial experience from top-flight European leagues, its chosen isolation may be to its detriment.

HERVE RENARD—A BRIEF COACHING PORTRAIT

Hervé Renard—born in 1968 in France—has taken the job of coach. And this is a serious job. The passion in Arabic nations for soccer is extreme. To coach Morocco, Algeria, Tunisia, Egypt, or Saudi Arabia is a big deal that carries a lot of weight and expectations. These are nations that are widely keen on making waves in World Cup competition. By and large, Renard could prove what many Saudi Arabian fans already assume, that it's time to leapfrog into the final of a FIFA World Cup! Don't worry, it probably won't happen any time soon. But with a little tweak here and there, Renard has a program replete with talent. On Renard's journey, he'll be forced to tackle challenges head on. In the group stage, he'll have a small window to annotate thoughts around his game plan. By this stage in his career, he's familiar with coaching high-level teams—Zambia, Angola, Ivory Coast, Lille, and Morocco—and he should be able to move on the fly with respect to fluctuating challenges, improvements, and substitutions. At long last, he may be the man to place Saudi Arabia alongside the other great international sides.

KEY PLAYERS AND THEIR CHARACTERISTICS

Fahad Al-Muwallad—born in 1994 in Saudi Arabia—is a well-rounded, 5'6" midfielder and forward who will be pivotal for Saudi Arabia. For Al-Ittihad, he has been a gamer with more than 190 games under his belt and over 55 goals. He is a leading scorer for Saudi Arabia, with over 15 goals and counting.

    Salem Al-Dawsari—born in 1991—keeps things interesting as a 5'8" winger with experience at Al-Hilal where he's gathered 200-plus games with over 45 goals. He's a veteran with Saudi Arabia. His debut came in 2011, and he's since gathered 60-plus caps with over 15 goals—a team leader.

    Saleh Al-Shehri—born in 1993—stands at 6'0" and is a forward who has done well with Al-Hilal in recent years, hitting the 10-goal mark with more around the corner. He's a recent addition to Saudi Arabia's national team, as he first made an appearance in 2020. His fortunes have been good so far, with around 10 goals. As 2022 winds down, don't be surprised to see him with 20 goals as a forward in his prime.

A multi-equipped defender and midfielder found out wide that brings a lot of experience to his team is **Yasser Al-Shahrani**. At 5'7", Yasser has played in over 210 games for Al-Hilal, while he's attained over 65 caps for Saudi Arabia since his national team debut in 2012. As a veteran, he'll use his quickness and wisdom to keep the defense strong and supplement the attack with runs down the wing.

Abdullah Al-Hamdan—born in 1999—joined Al-Hilal in 2021 after switching over from Al-Shabab. The 6'1" forward should add youth, speed, and aggressiveness to Saudi Arabia's attack. Since 2019, he's had a handful of goals for his nation, and World Cup 2022 will provide the largest stage of all for him to tally up a few more. Still in his early 20s, he could end up being Saudi Arabia's all-time leading scorer.

Firas Al-Buraikan—born in 2000—will help guide Saudi Arabia's attack as an up-and-coming star with speed, quickness, and a good eye for goal. As a 5'11" forward, he joined Saudi Arabia's senior national team in 2019. Like Abdullah Al-Hamdan, Firas has many years left to play, and you might be looking at a future Saudi legend when he takes his boots off for the last time. At that point, his goal tally could very well be extremely high.

Assuming he's free of injuries, you should see **Salman Al-Faraj** guiding the way from center mid with an eye for distributing the ball throughout the field during counterattacks and stints of possession. With craft and skill, he'll be a huge factor for Saudi Arabia as it moves forward in the tournament. Much of its success will lean on his handling of the ball. He's a big-time veteran with Al-Hilal, having played his first game for the club back in 2008. The 5'11" field general has been with Saudi Arabia's national team since 2012, where he's gone over 65 caps.

OVERALL PLAYER RATING

Fahad Al-Muwallad: 9.2   Abdullah Al-Hamdan: 8.9

Salem Al-Dawsari: 9.2   Firas Al-Buraikan: 8.9

Saleh Al-Shehri: 8.9   Salman Al-Faraj: 8.9

Yasser Al-Shahrani: 9.1

KEY PLAYER STATS

(Total career goals for their country)

	Games Played	Goals
Fahad Al-Muwallad	70	17
Salem Al-Dawsari	65	17
Saleh Al-Shehri	16	8
Yasser Al-Shahrani	69	2
Abdullah Al-Hamdan	20	5
Firas Al-Buraikan	22	6
Salman Al-Faraj	68	8

WHAT TO WATCH FOR ON TV

Leading up to and during Asian qualifiers for World Cup 2022, Saudi Arabia had a resolute team that included **goalkeepers** Mohammed Al-Rubaie, Fawaz Al-Qarni, and Mohammed Al-Owais; **defenders** Saud Abdulhamid, Mohammed Al-Breik, Ali Al-Bulaihi, Sultan Al-Ghanam, Ziyad Al-Sahafi, Abdulelah Al-Amri, Yasser Al-Shahrani, Abdullah Madu, Mohammed Al-Khabrani, and Hassan Tambakti; **midfielders** Turki Al-Ammar, Ayman Yahya, Fahad Al-Muwallad, Salman Al-Faraj, Salem Al-Dawsari, Mohamed Kanno, Abdulellah Al-Malki, Abdulrahman Ghareeb, Sami Al-Najei, Ali Al-Hassan, Mohammed Al-Kuwaykibi, and Abdullah Otayf; and **forwards** Firas Al-Buraikan, Abdullah Al-Hamdan, and Saleh Al-Shehri.

Saudi Arabia maneuvered through the 2022 World Cup qualifiers in Asia in Group B that included Australia, Japan, Oman, Vietnam, and China.

As a team whose players represent Saudi clubs, it is going to be fascinating to watch! Can Saudi Arabia prove, once and for all, that a team with home-grown talent can win a World Cup? Acting as guide, Hervé Renard will wave his magical wand so that Saudi fans can gain as much satisfaction as possible from the international soccer stage. With the lights focused on the green-and-white uniforms of the Green Falcons, every moment will be crucial as drama unfolds. Minus a World Cup title, this venture could be seen as successful in so far as Saudi Arabia finds itself in the quarter-finals. With only a Round of 16 achievement in 1994, this program is desperately in need of a quantifiable result.

The players are very familiar with each other's skills. You've got sly ballhandlers, passing that flows from wing to wing (with a French touch), speed, and a fervent attack.

As with four years ago, Saudi Arabia's defenders could stand to improve owning possession of the ball and adding positive—dangerous—runs in the attack. Furthermore, can Saudi Arabia control the simple mistakes? Petty errors around its own goal will be cause for concern. For a group of players that play club ball in Saudi Arabia, this lack of exposure to European and South American talent on a regular basis presents real stumbling blocks for the defense.

On offense, can Saudi Arabia find a consistent source of goals? This will likely be the team's undoing. Saudi Arabia needs to find goals and lots of them. Easier said than done.

For a tournament that has so much talent, it's hard to pick a single team to watch. As such, Saudi Arabia is tied for first on the list of must-see teams that aren't top brass glamour sides.

SOUTH KOREA
World Cup titles: 0
Overall Team Rating: 8.7

A BRIEF TEAM HISTORY
Let's take a quick glance at the World Cup record of South Korea.

1930: South Korea didn't compete.

1934: Didn't compete.

1938: Didn't compete.

1950: Didn't compete.

1954: Couldn't escape its group.

1958: Didn't compete.

1962: Didn't qualify.

1966: Didn't compete.

1970: Didn't qualify.

1974: Didn't qualify.

1978: Didn't qualify.

1982: Didn't qualify.

1986: Couldn't escape its group.

1990: Couldn't escape its group.

1994: Couldn't escape its group.

1998: Couldn't escape its group.

2002: South Korea co-hosted and earned fourth overall. In this amazing World Cup, South Korea's fans chanted like few other nations ever have, with a ferocity, consistency, and organization that was spectacular!

2006: Couldn't escape its group.

2010: Made the Round of 16.

2014: Couldn't escape its group.

2018: South Korea couldn't escape its group.

ASIAN COMPETITIONS
South Korea won the AFC Asian Cup in 1956 and 1960. It won the EAFF Championship (AKA the East Asian Football Championship) in 2003, 2008, 2015, 2017, and 2019.

FACTS ABOUT THEIR COUNTRY

The capital of South Korea is Seoul. You'll find amazing BBQ there along with an assortment of green teas. Green tea is one of the best around; it has less of a taste and more of a momentary essence. Once upon a time, Cecilia Hae-Jin Lee wrote an apt description in the *Los Angeles Times*: "Green tea is the most popular in Korea, and the people in the Boseong area have incorporated the leaves into everything. They make beauty products with green tea, put green tea in their noodles and even have hot springs where you can soak in mineral waters infused with green tea."[19] How perfect is that for armchair reading? We'll get to the beer in a second!

South Korea's current population is about 51.7 million people, and its GDP is around $1.8 trillion.

A few soccer rivals for South Korea include Japan and Australia. Cha Bum-kun (1972-86) and Hong Myung-bo (1990-2002) are tied for the most South Korean caps, with 136.

Who has the most goals in the history of South Korea's national team?
1. Cha Bum-kun (58)   2. Hwang Sun-hong (50)

Some beer you might find in South Korea?
Gorilla Hop Bomb   Hite
Amazing Brewing Company   Cass
Maloney's Combat Zone   OB Lager

Count on these, and others, making an appearance or two as South Korea competes in Qatar.

WHERE THE TEAM IS TODAY—TACTICS AND STRATEGIES

Though its World Cup record would suggest that South Korea isn't going to go anywhere, most opponents wouldn't call South Korea an easy win. It's a team that usually brings the thunder in terms of elbows, knees, shoulders, and any extra something'-something' that sounds like "thump!" and feels like "ow!" following a slide-tackle from all directions. South Korea has been accused of rough—bordering on outright dirty—play from time to time. Just think of the 1986 FIFA World Cup against Argentina and the 2002 FIFA World Cup against Italy. Those matches became a sort of who's who of scattered bodies lying on the ground, attended to by medical staff. South Korea is like the UFC of teams.

Questionable tactics aside, you should also keep South Korea in mind as it has been known to field quality teams, including the 2002 FIFA World Cup side—Lee Woon-jae, Choi Jin-cheul, Hong Myung-bo (captain), Kim Tae-young, Song Chong-gug, Kim Nam-il, Yoo Sang-chul, Lee Young-pyo, Park Ji-sung, Ahn Jung-hwan, and Seol Ki-hyeon—that was orchestrated by Dutch coaching wiz, Guus Hiddink. In retrospect, this team out of all the South Korean teams in its history had the best chance to win that year's World Cup outright, if not for an unlucky 1-0 loss to Germany in the semis. This team led by Hong Myung-bo, who was named to Pele's FIFA 100 list in 2004, was a legit contender to win that tournament.

Now, 20 years later, South Korea has a chance to make up for lost time with a blastoff performance for the ages. Players Son Heung-min, Lee Jae-sung, Hwang Ui-jo, Hwang Hee-chan, Hwang In-beom, and Jung Woo-young will help push the team forward.

Tactics and strategies: South Korea will likely use the 4-2-3-1 formation it used during qualifiers.

Defensively, South Korea is skilled at collapsing on the ball with multiple players that like to body opponents off-balance, both subtly and overtly. A team can't play South Korea without expecting body contact. Structurally, South Korea is hard to break down; it's a very disciplined team, one intent on keeping scores low.

Offensively, its players check in and out, opening up for the ball regularly. Typically, you'll see South Korea move the ball from wing to wing, either with a well-placed long ball or short passes with sharp movement.

There are three areas of concern for South Korea. One, South Korea lacks offensive confidence against top-level sides, particularly confidence in prime-time games. Two, despite the presence of Son Heung-min (Tottenham Hotspur fame), overall players lack individual ingenuity. A lack in individual ingenuity lowers the chances of interesting play around the field and box. South Korea definitely puts forth a team effort, but sometimes South Korea's attack is a little robotic. Three, South Korea tends to be a little bit impatient when they have possession. It tends to get shots off early around goal, rather than waiting for a moment or two to pass with further possession. If South Korea rushes to shoot, then the shots tend to be lower quality, versus opting for longer stints of possession that should inevitably increase the quality of shots, which is more ideal.

As an upper middle-of-the-pack team, South Korea's chances of winning the World Cup are slim. While it has a higher chance of winning than others, South Korea is nowhere near being a favorite. However, this is a strong-willed contender that might be a very high choice for someone's tournament dark horse.

PAULO BENTO—A BRIEF COACHING PORTRAIT

Paulo Bento—born in 1969 in Portugal—had an eventful career as a defensive midfielder for Benfica, Oviedo, Sporting CP, and he played with Portugal's national team from 1992-2002 where he gathered 35 caps. He's coached Sporting CP, Portugal, Cruzeiro, Olympiacos, Chongqing Liangjiang Athletic (China), and in 2018 he accepted the job with South Korea.

KEY PLAYERS AND THEIR CHARACTERISTICS

South Korea's leading gun is **Son Heung-min**. Born in 1992, he is a 6'0" versatile forward and winger who has suited up with Hamburger SV (20 goals), Bayer Leverkusen (21 goals), and Tottenham Hotspur (over 90 goals). He joined Tottenham in 2015 and really made a name for himself. Dating back to 2010, he's now a veteran force with South Korea where he's surpassed 100 caps, while he's hit the 30-goal mark.

You might think of attacking mid and winger **Lee Jae-sung** as part of a flurry of punches coming from South Korea's arsenal of weapons. At around 5'11" he joined Mainz 05 in 2021, and since 2015 he's represented South Korea's senior national side with over 60 appearances and a handful of goals to boot.

Hwang Ui-jo—born in 1992—is a 6'1" forward with success at Bordeaux. Since he joined in 2019, he's scored over 25 goals. He'll provide depth and a little punch up front for South Korea during World Cup 2022. With his national team, where he first made an appearance in 2015, he's a leading scorer with over 15 goals and counting.

Hwang Hee-chan—born in 1996—helps South Korea's attack at forward with a range of experience from Red Bull Salzburg, Hamburger SV, RB Leipzig, and Wolverhampton Wanderers. He's played with South Korea's senior national team since 2016. He's done well so far with over 45 caps, and he'll put a few goals in from time to time.

Hwang In-beom—born in 1996—plays midfield and was seen from 2019-20 with Vancouver Whitecaps where he tallied up 40 games and three goals. As of 2020, he joined Rubin Kazan (Russia) for the next step in the progression of his career. In 2022, he switched to FC Seoul. With South Korea, he's been a regular performer since 2018 with 30-plus caps and a few goals to his name. He's not a huge scorer, but he'll add to the flow of play from midfield as South Korea launches its attack in Qatar.

Jung Woo-young—born in 1989—is 6'1" and keeps the ship steady at defensive midfield. Prior to turning pro, he went to Kyung Hee University. In 2018, he joined Qatari club Al-Sadd and has appeared in over 75 games, with a few goals. Don't count on him for mega-scoring, but do look to him for strong defensive stops and distribution in transition. He's become a veteran with South Korea since 2015, with over 60 caps to date.

OVERALL PLAYER RATING

Son Heung-min: 9.3   Hwang Hee-chan: 9

Lee Jae-sung: 9   Hwang In-beom: 8.9

Hwang Ui-jo: 9   Jung Woo-young: 8.9

KEY PLAYER STATS

(Total career goals for their country)

	Games Played	Goals
Son Heung-min	102	33
Lee Jae-sung	63	9
Hwang Ui-jo	47	16
Hwang Hee-chan	47	8
Hwang In-beom	34	4
Jung Woo-young	63	3

WHAT TO WATCH FOR ON TV

Leading up to and during Asian qualifiers for World Cup 2022, South Korea had an experienced group that included **goalkeepers** Kim Seung-gyu, Jo Hyeon-woo, Gu Sung-yun, and Kim Jin-hyeon; **defenders** Lee Yong, Kim Jin-su, Kim Min-jae, Hong Chul, Park Ji-soo, Jung Seung-hyun, Kwon Kyung-won, Kim Tae-hwan, Kim Young-gwon, Kim Moon-hwan, Won Du-jae, and Park Joo-ho; **midfielders** Jung Woo-young, Hwang In-beom, Son Heung-min, Paik Seung-ho, Lee Jae-sung, Hwang Hee-chan, Song Min-kyu, Lee Dong-gyeong, Na Sang-ho, Kwon Chang-hoon, Ju Se-jong, Son Jun-ho, Nam Tae-hee, Yoon Bit-garam, and Lee Kang-in; and **forwards** Cho Gue-sung, Hwang Ui-jo, Kim Shin-wook, Jung Sang-bin, and Lee Jeong-hyeop.

South Korea worked its way through the 2022 World Cup qualifiers in Asia in Group A that included Iran, United Arab Emirates, Syria, Lebanon, and Iraq.

In Qatar, South Korea is not a favorite. Still, South Korea is marching into Qatar with focus and dedication. South Korea's attention to detail, immaculate. Its organization, steadfast. Its eye for perfection, perfect. Don't think South Korea's going down without a fight. This team secretly wants to win the World Cup. It's a team with a vibe that says "we want to upset every team here who thinks it's better than us." This team is ready for action.

Still, South Korea must first prove that it can find the goals. It will be competitive and relevant in all its games, but will goals happen? This is a big question heading into the 2022 World Cup. Essentially, South Korea is a superstar or two shy of consistently being the elite team it wants to be. Sure, currently, Son Heung-min is the team's superstar, but how can future teams produce more superstars, that exude highly creative dribbling skills and the ability to create high-quality shots?

In addition, if South Korea can get some goals, can it hold on to a lead? Up to this point, it's struggled to do so.

All the same, this current squad will do what it can to produce moments of brilliance, flair, and strong attacks from all angles. Rest assured, this World Cup will see a South Korean team that goes all in on effort, tackles, fun-to-watch slide-tackles, aggressive play, strong passing combinations, overlapping runs, and blazing attacks.

QATAR
World Cup titles: 0
Overall Team Rating: 8.4-8.9

A BRIEF TEAM HISTORY

Let's take a quick glance at the World Cup record of Qatar.

1930: Qatar didn't compete.
1934: Didn't compete.
1938: Didn't compete.
1950: Didn't compete.
1954: Didn't compete.
1958: Didn't compete.
1962: Didn't compete.
1966: Didn't compete.
1970: Didn't compete.
1974: Didn't compete.
1978: Didn't qualify.
1982: Didn't qualify.
1986: Didn't qualify.
1990: Didn't qualify.
1994: Didn't qualify.
1998: Didn't qualify.
2002: Didn't qualify.
2006: Didn't qualify.
2010: Didn't qualify.
2014: Didn't qualify.
2018: Qatar didn't qualify.

ASIAN COMPETITIONS

Qatar won the AFC Asian Cup in 2019. Recently, Qatar placed third in the FIFA Arab Cup in 2021.

FACTS ABOUT THEIR COUNTRY

The capital of Qatar is Doha. As you probably know, Qatar is a tiny country in the Persian Gulf in the Middle East. Its neighbors are Saudi Arabia, Bahrain, United Arab Emirates, Kuwait, Iran, and Oman. Qatar's population is around 2.7 million people, and their GDP is approximately $183 billion. It's an oil-rich nation that loves soccer.

Who is the top scorer in the history of Qatar's national team?
1. Mansour Muftah (44)

Also high on the list are Mubarak Mustafa (41), Sebastian Soria (39), and Almoez Ali (39).*

Looking for beer in Qatar? Good luck! Palko Karasz pointed out in *The New York Times* that, "Getting a beer has never been easy in Qatar."[20] This was a concern, around the world, by many fans eager to experience Qatari culture at the 2022 FIFA World Cup. Karasz added, "Many countries have tried to regulate alcohol consumption by making drinking expensive. But Qatar, a predominantly Muslim country that has long had strict limits on the purchase and consumption of alcohol, has essentially doubled the cost overnight."[21] That's noteworthy. "A 100 percent tax, calculated on the previous sales price, has been imposed on all alcohol imports, the country's sole liquor retailer, the Qatar Distribution Company, told customers in a letter."[22] What on earth could the cost for customers be? "This brings the price of a 24-pack of beer to 382 Qatari riyals, or about $104, and a one-liter bottle of gin (roughly 33 ounces) to 304 riyals, according to news reports."[23] Oh boy. If those prices stand, that ain't cheap!

Interestingly, "The new prices apply only to foreigners living in Qatar who have valid permits to buy alcohol.

Visitors who want an alcoholic beverage have limited options. The authorities confiscate alcohol at Doha Airport, and drinking in public is banned. A few bars in international hotels do serve foreign visitors, selling beers for around 50 riyals.

The price increases that went into effect on Tuesday are likely to be a delicate subject as Qatar prepares to host the men's soccer World Cup in 2022, when a country of 2.6 million people will open its doors to an expected 1.5 million international

---

* Still active and this number will likely increase.

visitors. Many have wondered how much Qatari society might bend to accommodate guests who view drinking as a central part of the World Cup experience.

Qatari officials have said that alcohol consumption would be more restricted than in other World Cups. They have suggested that some drinking would be allowed in designated zones, and that the country's courts would deal more gently with visiting fans who consume more alcohol than usual."[24]

Let's see: "More alcohol than usual?" That *is* the World Cup experience! Get ready, World Cup travelers, for possible court time, apparently! It sounds like the worlds of alcoholic and non-alcoholic drinks are about to collide! Will English, German, and American fans be in direct competition for "most court appearances?" Such off-field shenanigans could get interesting. No one ever said a World Cup experience only takes place between the lines! It should be a spectacle!

WHERE THE TEAM IS TODAY—TACTICS AND STRATEGIES

Don't be too dismissive when it comes to Qatar. Qatar will stop opponents in their tracks with strong possession and technical play. The coach, Félix Sánchez, spent many years coaching in the youth system of Barcelona, which should tell you that this team is skilled in possession. Its roster is full of players that are part of Qatar's professional league, the Qatar Stars League. As such, this league essentially acts as an incubator for the national team. Qatar, as most know, is a very oil-rich nation. There are smart people behind the scenes that are dedicated to making their backyard a soccer paradise. The national team players stay at home (as opposed to joining European leagues, for example). They are trained under elite supervision in a controlled environment, then are unleashed to test this "experiment" by way of the national team.

In recent times, the results have been good. For instance, Qatar placed third in the very competitive 2021 FIFA Arab Cup.

When you watch Qatar perform you quickly realize it's a good, well-trained team that can handle itself.

Yet, Qatar's chances of winning the 2022 World Cup are not too good. It's a group somewhere in the middle of the pack. Anything's possible, though. The vibe of Qatar's play is a little reminiscent of Iceland in recent years. A small country you don't expect much from, yet, with short passing on its side, coupled by calm confidence, it moves forward at a blasé pace a little too confident for its own good. Chances are created with a lot of patience. Qatar has a way of hanging in there. It wouldn't be too surprising to see Qatar traverse deep into the elimination rounds. It's not guaranteed by any stretch of the imagination, but there's always a chance!

Tactics and strategies: Leading up to this 2022 FIFA World Cup, Qatar was seen using a 3-5-2, 5-3-2, and 5-4-1.

Qatar has a few players it leans on who will, hopefully, for the sake of Qatar fans, lead the way to a triumphant result! These players are Almoez Ali, Hassan Al-Haydos, Akram Afif, Mohammed Muntari, Abdulaziz Hatem, Ali Assadalla, Boualem Khoukhi, and Abdelkarim Hassan.

Defensively, Qatar keeps good team shape and plays together as a unit. The way in which the organization comes together to pry loose the ball from opponents is reminiscent of Spain. In addition, Qatar has a lot of quickness and fortitude. One fallback is that Qatar is seen as an underdog. It's not so much that it's *seen* as an underdog, it's that it *is* an underdog. This should act as motivation, as Qatar has nothing to lose. In essence, if the defense can hold its own Qatar has a chance thanks to its offense, which is surprisingly good.

Offensively, the Qatari players distribute the ball with a surprisingly deft touch, confidence, and organization from wing to wing. As such, Qatar has a sneaky way of establishing its presence from the first whistle.

Keep in mind, this is the first World Cup for Qatar. Aside from the typical glamour teams—Brazil, Argentina, Germany, France, and England—there are some other interesting sides to watch, such as the United States, Mexico, Iran, and South Korea, that will bring a ton of excitement to the atmosphere with every touch of the ball. And these teams bring drama as the level they might reach is always uncertain. In the case of host-nation Qatar, will it be able to shake the international fabric of soccer in its debut World Cup appearance? Here's why this question is interesting: Qatar has a chance to move the meter a bit. Will Coach Sánchez, with his Barcelona approach that emphasizes short-passing combinations, possession, and technique, be able to prove that his way works? What if, by some crazy turn of events, Qatar finds itself in the semi-finals? Whether you believe in small nations with zero World Cup experience or not, this team might surprise the hell out of you.

FELIX SANCHEZ—A BRIEF COACHING PORTRAIT

Félix Sánchez—born in 1975 in Spain—coached at the youth level at Barcelona (1996-2006), the Qatari sports academy known as Aspire Academy, the U19 and U23 Qatari national teams, and finally Qatar. He accepted the big job for Qatar in 2017 and led the team to the AFC Asian Cup championship in 2019. He also produced a strong result at the FIFA Arab Cup in 2021 with a third-place finish. His time with Barcelona's youth system is evident as Qatar approaches the pitch with technical passing; a calm, confident, nature; and a refined flow of play. With Qatar serving as host, he'll have a lot of extra attention on his every move, and the team will be under a lot of scrutiny as things unfold. Will Sánchez be able to reduplicate his AFC Asian Cup success at this, the highest level? Good question. Luckily, he has a strong group of players to guide forward.

KEY PLAYERS AND THEIR CHARACTERISTICS

The head honcho within the scoring ranks of Qatar would be none other than **Almoez Ali**. He won the Golden Boot at the 2021 CONCACAF Gold Cup and also made the Best XI for that tournament. He was top scorer in the AFC Asian Cup in 2019. Born in 1996, he's in the prime of his athletic career with a World Cup to make a big stand. At 5'11", he's a versatile forward and winger who spent time at Qatar's Aspire Academy, and eventually he transitioned to Al-Duhail in 2016 where he's played in 110-plus games, with over 35 goals. He's been a mega-star with Qatar's national team, where he debuted in 2016, with over 35 goals scored, and he's got a ways to go.

 Hassan Al-Haydos—born in 1990—is a top forward for Qatari club Al Sadd, with more than 260 appearances, and over 80 goals. With Qatar the 5'7" sensation is a solid leader in the category of caps with over 160 and counting. He also has over 30 goals for his national team. He's like the iron man for Qatar, one to depend on.

 Akram Afif—born in 1996 in Qatar—won the Asian Footballer of the Year in 2019. The 5'10" winger, typically found on the left side, has done well with Al Sadd, having scored over 50 goals since 2018. With Qatar's senior national team, he's a big scorer, with over 20 goals and counting. Representing his nation, he made the Best XI for the 2021 CONCACAF Gold Cup. He's a force, and he strengthens Qatar's offense that already features the scoring threats of Almoez Ali and Hassan Al-Haydos.

 Mohammed Muntari—born in 1993—is a 6'4" striker who's been with Qatar since 2014. The veteran has surpassed 40 caps, with over 10 goals to date. He provides an aerial presence up top for the squad, along with holdup play as things develop in the attack.

 Watch out for the 5'9" midfielder **Ali Assadalla** who has played in more than 155 games for Al Sadd, with over 20 goals to his credit. For his national team, he's a veteran presence with over 45 caps and 10-plus goals to date. Keep an eye on him as he facilitates passing throughout the channels and gets his teammates in position to score.

Boualem Khoukhi—born in 1990—adds experience and wisdom to the roster as a versatile 6'0" defender and midfielder. He's represented Qatar since 2013, with more than 90 caps, while he's also hit the 20-goal mark. He's one to make a difference for Qatar.

Abdelkarim Hassan—born in 1993 in Qatar—won the Asian Footballer of the Year in 2018. At 6'1", he's a left-back who scores often. Since 2010, he's appeared in more than 115 games for Qatar, with over 10 goals. He's a veteran that will be expected to keep things calm for Qatar while adding some zing to its offense.

OVERALL PLAYER RATING
Almoez Ali: 9.2   Ali Assadalla: 9
Hassan Al-Haydos: 9.2   Boualem Khoukhi: 9.1
Akram Afif: 9.2   Abdelkarim Hassan: 9.2
Mohammed Muntari: 8

KEY PLAYER STATS
(Total career goals for their country)

	Games Played	Goals
Almoez Ali	74	39
Hassan Al-Haydos	163	33
Akram Afif	83	24
Mohammed Muntari	43	12
Ali Assadalla	48	12
Boualem Khoukhi	98	20
Abdelkarim Hassan	117	15

WHAT TO WATCH FOR ON TV

Leading up to World Cup 2022, Qatar had an experienced group that included **goalkeepers** Saad Abdullah al-Sheeb, Yousef Hassan, and Meshaal Barsham; **defenders** Ró-Ró, Abdelkarim Hassan, Tarek Salman, Musab Kheder, Homam Ahmed, Bassam Al-Rawi, Boualem Khoukhi, and Salem Al-Hajri; **midfielders** Abdulaziz Hatem, Mohammed Waad, Ali Assadalla, Karim Boudiaf, Abdullah Al-Ahrak, Assim Madibo, Ahmed Fatehi, and Moayad Hassan; and **forwards** Akram Afif, Ahmed Alaaeldin, Mohammed Muntari, Hassan Al-Haydos, Ismaeel Mohammad, Almoez Ali, and Yusuf Abdurisag.

Qatar received a free entry as host of the 2022 World Cup. As a result, to stay ready, it played a bunch of friendlies and did well in the 2021 FIFA Arab Cup, where it earned third place.

Do not underestimate this group. Qatar has a strong team that checks off a lot of boxes: It is full of detail-oriented passers. It has skillful players. It has confident players. It has well-trained players. It has invested tons of money into coaching. It has experienced players. It has the momentum of being the host; the crowd is behind the team. It is certainly an underdog. Being an underdog is tricky. It's tough because you're expected to lose. However, there's an added benefit because you can play with nothing to lose. The bottom line is that Qatar is good. Almoez Ali, Hassan Al-Haydos, Akram Afif, Mohammed Muntari, Abdulaziz Hatem, Ali Assadalla, Boualem Khoukhi, and Abdelkarim Hassan are ready to show you how good. It's a team to be reckoned with.

All things considered, despite Qatar being a team that might surprise you, the idea of Qatar placing last in its group is basically what most people would bet on. That's the crazy thing about Qatar. If you look at its World Cup record, which is something that can be done in Planck time, it's easy to shrug off the host as a group-stage bust. At the same time, this team is unpredictable!

THE TEAMS FROM OCEANIA (1/2)

The teams from Oceania received "half a berth" of a chance for World Cup 2022. Yes, Oceania has qualification rounds like the rest of the world. FIFA refers to it as "Preliminary Competition," and when it comes to Oceania the competition is, well, let's just say less than ordinary. Usually, Oceania fails to qualify a team. Essentially, just one team from Oceania has the honor of a playoff—known as an inter-confederation playoff—with a team in dire straits from CONCACAF or South America. If that lone Oceania team can best a far-superior Goliath, then it is granted a seat in the World Cup.

At the end of 2017, for example, New Zealand qualified to a playoff with the South American representative, Peru.* Peru ended up walking away victorious in the two-game playoff. (The first game was 0-0 and in the second match Peru won 2-0.) Thus, New Zealand lost its final opportunity to attend the 2018 FIFA World Cup.

As for the 2022 FIFA World Cup, Oceania was busy with qualifiers, completely off the grid, as usual. But you've got to appreciate how Oceania keeps plugging away! As of February 9, 2022, here's how the World Cup 2022 Oceania qualifiers looked:

---

* The games were held on November 11, 2017, in New Zealand, and November 15, 2017, in Peru.

Group A
1. Solomon Islands
2. Tahiti
3. Vanuatu*
4. Cook Islands

Group B
1. New Zealand
2. New Caledonia
3. Fiji
4. Papua New Guinea

Unfortunately, Oceania failed to qualify a team for the 2022 World Cup. Despite the mad skill they were throwing around, it just wasn't meant to be. When news hit the stands, it was sure to have been followed by a perfunctory nod at FIFA headquarters. While rugby is huge in the Pacific Islands, soccer is still on the rise in terms of reaching the high standards of the modern soccer-playing world.

With that, you have the 32 teams of the 2022 FIFA World Cup!

For some teams, such as those from Oceania, it may seem like an Egyptian Great Year of 25,920 years to compete in a World Cup. For others, it's a matter of finding that miraculous game whereby a great upset rocks the world. While for others still, such as Brazil and Argentina, expectations are high, and such teams have all the pressure in the world to win each and every World Cup.

One of the things that makes the World Cup so fascinating is the juxtaposition of world elites with up-and-coming nations (the upset bringers!). The group stage usually works this out; then the elimination rounds increase with excitement, drama, and nerve-wracking tension. Every game is worthy of attention. Every game is historic. Every team involved represents not just elite athletes, but also ambassadors of each respective nation.

---

* Vanuatu is not to be taken lightly. Its biggest win came over Kiribati by a score of 18-0 in 2003!

Kids watching for the first time become accustomed to different names from various parts of the world, along with the unique colors of each nation by way of the different uniform designs; adults that are watching for the umpteenth time are reminded of such things yet again.

You can't think of this World Cup in normal soccer terms. First off, you have a nation, Qatar, shrouded in mystery as to how it got the hosting gig in the first place. Still, Qatar is hosting the World Cup for the first time ever in the Middle East. History is being made. What's more, you have a world that is recovering from the COVID-19 pandemic. And some three years later, the international community of soccer fans, over a billion people, are still facing this lingering threat. Precautions have been taken by every entity involved with the organization of this tournament, yet still it is part of the story, struggle, and process of bringing the world its most beloved athletic tournament.

The exotic land of Qatar will be remembered in so many ways as a very unique World Cup experience!

WORLD CUP HISTORY

A BRIEF OVERVIEW OF EACH WORLD CUP FROM 1930 TO TODAY

1930
Host: Uruguay*
Champions: Uruguay!
Uruguay overwhelmed Argentina 4-2 in the final, with goals from Pablo Dorado, Pedro Cea, Santos Iriarte, and Héctor Castro.

1934
Host: Italy
Champions: Italy!
Italy bested Czechoslovakia 2-1 in the final, with goals from Raimundo Orsi and Angelo Schiavio.

---

*   Under the direction of Coach Alberto Suppici, Uruguay brought home the first trophy ever. At this tournament, it could be safely assumed that no one envisioned the grand parade that we see today. Back in 1930, the shorts were huge and baggy. The shoes came in one design: black. In terms of style, the overall vibe from the uniforms resembled the Ford Model T. By comparison, shoes and uniforms today look like they were designed on spaceships. Thanks to brands like Adidas, Nike, Puma, Lotto, New Balance, and others, the uniforms over the years have morphed into a pleasant change of pace. Over time, the shoes and ball have progressed drastically. But we have to remember that the World Cup started in a different era!

1938

Host: France

Champions: Italy!

Italy outdid Hungary 4-2 in the final, with goals from Gino Colaussi (2) and Silvio Piola (2).

1950

Host: Brazil

Champions: Uruguay!

Uruguay defeated Brazil 2-1 for the championship, with goals from Juan Alberto Schiaffino and Alcides Ghiggia.

1954

Host: Switzerland

Champions: West Germany!

West Germany stepped past Hungary 3-2 for the championship, with goals from Max Morlock and Helmut Rahn (2).

1958

Host: Sweden

Champions: Brazil!

Brazil trounced Sweden 5-2 in the final, with goals from Vavá (2), Pelé (2), and Mário Zagallo.

1962

Host: Chile

Champions: Brazil!

Brazil defeated Czechoslovakia 3-1 in the final, with goals from Amarildo, Zito, and Vavá.

1966

Host: England

Champions: England!

England triumphantly defeated West Germany 4-2 in the final, with goals from Geoff Hurst (3) and Martin Peters.

1970
Host: Mexico
Champions: Brazil!
Brazil walked all over Italy 4-1 in the final, with goals from Pelé, Gérson, Jairzinho, and Carlos Alberto.

1974
Host: West Germany
Champions: West Germany!
West Germany narrowly defeated Netherlands 2-1 in the final, with goals from Paul Breitner and Gerd Müller.

1978
Host: Argentina
Champions: Argentina!
Argentina defeated Netherlands 3-1 in the final, with goals from Mario Kempes (2) and Daniel Bertoni.

1982
Host: Spain
Champions: Italy!
Italy took down mighty West Germany 3-1 in the final, with goals from Paolo Rossi, Marco Tardelli, and Alessandro Altobelli.

1986
Host: Mexico
Champions: Argentina!
Argentina defeated West Germany 3-2 in the final, with goals from José Luis Brown, Jorge Valdano, and Jorge Burruchaga.

1990

Host: Italy

Champions: West Germany!

West Germany beat Argentina 1-0 in the final, with a goal from Andreas Brehme.

1994

Host: United States

Champions: Brazil!

Brazil beat Italy 3-2 in a penalty-kick shootout in the final, with goals from Romário, Branco, and Dunga.

1998

Host: France

Champions: France!

France knocked off Brazil 3-0 in the final, with goals from Zinedine Zidane (2) and Emmanuel Petit.

2002

Hosts: South Korea and Japan

Champions: Brazil!

Brazil soundly defeated Germany 2-0 in the final, with goals from Ronaldo (2).

2006

Host: Germany

Champions: Italy!

After a 1-1 tie, Italy took down France 5-3 in a penalty-kick shootout in the final, with goals from Andrea Pirlo, Marco Materazzi (2),* Daniele De Rossi, Alessandro Del Piero, and Fabio Grosso.

---

* Materazzi scored one goal in regulation time and one goal in the shootout.

2010
Host: South Africa
Champions: Spain!
Spain stepped past Netherlands 1-0 in the final, with a goal from Andrés Iniesta.

2014
Host: Brazil
Champions: Germany!
Germany emerged victorious over Argentina 1-0 in the final, with a goal from Mario Götze.

2018
Host: Russia
Champions: France!
France easily walked all over Croatia 4-2 in the final, with goals from Mario Mandžukić (own goal), Antoine Griezmann, Paul Pogba, and Kylian Mbappé.

In the grand history of the World Cup, only a few nations run the show. Germany is the leader in World Cup finals appearances with eight.* This is enormously impressive. After all, it's extremely difficult to reach the final, let alone to do it eight times!

For other nations that are trying, desperately, to get to a final, it becomes clear that a lot of the difficulty has to do with iconic teams, such as Germany, Brazil, Italy, Argentina, France, England, and Spain, standing in the way. Then there's a traditional power like Uruguay. Don't forget Netherlands. All in all, just getting to the semi-finals is a feat unto itself.

Teams that have reached the finals of the illustrious World Cup are Germany, Brazil, Italy, Argentina, Uruguay, France,

---

*   As of 2014, Brazil was second with a total of seven World Cup finals appearances.

England, Spain, Holland, Czech Republic, Hungary, Sweden, and Croatia. Game over. That's it.

The coveted World Cup champion list includes:

Brazil (5)	Uruguay (2)
Germany (4)	France (2)
Italy (4)	Spain (1)
Argentina (2)	England (1)

Outside of these champions, there are a few other dominant teams that flourished early on only to drift in and out of standing. Some teams that were once very relevant seem to have disappeared altogether. For example, World Cups after 1960 have not been overwhelmingly great for Uruguay, Czech Republic, and Hungary. Uruguay, of all teams, has two titles from 1930 and 1950—which is very relevant on paper. However, millions would agree that since around 1950 Uruguay has lost its left hook.

True to form, Czech Republic and Hungary have second-place finishes, which is noteworthy, but there's been an absence of success in recent times. As such, few people, if any, would consider either nation elite at this point.

England won the World Cup once in 1966, the year it hosted, and that's been it. Since then, England has had a difficult time, to say the least. However, England is always a major threat, and it remains one of the elite teams in the world.

Uruguay, Czech Republic, Hungary, and Sweden, for instance, remain tough opponents, but deep down everyone knows that it will take a lot for one of these teams to make a major push forward in World Cup competition. You can add Denmark—and many others—to the list. Having said that, soccer is unique as there is a lot of parity compared to, say, basketball. With basketball there are but a handful of nations that compete—realistically—for the Olympic gold. With soccer, on the other hand, there is strong competition across the board. This, in part, adds to the popularity of soccer worldwide. While the World Cup championship tends to be taken up by an elite few, the overall competitive nature in the field of talent gives way to many. Of the many teams in question, there's always a feeling that one of them will be a dark horse that changes history forever.

For all intents and purposes, the World Cup is cyclical. New coaches and players emerge, stories abound, drama lurks, and every four years the big party starts all over again! To some, the four-year wait might seem like an eternity, and some have thought of changing it to every three years. However, four makes it grand. Four makes it just the right amount of time for every last fan around the world—over a billion strong—to plug in their battery chargers, so to speak, and get ready all over again. And then before you know it, another champion is crowned. Then, soon after, qualifications begin again for the next one. To have this tournament annually would diminish this unique anticipation of waiting four years. True, some critics are correct in that star players will only have a few opportunities to showcase their worth. Not to mention, in four years there is ample time to accumulate injuries. Yet to have the World Cup every year—or two years—would make the whole thing seem trite. The four-year cycle is special.

In this era of big salaries and $100 million-dollar deals, and, in the case of Cristiano Ronaldo, a $1 billion-dollar lifetime deal with Nike, it's easy to forget the first rudimentary tournament back in 1930 in the small South American nation of Uruguay. At that time, newspapers were huge. Smart phones didn't exist. TV was starting to emerge. In fact, newspapers and radio delivered the news. Deep in the heart of South America, in a city called Montevideo, fans and players gathered together for the first tournament that had so much potential. Newspapers and radio spread the news of the first champions, Uruguay. Second place went to Argentina. Third place, the United States.

And so it was. The World Cup left its humble beginnings behind to become the major sporting event we know today.

ORGANIZING THE WORLD CUP

A LOOK AHEAD TO WORLD CUP 2026
"32 Teams Will Increase to 48"

World Cup 1930
13 teams competed.

World Cup 1934
16 teams competed.

World Cup 1938
15 teams competed.

World Cup 1950
13 teams competed.

World Cups 1954-1978
16 teams competed.

World Cups 1982-1994
24 teams competed.

World Cups 1998-2022
32 teams competed.

World Cup 2026
48 teams will compete! This is new!

This maverick idea, to have 48 teams compete, is the plan! In a story for CNN, James Masters and Chris Murphy explained that beginning in 2026, "FIFA, soccer's world governing body, has approved a grand plan to revolutionize the World Cup by increasing the number of teams from 32 to 48."[25] One might wonder why? "This latest tweak would pull in close to an extra $1bn in revenue, according to FIFA estimates."[26] Interesting. What would be the actual tournament format? "The addition of 16 more teams will mean groups are reduced from four to three sides, with swifter progression to the knockout stages."[27] In addition, "Each nation will play the others in its group once, with the top two progressing to an enlarged knockout round comprising 32 teams. The number of games will rise from 64 to 80 but the competition will remain at 32 days in length."[28] Another interesting point: "On the possibility that three-team groups might give rise to teams conspiring to produce a result that sees both go through, the FIFA president suggested drawn games could be settle [sic] by penalty shootouts or that rankings could be used to determine qualifiers if some nations finish with identical records."[29] An important final point would be the following: "Teams who reached the semifinals in 2026 would still play seven matches, like those who made the last four in 2014."[30]

In whatever way you look at it, 48 teams is a lot. At first, it seems like a crazy idea, right? As you can imagine, there are opposing voices. Some critics feel this format would water down the competition.

As things stand, the qualifiers are the World Cup in motion, so to speak, so essentially many teams are already competing by way of the qualifiers. Having said that, qualifiers represent distinct areas of the world; some of these areas don't have the best soccer when compared with the 32 teams that have made the tournament since 1998. It could be argued that qualifiers linger, and some weaker teams stick around because of the longer qualification process. When the World Cup competition begins, it's an accelerated race to the finish. So therefore, why should weaker teams—that likely wouldn't make the format with 32 teams allowed—be able to disrupt the play of a superior team with a lucky win here and there?

Even with this change, the top teams should still remain dominant. The plus to this whole thing is that weaker nations will, at least, have an opportunity to take place in the historic World Cup.

For some, it would appear that FIFA has foisted this idea onto the masses. Naysayers feel the World Cup experience will soon be in disrepair. Be that as it may, get used to 48 teams! With that in mind, the number of teams has fluctuated over the years. Will it change someday and revert back to a, one might say, respectable number of 32 teams? It might happen. But for now the grand experience of the World Cup just got a little grander.

THE 2026 FIFA WORLD CUP

CANADA–MEXICO–UNITED STATES!

Various news outlets reported on April 10, 2017, that Canada, Mexico, and the US were making a joint bid for World Cup 2026. Since then, it has been confirmed! The 2026 FIFA World Cup will be hosted by Canada–Mexico–United States!

Canada has not yet hosted a men's World Cup. This will be a first. However, Canada did host a successful women's World Cup in 2015. Mexico has hosted two previous World Cups: 1970 and 1986. Both came off in legendary fashion.

The United States brings a lot to the table. For starters, it hosted the World Cup once already, in 1994. In 2017, the US Soccer president, Sunil Gulati, told listeners on NPR affiliate WBEZ Chicago (91.5FM) that the US is the most successful host nation in World Cup history, with respect to average attendance and total attendance. A lot of this had to do with the quality of transportation, hotel accommodations, restaurants, shopping options, and elite stadiums. These factors were evident in 1994 and remain so for 2026. Gulati elucidated how the proposal put forward (for FIFA's consideration) described a shared game outline, with Mexico and Canada receiving fewer glamour games.* As a result, the US would take the lead and host the big games, such as those from the semi-finals onward.

FIFA considered and approved the plan. The unique idea of Canada, Mexico, and the US hosting concurrently is going to make history. Finally, this long process of planning, meeting, organizing, and waiting came to fruition. The World Cup is back in North America! There's a lot around the corner as the 2026 FIFA World Cup draws near!

2022 WORLD CUP QUALIFICATIONS EXPLAINED

THE HASTENED FRENZY OF QUALIFYING IN A PANDEMIC!

Because of COVID-19, the World Cup qualification process was paused and then expedited in September 2021 to get things back on track! Each region—Europe, South America, North America, Africa, Asia, and Oceania—pulled together a valiant effort to allow teams to compete in a shortened amount of time.

Think of the FIFA World Cup qualification rounds like a marathon. It's usually drawn out over three years, and the average fan can struggle to keep track one phase to the next. The COVID-19 pandemic accelerated the process. By way of the accelerated process, each continental confederation of FIFA went through qualifiers, and the teams got dwindled down through a series of games that took place in group competition.

---

*   This refers to teams that carry more weight based on their current ranking, past record, popularity at large, and star players. A few obvious examples include Brazil, France, Italy, and Germany. It also refers to elimination games.

A little more than a year before the 2022 FIFA World Cup, on September 10, 2021, here's how it looked around the world. Keep in mind, these rankings fluctuated over time. (The teams in **Bold** eventually qualified.)

NORTH AMERICA
2022 FIFA World Cup Qualifiers
Octagonal

1. **Mexico**	5. **Costa Rica**
2. Panama	6. Honduras
3. **Canada**	7. El Salvador
4. **United States**	8. Jamaica

SOUTH AMERICA
2022 FIFA World Cup Qualifiers

1. **Brazil**	6. Paraguay
2. **Argentina**	7. Peru
3. **Uruguay**	8. Chile
4. **Ecuador**	9. Bolivia
5. Colombia	10. Venezuela

EUROPE
2022 FIFA World Cup Qualifiers

Group A

Portugal	Ireland	Azerbaijan
Serbia	Luxembourg	

Group B

Spain	Greece	Georgia
Sweden	Kosovo	

Group C

Italy	N. Ireland	Lithuania
Switzerland	Bulgaria	

Group D

France	Finland	Kazakhstan
Ukraine	Bosnia	

Group E

Belgium	**Wales**	Estonia
Czech Republic	Belarus	

Group F

Denmark	Israel	Faroe Islands
Scotland	Austria	Moldova

Group G

Netherlands	Turkey	Latvia
Norway	Montenegro	Gibraltar

Group H

Croatia	Slovakia	Malta
Russia	Slovenia	Cyprus

Group I

England	**Poland**	Andorra
Albania	Hungary	San Marino

Group J

Germany	Romania	Iceland
Armenia	N. Macedonia	Liechtenstein

AFRICA
2022 FIFA World Cup Qualifiers

Group A
Algeria	Niger
Burkina Faso	Djibouti

Group B
Tunisia	Equatorial	Mauritania
Zambia	Guinea	

Group C
Nigeria	Cape Verde
Liberia	Central African Republic

Group D
Ivory Coast	Malawi
Cameroon	Mozambique

Group E
Mali	Uganda
Kenya	Rwanda

Group F
Libya	Gabon
Egypt	Angola

Group G
South Africa	Ethiopia
Ghana	Zimbabwe

Group H
Senegal	Congo
Namibia	Togo

Group I
Guinea-Bissau	Guinea
Morocco	Sudan

Group J
Tanzania	DR Congo
Benin	Madagascar

ASIA
2022 FIFA World Cup Qualifiers

Group A
1.	**Iran**	4.	Syria
2.	**South Korea**	5.	Lebanon
3.	United Arab Emirates	6.	Iraq

Group B
1.	**Australia**	4.	Oman
2.	**Saudi Arabia**	5.	Vietnam
3.	**Japan**	6.	China

Qatar*

OCEANIA
2022 FIFA World Cup Qualifiers
    As of February 9, 2022, here's how the World Cup 2022 qualifiers looked in Oceania:

Group A
1.	Solomon Islands	3.	Vanuatu
2.	Tahiti	4.	Cook Islands

---

*   As host nation, Qatar automatically qualified.

Group B

1. New Zealand
2. New Caledonia
3. Fiji
4. Papua New Guinea

2022 WORLD CUP POTS

Qualified Teams: 4 Pots!
Prior to the 2022 World Cup, the teams were placed in four pots, based on rankings. From this point, the World Cup groups were determined at the final draw on April 1, 2022, in Qatar.

POT 1

Qatar	France	Spain
Brazil	Argentina	Portugal
Belgium	England	

POT 2

Mexico	Germany	United States
Netherlands	Uruguay	Croatia
Denmark	Switzerland	

POT 3

Senegal	Morocco	South Korea
Iran	Serbia	Tunisia
Japan	Poland	

POT 4

Cameroon	Saudi Arabia	Costa Rica
Canada	Ghana	Australia
Ecuador	Wales	

2022 WORLD CUP FINAL DRAW
The Final Draw in Qatar!
Announced on April 1, 2022, in Doha, Qatar.

GROUP A
Qatar	Senegal
Ecuador	Netherlands

GROUP B
England	United States
Iran	Wales

GROUP C
Argentina	Mexico
Saudi Arabia	Poland

GROUP D
France	Denmark
Australia	Tunisia

GROUP E
Spain	Germany
Costa Rica	Japan

GROUP F
Belgium	Morocco
Canada	Croatia

GROUP G
Brazil	Switzerland
Serbia	Cameroon

GROUP H
Portugal	Uruguay
Ghana	South Korea

STADIUMS IN QATAR AND LOCAL HISTORY

Here we go, let's take a look at the stadiums! The amazing cities that will host:

Doha   Al Khor   Al Wakrah
Lusail   Al Rayyan

Will the famous vuvuzela make an appearance in each and every stadium, ringing out like a dying wh ale? Likely not! Most people are hoping that Qatar does not present a World Cup experience like that of South Africa in 2010 whereby the vuvuzela—which some tried to ban before the competition—echoed throughout the stadiums, a cacophony of annoying. Qatar should be, as they say, smooth sailing. (All stadium capacities are approximate.)

DOHA, QATAR
Stadium 974
Capacity: 40,000
Who usually plays here? Built for the 2022 World Cup!

Historical Overview
Doha, the capital of Qatar, has a lot of activity. The Doha area is providing multiple stadiums: Stadium 974, Khalifa International Stadium, and Al Thumama Stadium. We'll get to Khalifa International Stadium and Al Thumama Stadium momentarily.

First things first, Stadium 974! When construction for Stadium 974 started back in 2018, things began moving quickly as it reached completion and opened in 2021. This stadium was brought to fruition by what's called the Supreme Committee for Delivery and Legacy. Allegedly, throughout the long history of the FIFA World Cup, this stadium is the first that could be, if so desired, deconstructed. It could prove a fascinating model for further stadium builds. The first game played here was for the FIFA Arab Cup on November 30, 2021.

DOHA, QATAR
Khalifa International Stadium
Capacity: 45,416*
Who usually plays here? Qatar's national team and various events!

Historical Overview
Khalifa International Stadium is listed in both Doha and Al Rayyan, Qatar. A bit confusing, but both Doha and Al Rayyan are right next to each other. Khalifa International Stadium first opened in 1976. It took on renovations in 2005 and then from 2014-17. Of all the stadiums in Qatar for this 2022 World Cup, this one has the oldest roots. This stadium has very special significance as it honors a previous Emir of Qatar, the one and only: Khalifa bin Hamad Al Thani.

DOHA, QATAR
Al Thumama Stadium
Capacity: 40,000
Who usually plays here? Built for the 2022 World Cup!

Historical Overview
Work for Al Thumama Stadium began in 2017. It opened very recently in 2021. It takes the shape of a circle, with a circular

---

*   For the 2022 FIFA World Cup organizers wanted to make room for more capacity, perhaps to 68,000.

opening on its roof. From an aerial viewpoint, it looks like a fancy, off-white bowl, or perhaps a UFO.

A Little Backstory on Doha
Prior to Doha was Al Bidda. Perhaps the first account of Al Bidda from Westerners comes from 1681 AD (by way of the Carmelite Convent).

In 1801, David Seaton—a political representative for the British—expressed his opinion that the inhabitants of Al Bidda* were of the pirate persuasion.

After friction between the East India Company (a branch of London, Great Britain) and the residents of Al Bidda—who were accused of taking part in piracy—there were "disputes" in 1821. A vessel from the East India Company launched attacks, and locals relocated to nearby islands.

Subsequently, in the 1820s, Doha came about by way of Buhur bin Jubrun, who is said to be Doha's founder. As it turns out, Doha was in the same general area as Al Bidda. Being so close, often both were mixed together in written accounts. Back in the 1820s, amid drama, murder, imprisonment, and violence between local factions, the town became a nesting place for the unseemly behavior of stewards of piracy.

As of 1847, with Mohammed bin Thani leading the way, the Al Thani family took control of Doha. Hence, the influence and leadership of the Al Thani family guided Doha and Qatar to where they are today.

Representing Qatar, we have the following Emirs:

* Sheikh Thani bin Mohammad
* Sheikh Mohammed bin Thani, Emir of Qatar (1851–1878)
* Sheikh Jassim bin Mohammed Al Thani, Emir of Qatar (1878–1913)

---

* He apparently called the town Bedih.

- Sheikh Ahmad bin Mohammed Al Thani, Ruled Qatar between 1898 and 1905 (*after his brother abdicated in favor of him*) until he was killed in 1905
- Sheikh Mohammed bin Jassim Al Thani, Emir of Qatar (1913–1914)
- Sheikh Abdullah bin Jassim Al Thani, Emir of Qatar (1914–1949)
- Sheikh Ali bin Abdullah Al Thani, Emir of Qatar (1949–1960)
- Sheikh Ahmad bin Ali Al Thani, Emir of Qatar (1960–1972)
- Sheikh Khalifa bin Hamad Al Thani, Emir of Qatar (1972–1995)
- Sheikh Hamad bin Khalifa Al Thani, Emir of Qatar (1995–2013)
- Sheikh Tamim bin Hamad Al Thani, Emir of Qatar (2013–present)[31]

Under today's guidance, the success of the World Cup arriving in Qatar, along with the splendor, glitz, and pageantry the world will see, is in large part thanks to the leadership, guidance, affluent taste, and influence of the House of Thani.

LUSAIL, QATAR
Lusail Iconic Stadium
Capacity: 80,000
Who usually plays here? Built for the 2022 World Cup!

Historical Overview
Lusail Iconic Stadium—AKA Lusail National Stadium—is the big-gun stadium that will showcase the opening game and the final.

This stadium is extremely new as it began construction back in 2017 and reached completion in 2021. The actual look—its design—is meant to incorporate the dhow, a smaller-sized boat that tourists will likely see a lot of. This is the largest of the World Cup stadiums in Qatar, with a capacity of 80,000.

Lusail is located on the east coast of Qatar and dates to the early 1900s. John Gordon Lorimer—an interesting British historian and diplomat who lived from 1870-1914—recorded the early beginnings of Lusail. As presented by *Wikipedia*, we find that: "Sheikh Jassim first settled in Lusail in 1903 with a few allied tribes"[32] and he had a fort that was "known as the 'Founder's Fort'"[33] and this served as "his base of operations and is recognized as an important cultural icon of Qatar."[34] From humble beginnings, Lusail is currently one of Qatar's major cities, with a population of 250,000.

Lusail is just a short drive north of Doha. The easy travel between the two will help create an exciting atmosphere for the games!

AL KHOR, QATAR
Al Bayt Stadium
Capacity: 60,000
Who usually plays here? Built for the 2022 World Cup!

Historical Overview
Construction here began in 2014 and finished in time for the opening in 2021. From the outside, it looks like a grand royal tent. After the World Cup, the thought is to reduce the capacity of the stadium for other purposes.

The city of Al Khor—which rests on the Northeast coast of modern Qatar—took shape around the close of the 1700s AD by way of a tribe called Al Muhannadi. After finding a suitable water outlet, which was around the coast, the Ain Hleetan Well—which some believed to have had special health benefits—became a prominent feature that was of great value to the locals. As such, to protect this vital source of water, a little something called the Al Khor Towers came to fruition in approximately 1900.

AL RAYYAN, QATAR

Education City Stadium
Capacity: 45,350
Who usually plays here? Built for the 2022 World Cup!

Historical Overview
Construction started in 2016, and things opened in 2020. The design, as seen from the outside, is off-white with diamond-like shapes encompassing its outer walls that create a flow of motion. Lo and behold, its nickname is "Diamond in the Desert." Its construction allegedly followed environmentally-friendly standards as it used approximately 20% green materials.

The location of Education City Stadium resides a tad bit west of Doha.

AL RAYYAN, QATAR

Ahmed bin Ali Stadium
Capacity: 40,740
Who usually plays here? Al-Rayyan SC!

Historical Overview
With a scoreboard equipped, Ahmed bin Ali Stadium is fitted and suited to marvel crowds from far and wide. This little flower in the desert is a bit older than its cohorts as it first took shape in 2001 and opened for business in 2003. This was the older version of what now stands. A "tear it down" crew was summoned in 2015. Shortly after, in 2016-20, renovations took off. Back in business!

Al Rayyan is known for two sections, one being Old Al Rayyan located in the north and another being New Al Rayyan located in the south. Once upon a time, when Al Rayyan wasn't as big as it is today, the Old Al Rayyan area had older villages while New Al Rayyan reflected larger estates belonging to those in charge of Qatar.

AL WAKRAH, QATAR
Al Janoub Stadium
Capacity: 40,000
Who usually plays here? Al-Wakrah SC!

Historical Overview
Construction efforts for Al Janoub Stadium—the single venue used to represent the city of Al Wakrah in this World Cup—began in 2014, and it opened in 2019. Zaha Hadid served as architect for this design. Inside the stadium there is a very interesting blue-and-white design on the seats, a ribbon-like feature—perhaps a wave from the ocean—that sways across the first and second tiers. A digital scoreboard is included. The grass on the field is a vibrant light-medium green.

As the story goes, the name of Al Wakrah has to do with a hill in the area that was home to the nesting place of different birds. In the past, this was the epicenter of Qatar for pearling, the practice of fishing for pearls. In the old days, when you have valuable items such as pearls moving around, along with a waterway that is highly trafficked, you also have a prime opportunity for piracy. In the late 1800s, Al Wakrah was part of what some called the Pirate Coast (a name ascribed by the British that essentially dates to the 17th century). The Pirate Coast essentially encompassed areas from modern-day Bahrain, Qatar, United Arab Emirates, and Oman in the waterway of the Persian Gulf; on the opposite side of the water would be modern-day Iran. According to legend, these pirates were bloodthirsty zealots that reveled in atrocious attacks. For instance, Hermann Burchardt—who lived from 1857-1909—came from Germany and was a photographer and explorer who was known for his pictures of this part of the world. One of his still shots captures a quiet seaside moment from Doha in 1904—a few people next to a few boats docked in the sand next to water—in black and white. Regarding the overall area, he provided insight that the pirates were quite intimidating.

During the timeframe of 1920-25, Al Wakrah was estimated by American and British reports to have between 250-300 boats for use.

This mysterious city, Al Wakrah, represents but a tiny section of the overall legends of piracy in the region.

General Note on Stadium Controversies

Amnesty International and others have raised concerns about labor rights during construction of some stadiums, and there are high numbers of reported deaths of the workers. While the names of the stars of this 2022 FIFA World Cup will be remembered, the names of the workers that built the stadiums might be forgotten, but without their efforts, the stadiums would not exist. For more information on the topic, visit Amnesty International at www.amnesty.org.

CLOSING WORDS

So many previous FIFA World Cups that have featured legendary champions—such as Pelé and Maradona—will be compared to this once-in-a-lifetime shot at greatness, the 2022 FIFA World Cup. From bars, cafes, and smartphone communications, fans will analyze the players, teams, and winners from every possible angle. The host nation will only add to the spectacle, as it always does.

Qatar. This is where palaces meant for kings remain with a touch of old-world charm. The final touch, a signature of modern civilization in the skyscrapers in beautiful Doha.* Though someday these, too, may be lost to history. It's like a welcome mat to visitors for a desert sprinkled with palm trees, camels, and stories of long-lost battles that blow in the wind around places like the broken down, dilapidated, stone fort and ruins in Zubarah.** Despite its small size, there's a lot in Qatar, both past and present. Largely speaking, fans will gravitate to hotels, shops, restaurants, stadiums, and soccer games. Credit cards and purchasing apps on smartphones will be ready to go.

As planes touch down, the world's elite athletes will step off and make their way to hotels for meals, gameplans, and meetings with the press before heading off to practice facilities and eventually taking center stage. As the cameras bounce light around the stadiums, Messi, Suarez, Lewandowski, Werner, and a slew of stars will dash around in $300 dollar cleats of different colors—fluorescent green, orange, pink, yellow, and even black—as the famous FIFA World Cup Trophy awaits a new champion.

Who can conquer the world without style, a method, a formula, an approach? In fact, most teams today employ highly structured approaches to each game. The giants of possession,

---

* The West Bay area.

** Found in northwest Qatar with roots that date back to 1627 and 1732.

Spain, are leaders of the pack. When Tiki-Taka rages on, it's a thing of beauty. This approach by Spain most definitely satisfies those fans that appreciate detail, theory, style, and analytics.

While, on the other end of the spectrum, is the open style of free-flowing soccer. In its most basic form, free-flowing soccer is best exhibited by newer teams, those with the least amount of experience at the World Cup level.

Will this be the last stand for Portuguese giant, Ronaldo? Or the Argentinian wonder, Messi? Can France hold serve for a repeat? Will Germany remind the world that it has been in charge all this time? Can England escape its longstanding stint of World Cup bad luck? Is it Neymar's calling to guide Brazil back to the first-place pedestal exactly 20 years after World Cup 2002?

So many are watching. This is the new era of soccer. The game can be watched not just on TV but also on superpowered phones and computers that have more capability than the fledgling computers that helped guide the first astronauts to the moon! People congregate at mega-screen viewings in packed bars and large public spaces that come across as rock concerts.

This tournament—organized by FIFA for close to 100 years—has taken over the planet's imagination. It has brought the world together with over a billion strong glued to TVs and other viewing devices to catch glimpses of the best athletes in motion.

The world's greatest trophy has floated from tournament to tournament—Chile 1962, West Germany 1974, Italy 1990, Brazil 2014, along with all the others—with security and a watchful eye. Qatar 2022 joins the mix. Next stop: Canada-Mexico-United States 2026!

From all the greats who have hoisted the magnificent trophy—Pelé, Garrincha, Beckenbauer, Rossi, Maradona, Matthaus, Romario, Zidane, Ronaldo, Cannavaro, Iniesta, Schweinsteiger, and Griezmann—it's a remarkable ongoing story.

BONUS MATERIAL

STAY'S TOP 5 TEAMS OF WORLD CUP QATAR!
(Based on recent records, FIFA rankings, star power, and style of play)

1. Brazil
2. France
3. Argentina
4. Belgium
5. England

STAY'S ALL-11
The 2022 FIFA World Cup!
(Based on overall offensive contribution to the field of play)

1. Messi (Argentina)
2. Neymar (Brazil)
3. Cristiano Ronaldo (Portugal)
4. Eden Hazard (Belgium)
5. Griezmann (France)
6. Lewandowski (Poland)
7. Modric (Croatia)
8. Bale (Wales)
9. Kane (England)
10. Suarez (Uruguay)
11. Neuer (Germany)

Second Team: Muller (Germany), Timo Werner (Germany), Corona (Mexico), Koke (Spain), Pulisic (United States), Casemiro (Brazil), Virgil van Dijk (Netherlands), Kyle Walker (England), De Bruyne (Belgium), and Minamino (Japan).

STAY'S "ALL-TIME" ALL-11
The FIFA World Cup Champions List!

Ronaldo   Pele   Maradona
Ronaldinho   Zidane   Garrincha
Paul Breitner   Beckenbauer   Cannavaro   Jorginho
Buffon

10 FUN FACTS ABOUT THE 2022 FIFA WORLD CUP

1. This is the third FIFA World Cup in which goal-line technology will be used. (The first was Brazil 2014.)
2. Teams from Africa, Asia, and North America have never won a FIFA World Cup.
3. This is the first time Qatar has hosted a FIFA World Cup.
4. Brazil entered Qatar as the heavyweight champ with five previous FIFA World Cup championships.
5. As usual, the official ball will be provided by Adidas.
6. This FIFA World Cup runs from November 21 to December 18, 2022.
7. This is the first time a Middle Eastern country will host.
8. The majority of Qatar's World Cup stadiums hold around 40,000 people.
9. Each stadium in Qatar is located in the eastern part of the country.
10. The city of Lusail, Qatar, has the biggest stadium, Lusail Iconic Stadium, which seats around 80,000.

To access even more bonus material, scan the QR code! Read about the leading scorers from past World Cups and background information on FIFA and Qatar. Discover the interesting role corner kicks play in matches and which are the "top flopping" teams. Finally, for those interested in esports, there is a brief bonus section on FIFAe.

AUTHOR'S NOTE

All information in this book was current at publication. Sometimes, teams change at the last minute, or even during the World Cup. Still, every effort was made to keep all information in this book as up to date as possible.

The GDPs listed reflects totals from the GDP nominal and not the GDP PPP (Purchasing Power Parity). All estimates are approximate.

All team formations are subject to change. This is based on a number of factors that revolve around coaching decisions that usually include team chemistry, player suspensions, player performance, issues with another team, and injuries. Having said that, most teams stay with the same formation, but, up to the last minute prior to a game, a coach may change things up.

Each team's "Overall Team Rating" is on a scale of 10. Each team's rating (or score, if you will) is based on factors that include as much of the following as possible: the team's FIFA ranking (as of 2022), recent record (which includes the past two World Cups, smaller tournaments, and friendlies), historical results,* star players, style of a play, chemistry between players, and a good old-fashioned hunch.

It was an honor to write about this 2022 FIFA World Cup. It will go down as a very special tournament, as Qatar might be the last solo nation to host. Thanks to everyone involved with this book, including Meyer & Meyer Sport and Cardinal Publishers Group.

---

* This one is tricky, as the matter of past teams endowing their qualities to new generations of players is in part due to coaching, and, not to mention, fascinating psychological factors that potentially get muddled in pseudoscience. Yet, many teams follow the same trends that were established by their predecessors many years ago.

ENDNOTES & CITATIONS

1 Mike Ozanian, "Adidas Would Never Let Messi Stop Playing For Argentina," *Forbes*, published June 27, 2016, accessed September 15, 2021, https://www.forbes.com/sites/mikeozanian/2016/06/27/adidas-would-never-let-messi-stop-playing-for-argentina/?sh=2c6a2b904233

2 Thoraya Abdulkarim Abdullahi, "Neymar Finalizes Endorsement Deal With Puma," *Forbes Middle East*, published September 12, 2020, accessed September 15, 2021, https://www.forbesmiddleeast.com/lifestyle/sports/neymar-finalizes-endorsement-deal-with-puma

3 Ibid.

4 Ibid.

5 Ibid.

6 *Wikipedia, The Free Encyclopedia*, s.vv. "Harry Kane," accessed August 15, 2021, https://en.wikipedia.org/wiki/Harry_Kane

7 Jeff Scott, "8 ways to 'go Dutch,'" *CNN*, published July 12, 2017, accessed October 21, 2019, https://www.cnn.com/travel/article/netherlands-go-dutch/index.html

8 Guy De Launey, "What is Croatia's secret to sporting success?" *BBC News*, published May 2, 2013, accessed September 19, 2021, https://www.bbc.com/news/world-europe-22338370

9 Ibid.

10 Christina Settimi, "The World's Highest-Paid Soccer Players 2017: Cristiano Ronaldo, Lionel Messi Lead The List," *Forbes*, published May 26, 2017, accessed October 1, 2021, https://www.forbes.com/sites/christinasettimi/2017/05/26/the-worlds-highest-paid-soccer-players-2017-cristiano-ronaldo-lionel-messi-lead-the-list/?sh=57fb2375210e

11 Mary Novakovich, "60 SECOND VACATION," "11 best places to visit in Serbia," *CNN*, updated November 26, 2018, accessed November 6, 2021, https://edition.cnn.com/travel/article/serbia-best-places-to-visit/index.html

12 Ibid.

13 Maziar Motamedi, "10 dead in Iran after drinking homemade alcohol," *Al Jazeera Media Network*, published May 8, 2022, accessed June 24, 2022, https://www.aljazeera.com/news/2022/5/8/ten-dead-of-poisoning-in-iran-after-drinking-homemade-alcohol

14 Somayeh Malekian, "Iran confronts deadly alcohol crisis in midst of dealing with coronavirus," *ABC News*, published March 27, 2020, accessed June 24, 2022, https://abcnews.go.com/Health/iran-confronts-deadly-alcohol-crisis-midst-dealing-coronavirus/story?id=69842613

15 Mario Cacciottolo, "Saudi Arabia drinking: The risks expats take for a tipple," *BBC News*, published October 13, 2015, accessed December 22, 2021, https://www.bbc.com/news/uk-34516143

16 Ibid.

17 Ibid.

18 Ibid.

19 Cecilia Hae-Jin Lee, "Green tea is more than a way of life in South Korea," *Los Angeles Times*, published May 13, 2009, accessed December 17, 2021, https://www.latimes.com/food/la-fo-greentea13-2009may13-story.html

20 Palko Karasz, "*A 6-Pack of Beer for $26? Qatar Doubles the Price of Alcohol*," *The New York Times*, published January 1, 2019, accessed December 21, 2021, https://www.nytimes.com/2019/01/01/world/middleeast/qatar-tax-alcohol.html

21 Ibid.

22 Ibid.

23 Ibid.

24 Ibid.

25 James Masters and Chris Murphy, "FIFA gives go-ahead for expanded World Cup," *CNN*, updated January 10, 2017, accessed January 1, 2022, https://www.cnn.com/2017/01/10/football/fifa-world-cup-48-team-expansion/index.html

26 Ibid.

27 Ibid.

28 Ibid.

29 Ibid.

30 Ibid.

31 *Wikipedia, The Free Encyclopedia*, s.vv. "House of Thani," accessed January 5, 2022, https://en.wikipedia.org/wiki/House_of_Thani

32 *Wikipedia, The Free Encyclopedia*, s.v. "Lusail," accessed January 4, 2022, https://en.wikipedia.org/wiki/Lusail#Sports

33 Ibid.

34 Ibid.